ALSO BY JONATHAN F. VANCE

A History of Canadian Culture

Bamboo Cage: The POW Diary of Flight Lieutenant Robert Wyse, 1942–1943

Unlikely Soldiers: How Two Canadians Fought the Secret War Against Nazi Occupation

A Gallant Company: The True Story of "The Great Escape"

Death So Noble: Memory, Meaning, and the First World War

Objects of Concern: Canadian Prisoners of War Through the Twentieth Century

ALSO OF INTEREST

The Oxford Companion to Canadian Military History
J.L Granatstein and Dean F. Oliver

A Little History of Canada
H.V. Nelles

MAPLE LEAF EMPIRE

Men of the Queen's Own Rifles at Aldershot in 1910. The toque and the striped beanie (upper right) were probably not official military-issue headgear.

MAPLE LEAF EMPIRE
Canada, Britain, and Two World Wars

JONATHAN F. VANCE

OXFORD

UNIVERSITY PRESS

Oxford University Press is a department of the University of Oxford.
It furthers the University's objective of excellence in research, scholarship,
and education by publishing worldwide. Oxford is a registered trade mark of
Oxford University Press in the UK and in certain other countries.

Published in Canada by
Oxford University Press
8 Sampson Mews, Suite 204,
Don Mills, Ontario M3C 0H5 Canada

www.oupcanada.com

Library and Archives Canada Cataloguing in Publication
Vance, Jonathan F. (Jonathan Franklin William), 1963–
Maple leaf empire : Canada, Britain, and two world wars / Jonathan F Vance.

ISBN 978-0-19-544809-2

1. Canada—Civilization—British influences. 2. Canada—Relations—Great Britain. 3. Great
Britain—Relations—Canada. 4. World War, 1914–1918—Canada. 5. World War, 1914–1918—Great
Britain. 6. World War, 1939–1945—Canada. 7. World War, 1939–1945—Great Britain. I. Title.

FC95.V355 2011   306.0971   C2011-903273-2

Cover image: VE Day Revelers in London © Hulton-Deutsch Collection/CORBIS

Oxford University Press is committed to our environment.
This book is printed on paper which contains 100% post consumer-waste.

Printed and bound in Canada.

1 2 3 4 – 15 14 13 12

CONTENTS

LIST OF ILLUSTRATIONS

Colour Plates

ACKNOWLEDGEMENTS

The idea for this book serendipitously emerged in a number of different quarters. Galen Weston Sr was interested in the context of his own family's life in Britain through two world wars, and the continuing impact of that experience. A friend of mine in the publishing business suggested Canadians in Britain during the 1940s as a possible subject, and one of my students asked me if there was a First World War equivalent to C.P. Stacey and Barbara Wilson's fine social history *The Half-Million: The Canadians in Britain, 1939–1946*. And while researching a previous book, I had encountered an enclave of Canadians who had made themselves at home in London in the 1930s, and yet never ceased to consider themselves Canadians.

A number of people were instrumental in helping to convert this idea into a book. George Goodwin has given freely of his time and expertise, and has been a great friend and advisor throughout the project. I am also indebted to Ramona Lumpkin, former principal of Huron University College, for her guidance, and to her successor Trish Fulton for helping to see the project through to the finish. Linda McKnight was, as usual, always available to sort through the fine details.

My gratitude goes out to a number of people who helped me to understand Canada's empire in Britain in one way or another. I am especially grateful to the children of Garfield W. Weston, whose family estate in Buckinghamshire was a home away from home for so many Canadians in uniform during the Second World War. Derrick Clements, the custodian of the Weston Corporate Archives, always had an answer when I contacted him for help, and usually had a document or a photo to back it up. Kim Sollis shared with me the letters and photos of Harry Sands, currently held by her grandmother, Audrey Sollis, and the younger generations of the McGregor family allowed me to use the account of Muriel McGregor's visit to Scotland in 1917.

As usual, the people at Oxford University Press have been a pleasure to work with. Jennie Rubio is truly an author's best friend, and Katie Scott and Stephanie Davidson have been tireless in sorting out the production issues that accompanied a tight publishing schedule.

Finally, I have benefited from the wise counsel of many friends and colleagues who have helped this project along, including Claire Campbell, J.L. Granatstein, Roger Hall, Steve Marti, Francine McKenzie, Desmond Morton, Amy Shaw, and Andrew Smith. I am particularly indebted to Neville Thompson, whose biography of Beverley Baxter will soon be published and who generously shared his research with me. Neville's remarkable knowledge of twentieth-century Britain has been an enormous time saver for me on many occasions. Various people have read and commented on parts of the manuscript, and for that I am grateful, but I would like to single out my son Gordon, whose suggestion for improving the last chapter solved a tiresome structural quandary in the draft.

MAPLE LEAF EMPIRE

The funeral of Roy Gzowski, Aldershot, 1910

INTRODUCTION

Aldershot Military Cemetery is an Edenic place, a garden of the dead with spreading boughs of oak, beech, and evergreen, gently sloping lawns, and sun-dappled paths that wind between the gravestones. The burials date back to the 1850s, and together they constitute a guide to modern British military history. There are field marshals and privates from the Crimean War to the Falklands War, soldiers and civilians, and over a hundred Canadians who died there during the two world wars, when Aldershot was a home away from home for Canada's expeditionary forces. There are a few burials from earlier Canadian visits, including the grave of a young lieutenant who died of typhoid fever while his militia unit was on manoeuvres in England in 1910. Twenty-year-old Roy Gzowski came from a distinguished family. Descended from the Polish nobility, his grandfather Casimir had emigrated to Canada in 1841, and eventually became one of the leading engineers in the Dominion. By the time Roy was born in 1890, the family had risen to the heights of the Toronto aristocracy; their opulent home—"The Hall"—became a favourite destination on the city's social circuit. Roy's uncle held an officer's commission, and his three aunts all married British Army officers. That he should join Toronto's leading militia regiment, the Queen's Own Rifles, was perhaps foreordained.

In 1910, thanks to the largesse of Sir Henry Pellatt, the unit's commander and the squire of Casa Loma, 600 men of the Queen's Own travelled to Aldershot, a military town in southern England that had been home to the British Army since the mid-1800s, to take part in the annual summer manoeuvres and to celebrate the regiment's fiftieth anniversary. But just a few days after arriving, the unit was struck by typhoid fever and eight soldiers were hospitalized. Anxious relatives rushed from Canada to keep vigil at sick beds but before any of them could arrive, a sergeant died and then, on 25 September 1910, Roy Gzowski. After an impressive funeral at which every British regiment in the vicinity was represented, he was buried in Aldershot Military Cemetery, beneath a headstone adorned with a short verse:

> Then lead, and your son will follow,
> Or follow and he will lead
> And side by side, though the world deride,
> We shall show by word and deed
> That you share with me my youthfulness
> And I with you your prime,
> And so it shall be till the sun shall set
> On the uttermost edge of time.

Had he lived, Roy Gzowski would almost certainly have fought with the Canadian Expeditionary Force during the First World War, and he might well have found himself commanding Canadian troops in Britain during the Second World War. His epitaph captures the ethos that surely would have guided his life: a profound faith in the British connection. It personifies Canada as the dutiful son of the British Empire, but the relationship is more equal than the parent/child metaphor might suggest. Either can take the lead, for they each have unique attributes— the youthful vigour of Canada, the sage experience of Britain. Together, they constitute a formidable force; their relationship is the foundation of the British Empire, upon which the sun never sets.

Gzowski's regiment was one of the most anglophile in the country, as were the social circles in which he travelled. Despite their decidedly un-English surname, the Gzowskis were thoroughly anglicized, pillars of Toronto's Church of England, *plus royaliste que le roi*. But the brand of nationalism encapsulated on Roy Gzowski's headstone was not confined to the milieu of Anglo-Canadian elites. It could be found in ranching communities in the British Columbia interior and fishing villages in the Maritimes, in farming towns of the prairie west and working-class neighbourhoods in central Canada. A good number of French Canadians were deeply sympathetic to the ideology, and Aboriginal leaders tended to identify more with the British Crown than with Canada's partisan governments. The two world wars affirmed how widely those views were held across Canada, and how eagerly they might be acted upon. Many motives impelled Canadian men and women to enlist, but an attachment to British ideals, to the British connection, was one of the most common.

Canada is a nation of immigrants. Once the First Nations peoples had been dispossessed of their ancestral lands and herded into reservations, the way was clear for successive waves of newcomers to lay out townships and counties, establish cities and villages, create farms and factories. But many of these nation-builders—Italian miners, Polish farm labourers, Chinese railway workers, Ukrainian lumbermen—were nothing more than a footnote to the historical narrative. Not until the 1970s did ethnic history catch the imagination of a young generation of historians, who began to draw the distinct experiences of different ethnic groups out of the shadows. Official multiculturalism, enshrined by Pierre Trudeau's Liberals in 1971, helped along the process by which the various ethnicities that make up the Canadian mosaic were described, studied, and celebrated. At the same time, the French fact found eager students and supporters in Quebec's universities and the provincial government. But Britishness was usually left out, for a number of reasons. For some writers, it had been the *only* ethnicity deemed worthy of notice for so long that nothing more need be said about it. Part of this conscious turning away from Britain stemmed from a belief that too much of what Canada had done in the past was a knee-jerk reaction to the British connection. When Britain called and Canada responded, so the thinking went, it usually got us into trouble. To celebrate that was somehow un-Canadian; it was to celebrate a time when Canada happily did Britain's bidding, in whatever cause, a time when national sovereignty was subordinated to British dictates and desires. Britishness became, in short, little more than a vaguely embarrassing adolescent stage that, once grown out of, was best forgotten.

Only recently have historians turned back to Britishness, seeing it as something more than a sign of youthful immaturity; only recently have writers started to show a renewed interest in the British connection without feeling the need to preface their remarks with an apology or an excuse. In their view, Britishness was not an unthinking attachment to anything and everything emanating from the British Isles, as its critics had often implied. On the contrary, it represented an affection for British liberal ideals and a belief that the "British inheritance" was both greater and more enduring than the political entity that is the United Kingdom of Great Britain and Northern Ireland, or even the British Empire. Britishness as it evolved in Canada was uniquely Canadian, quite distinct from the sentiment that evolved in Australia, New Zealand, South Africa, Newfoundland, or even Britain itself. To see it as an immature and reflexive obsessiveness, they argue, is to misunderstand it.

To see Britishness as a Canadian hybrid, however, allows us to appreciate and understand one of the great mass migrations of the twentieth century: the return of Canadians to Britain during the two world wars. Close to a million Canadians travelled to the United Kingdom to fight for the ideals that the British Empire was deemed to represent. It was a kind of reverse colonialism in which Canadians established modest outposts in Britain; as those outposts grew and became small settlements in their own right, parts of the country were Canadianized. It was, in a very real sense, a re-enactment in reverse of the process by which Britain had placed its imprint on Canada. In the eighteenth and nineteenth centuries, Britain came to Canada and helped to shape the nation as a critical part of the British Empire. In the twentieth century, Canada went to Britain and established, at least for a time, a Maple Leaf Empire.

THE SENIOR DOMINION

A bitter November wind whipped around the Quebec Citadel, tugging at the Union Jack on the flagstaff as a British officer in a forest-green uniform hauled down on the halyard. One hundred and twelve years earlier, his regiment, the 60th Rifles, had been on hand as the rulers of New France surrendered and had watched as the British flag was raised over the city. Now, on 11 November 1871, the Green Jackets watched as the Union Jack came down for the final time and the Canadian ensign went up in its place. The last British soldiers to garrison Quebec were leaving.

When the formalities were over, the men of the 60th marched from the Citadel towards St Andrew's Wharf, where they joined the blue-coated gunners of the Royal Artillery from the Palace Gate barracks. Crowds sang *Good-bye, Sweetheart, Good-bye* and *Auld Lang Syne*, and if we are to believe one journalist, some of the soldiers even had to wipe away tears as they filed aboard the steamer *Orontes*. There were more speeches, more rounds of applause, and then, as the transport edged away from the dock, one chapter in Canadian history came to a close and another opened. "And thus we are budding with national existence!" mused another journalist wistfully.[1] Over the next few days, Quebec's newspapers spoke of bitterness and disappointment at the departure of the British regulars, "who had proven not only benevolent, but also humane and disciplined. And modest and indulgent to the citizens." *L'Événement de Québec* observed that "the population . . . owes a show of esteem, a demonstration of the public sentiment, to the officers who last among us wore the English uniform and represented with such distinction and affability this noble army which is leaving here memories of honour and generous hospitality."[2]

The new Dominion owed a lot to the regiments of the British Army, and not just for a century-and-a-half of defending its borders. The fabric of Canadian life in 1871—its culture, its economy, its society, its infrastructure—bore the deep imprint of the British military. It was the British soldier, as much as the native chief, the habitant, or the Loyalist settler, who had made Canada what it was. It was a debt that would not soon be forgotten. "Never, never will Canadians say," observed the Toronto *Leader* a few days after the departure from Quebec, "that our allegiance is a whit endangered because of the departure of the Imperial soldiers." Canada would now have to shoulder its own defensive burden by taking over all the tasks, and more, that the British Army had done, but it would stay close to its roots in the process.

The first British regiment to set foot in Canada was probably a contingent of 500 marines, part of a force sent to recapture Nova Scotia from the French in 1709. Since then, the British North American colonies had become stops on the rotation through Britain's overseas garrisons, with the troop strength varying according to the international situation. In 1757, as the Seven Years' War spilled over into North America, three Highland Regiments—the 42nd (the Black Watch), the 77th (Montgomerie's Highlanders), and the 78th (Fraser's Highlanders)— came to Canada to fight the French. The Frasers had been raised specific- ally for service in North America; its 1,542 men, including five named Simon Fraser, arrived at Halifax in July 1757 to begin a long association with Canada. More than a dozen British regiments fought at Quebec and Montreal in 1759–60, and many more passed through British North America during the War of 1812. The British Army also found Canada a fertile recruiting ground in time of emergency, although native-born Canadians were not generally allowed to enlist in the ranks for fear of draining the colony of young men. Special regiments were occasionally raised in Canada to serve either at home or elsewhere in the Empire. When rumours circulated in 1855 that Britain would raise a Canadian volunteer unit for imperial service, applications poured in from eager volunteers like Pierre Levesque, who referred to the "tried loyalty and honorable bearing of his ancestors" to prove himself "ardently desirous to devote himself to the military profession."[3] In 1858, during the Indian Mutiny, the government of the Canadas allowed Britain to raise the

100th Royal Canadian Regiment of Foot. A young Charles Boulton, later a militia officer and senator, was a self-appointed recruiting sergeant:

> My father supplied me with what necessary funds I wanted, lent me his waggon and a pair of horses, and I engaged a friend who played the bagpipes, the only musical instrument I could procure in the neighbourhood for recruiting purposes. With an old-fashioned uniform, lent me by an officer who had early settled in the country, I started off to visit the neighbouring villages to recruit; and I need hardly say that I was the envy and admiration of every youth of my own age who witnessed my progress through the country.[4]

The regiment drew most of its 1,027 recruits from Canada West, a good number of them descendants of the men who had fought with the original 100th Regiment, which had been demobilized in Canada in 1810. The Royal Canadians went on to have a distinguished record, and eventually ended up in Ireland as the Prince of Wales' Leinster Regiment.

But soldiers were also needed out of uniform. Aware that the greatest threat to Upper and Lower Canada came from the south, the British government worked to settle the colonies with retired soldiers, who could be mobilized to turn back any invaders. So when Fraser's Highlanders were demobilized in December 1763, some 150 soldiers took up the offer of fourteen days' pay and a grant of land in lieu of transport back to Britain. In 1804, a whole regiment of the Glengarry Fencibles of the British Army settled along the St Lawrence River, not far from Montreal; around the same time, Colonel Thomas Talbot settled ex-soldiers on the north shore of Lake Erie at the equally vulnerable western end of Upper Canada. The 10th Royal Veteran Battalion was raised in 1806 from experienced soldiers in Britain who were willing to serve in Canada in exchange for eventual land grants—in fact, any ex-soldier had only to show his discharge certificate to claim a grant of free land. After the War of 1812 confirmed the need to defend the borders against American aggression, the program of assisted emigration continued. Despite the growing belief that land should be sold rather than given away, the Military Settling Department (which worked under the governor of Lower Canada until 1822) interpreted the will of the government loosely. A group of discharged soldiers was settled in the Bathurst district (around Ottawa) and "paid" for their grants with their willingness to accept land that was poor for farming but strategically important—between the US border and the route of the Rideau Canal.

The Rideau Canal was another British military project, as was much of Canada's early infrastructure. Most of Canada's early canals, such as the first St Lawrence canals above Montreal and the four Ottawa-Rideau military canals, were built by the Royal Engineers and paid for by the British government. The British Army was responsible for other critical transportation routes too: the Grand Communications Route, which for decades was the only winter link between Montreal and the Maritimes; the Governor's Road, the military highway between Toronto and London, Ontario; and the Cariboo Wagon Road North, built by the Royal Engineers to link Yale, British Columbia, with the gold-mining town of Barkerville. Canada's first significant bridge, across the Ottawa River, was built by the British Army to link Upper and Lower Canada without relying on the St Lawrence waterway, which was vulnerable to American interdiction.

The British Army was more than just a builder; it had also been good for the economy—as the kind of investor that makes twenty-first-century politicians go glassy-eyed. British regular regiments generated economic activity far beyond their numbers, creating employment and profit in the communities that housed them. There were regulations requiring the army to buy as much as it could in Britain and have it shipped over, but the vast majority of a garrison's needs could only be met locally. And that meant lucrative deals for local businesses. Fortresses were constantly in need of repairs or additions; complicated construction jobs were done by the Royal Engineers, but local contractors eagerly watched for advertisements like the one that appeared in the *Quebec Gazette* in 1832, asking for tenders to build a guard room, an orderly room, and work rooms at the Palace Gate barracks, "the Whole of the materials to be of the best quality, and to be executed in a Workmanlike manner." Auctioneers were commissioned to sell off surplus equipment. Cavalry and artillery units bought their horses locally, rather than transporting them from Britain. Ship owners competed for contracts to transport men and supplies between garrisons. In fortresses that had no accommodation for officers (such as Montreal), landlords could name their price. Town authorities sold water to the army. The Montreal garrison needed 2,750 cords of wood a year and 12,000 twelve-pound bundles of straw just to fill the soldiers' mattresses. Clearly, any heartfelt laments at the departure of British regulars had an economic motive as well.

The beginnings of a distinct Canadian culture also lay with the British regular soldier. Some of Canada's first artists were military officers, trained as draftsmen to record physical features in meticulous detail—the only means of capturing topography in the days before photography. The roots of many a local theatre troupe could be found in British garrison regiments, whose officers and men trod the boards in their idle hours. Only occasionally did things go wrong, like in Victoria in 1830, when a re-enactment of the Battle of Waterloo ended in disorder after a soldier/ actor was killed by a ramrod to the head. In many communities, the only music available was provided by military bands. They put on concerts of serious music for the more discerning—"Every evening during summer, when the weather is fine, one of the regiments of the garrison parades in the open place before the chateau, and the band plays for an hour or two, at which time the place becomes the resort of numbers of the most genteel people of the town," observed one visitor to Quebec[5]—and could be hired by any passing showman who wanted musical accompaniment for his circus; he could also rent artillerymen to provide sound effects or manufacture fireworks for a grand finale. Even Canadian literature owes its birth to the British Army, for some of the first lending libraries and reading circles were established in garrison towns with the support of local officers. *The History of Emily Montague* (1769), widely regarded as the first Canadian novel, was written by Frances Brooke while her husband was serving as chaplain to the garrison at Quebec. And although one theorizes about the roots of sport at one's peril, it is quite likely that British regular soldiers were responsible for the emergence in Canada of curling, horse racing, cricket, sailing, rowing, and fencing, either by bringing them in the first place or popularizing them here.

The British Army had become such an institution in Canada that few could imagine life without it. Who would play at the strawberry social if the regimental band was not there? Could the local theatre survive if the soldier/actors were withdrawn? What would become of the taverns that prospered on the business of thirsty British soldiers? But the Dominion government had more to be concerned with than Sunday concerts or pub profits. The British Army's real purpose in Canada was defence and as long as it remained there, the Canadian government had no reason to devote much money to defending itself. If British regulars, paid by the British taxpayer, would garrison the borders and sea approaches, why should the Canadian taxpayer do it? Furthermore, politicians lived under the spell of the militia myth, an abiding belief that a permanent standing army was unnecessary—Canada's young men were tough, resourceful, and brave enough that they could be called out in an emergency to hold the borders against any invader. Isn't that precisely why so many ex-soldiers had been settled in Canada? It made sense practically, and no one could ever accuse Canadian politicians of lacking in severe practicality.

But the British government was just as practical. To them, Canada was just one overseas possession of many that needed garrison troops; when tensions flared in one part of the world, regiments were withdrawn from another. During the 1850s, when Britain was at war in the Crimea, garrisons in Canada were stripped to send regiments to the battlefields, leaving only 2,300 regulars to defend all of British North America, and leaving colonial tavern-keepers with empty chairs and bare tills. In the 1860s, when the US Civil War brought Anglo-American relations almost to the breaking point and pro-Irish members of the Fenian Brotherhood launched raids across the border into Canada, the garrison strength in British North America grew to some 18,000 regulars. It would have been less annoying if Britain had received something from Canada beyond constant gripes about self-government. "An Army maintained in a country which does not permit us even to govern it!" lamented British Prime Minister Benjamin Disraeli. "What is the use of these colonial deadweights which we do not govern?"[6]

A new British government under William Ewart Gladstone had no good answer to Disraeli's question. It preached economy in military spending in the far reaches of the Empire and reacted warmly to any proposal to bring troops home to defend the British Isles. This new climate of austerity went hand in hand with a movement to reform the

British Army from the ground up. The Cardwell Reforms are best known for the abolition of flogging during peacetime but more important was the reduction of British garrisons around the world, as a way to save money and improve training standards. Canada, with its fractious government that balked at even the most modest military spending and large population of military-age men who were quite capable of soldiering, was an obvious target for cuts. In the years after Confederation, the Royal Navy pulled its last gunboats and sailors from the Great Lakes and withdrew everything to Halifax, which the British would continue to garrison as an imperial station. British infantry battalions and artillery batteries began withdrawing from garrisons across Canada—one by one, forts, citadels, and Martello towers were handed over to the Canadians, and by the end of September 1870 the last British regulars outside of Nova Scotia had been collected at Quebec. The *Globe* argued that Britain should leave its garrisons in Canada as proof that the Mother Country valued the imperial tie. The Dominion government used the same emotional argument to camouflage a fiscal one, but it would not alter the harsh reality that it could no longer avoid meaningful military spending. In November 1871, more than a century-and-a-half of British regulars in Canada came to an end, with a profound impact on communities. "With the departure of the garrison," recalled Montreal resident Adele Clarke, "the character of Montreal society . . . entirely changed . . . and was replaced by another society which has gradually developed itself, but on totally different lines, not united as in the old days, but broken into numerous sets, who scarcely meet each other and are occupied with thoughts and avocations quite dissimilar."[7]

The British left behind a few things that would get Canada started on the right foot. The imperial station at Halifax would continue to be garrisoned until 1906 (a second imperial station, at Esquimalt, was garrisoned from 1894 to 1906), and there were plenty of impressive fortifications to guard the approaches; some of them, like the forts at Lévis, were brand new. Perhaps the most important legacy, though, rested in the militia regiments established to defend the country, and in the officers and men who staffed them. There, British military traditions lived on, to be perpetuated and fostered by future generations of Canadian soldiers.

In the mid-nineteenth century, however, the Canadian militia was anything but impressive. On paper, in 1840 it consisted of 235,000 men in Upper and Lower Canada, a formidable force to be sure. But there was never a thought that they would actually serve; militia duty was only a statement of the *theoretical* obligation to serve. Few people took the militia seriously, and many who did viewed it only with scorn. The great event was the annual muster, when the men on militia rolls turned out to parade and perhaps even train to meet any future attack. But the typical muster was hardly an awe-inspiring show of force, if Anna Jameson's description of the scene at Erindale in 1837 is any indication:

> [T]here was no uniformity attempted of dress, of appearance, of movement; a few had coats, others jackets; a greater number had neither coats nor jackets, but appeared in their shirt-sleeves, white or checked, or clean or dirty, in edifying variety! Some wore hats, others caps, others their own shaggy heads of hair. Some had firelocks; some had old swords suspended in belts, or stuck in their waistbands; but the greater number shouldered sticks or umbrellas.

Far from frightening any potential invaders, Jameson admitted that "not to laugh was impossible, and defied all power of face."[8]

The Militia Act of 1855 aimed to improve the situation as cheaply as possible. It created an Active Militia of no more than 5,000 volunteers in the cavalry, artillery, and infantry; they would be equipped and trained for ten days a year, with pay. The first new units were created that year, artillery batteries in Montreal and Hamilton and the Governor-General's Body Guard; the first new infantry unit was the 1st Battalion Militia Rifles of Canada (later the Prince of Wales Regiment and, eventually, the Canadian Grenadier Guards), established in Montreal in 1860. Subsequent infantry units were numbered in order, according to when they were established, so that the pecking order was obvious. All other adult males could register and become part of the Sedentary Militia, which was supposed to muster annually for six days' training—although as the years passed, musters became less and less frequent. They were also no more threatening, at least according to a description of a muster shortly before Confederation:

> Colonel Axford was supreme. Dressed in the old uniform he wore in 1837, consisting of a long-tailed blue coat, with brass buttons, and gilt-cord shoulder straps, a pair of white duck trousers tucked into his high cavalry boots; while a shako and a pair of spurs completed his attire. . . . His appearance to me was anything but dignified, but to his troops he was the personification of military dignity and glory. His popularity was not diminished by the production of two kegs of whisky . . . The arms which the men had brought were of all sorts and conditions. Some had old Queen Bess muskets, with flint locks, others shot guns, a few rifles, while others, not to be entirely defenceless, had strapped scythe blades on pitch-fork handles, and considered themselves as well equipped as the regular lancers.[9]

Attempts to strengthen the militia usually came up against the brick wall of economy. In 1862 Minister of Militia Affairs John A. Macdonald proposed a force of 50,000 volunteers and 50,000 reservists, to be trained for twenty-eight days a year, as well as a regular force and a naval flotilla, but the Liberal opposition beat Macdonald's bill down to a paid militia of only 10,000 men. With the tensions that accompanied the US Civil War, a new act in 1863 boosted the number of volunteer militiamen to 35,000, and the first Militia Act of the new Dominion, in 1868, increased the Active Militia to 40,000 men and created a Reserve Militia of all able-bodied males between the ages of eighteen and sixty. In 1869, the government's books showed 37,170 enrolled in the Active Militia and 618,896 men listed as part of the Reserve Militia. Still, even Active Militiamen were obliged to do only eight to ten days of training a year, and their ability to train depended very much on money. For every wealthy urban unit, like Toronto's 2nd Queen's Own Rifles or Montreal's 5th Royal Highlanders of Canada, there were a dozen or more rural units (in 1891, seventy-three of the ninety-five infantry battalions were rural) where the situation hadn't improved much since the 1840s. They tended to be far under-strength (and even then, militia officers weren't above filling the rolls with the young, the aged, and the infirm), desperately short of equipment, and woefully ill-trained. The typical rural militia manoeuvres were less a military training exercise than equal parts family reunion, Boy Scout cook-out, and high school field trip.

Of course, it was difficult to get good soldiers without good officers, and here too there was much work to be done. The top of the military hierarchy in Canada remained in British hands. Fully aware that the militia could be a snakepit of political intrigue, the Dominion government created in 1874 the position of General Officer Commanding (GOC), to be held by a British officer. The fact that the GOC was an outsider would, the government hoped, free him from partisan politics and enable him to make unbiased and objective decisions. It was a shrewd move in theory (even if no GOC was immune from the blandishments of scheming politicians), although the system would have worked better if everything else—accounts, supply, arms, armouries, uniforms, equipment—had not remained in political hands and if the British hadn't occasionally used the post as a dumping ground for ineffective or troublesome officers.

Creating a Canadian officer corps posed different problems. There had never been a shortage of local worthies interested in commanding militia units (whether they were fit for command was another matter), and a good number of ambitious young men had joined the imperials and seen action in the Crimea or the Indian Mutiny. But because a stint at the British military academies at Sandhurst or Woolwich was not a viable option for many prospective officers, the government established the Royal Military College of Canada (RMC) in 1874. Unlike its British counterparts, it operated more like a normal undergraduate institution, with a four-year program—since military opportunities in Canada were so limited, it was decided that cadets should get a broad education for civilian life. But it promised a more efficient, more effective militia system (every cadet who graduated became a lieutenant in the Active Militia) and gave outstanding cadets the opportunity to secure commissions in the British infantry or engineers. For the first few years, the great beneficiaries of an RMC education were the railway companies, with their inexhaustible demand for young men trained in civil engineering.

Once a few years' worth of trained officers became available, the government bowed to military pressure and created a professional army, the Permanent Force, under the Militia Act of 1883. It was limited to 750 all ranks, but it was a start.

Few of these institutions were more than a decade old when Canada got its first opportunity to flex its military muscles and to repay Britain for some of the defence expenditure it had lavished on British North America over the years. Rickety Egypt had been teetering on the brink of collapse since the Suez Canal opened in 1869. The Egyptian viceroy embraced the odd notion that he could pay off his debts by borrowing money at higher interest rates, a practice that confounded the British government. But Whitehall cared less about the viceroy's finances than the route to India; because that was endangered, there was no choice but to be drawn ever deeper into Egypt's internal affairs. And just as the ship seemed to be righting itself, a different threat emerged far to the south, on the upper Nile. A messianic boat-builder named Muhammed Ahmad proclaimed himself the Mahdi, prophesied as the redeemer of Islam who would lead the faithful to peace. He was little more than a Sudanese separatist but he had a gift for mobilizing support and his devotees easily shattered attempts by the Egyptian government to crush the revolt. The British government was alarmed—the Egyptians were clearly not up to dealing with the Mahdi, and the threat to the Suez could not be ignored. In the end, Britain chose the best from a poor lot of options: pull the garrisons from Sudan and focus on defending Egypt itself.

To find out what was happening in the Sudanese capital, Khartoum, it was decided to send in one of the heroes of the Victorian age: Charles "Chinese" Gordon. Part missionary, part soldier of fortune, Gordon had come to fame in the 1860s, when he crushed a rebellion in China at the head of the quaintly named Ever Victorious Army. He embodied the kind of muscular Christianity that the Victorians adored, to the point that most people were willing to overlook his impetuousness. His Christian faith made him brave to the point of recklessness, so it was essential that he be given clear orders (although he still might ignore them). But there was confusion over what Gordon was supposed to do: simply look around Khartoum and report back to London, or evacuate all of the British and Egyptians in the city, some 6,000 soldiers and as many as 15,000 civilians? In the end, it didn't really matter. By May 1884 the Mahdists had him bottled up in the capital.

Whatever their private feelings, the government had no choice but to attempt a rescue; Gordon was too popular to be left to the tender mercies of the Mahdists. But Khartoum was not exactly convenient. There was a British garrison at Suakin, on the Red Sea, and military engineers proposed pushing a railway line from there through 300 miles of desert to the Sudanese capital. The plan made strategic sense, but the cost was frightening. So when Garnet Wolseley proposed a much cheaper plan to send a relief force up the Nile River to Khartoum, it immediately got the attention of the British government.

Wolseley was another great celebrity of the Victorian army, a skilled self-promoter who parlayed some stunning military successes into a place in popular culture. He was "the very model of a modern major-general" in Gilbert and Sullivan's operetta *The Pirates of Penzance*, and he even entered the language—if something was alright, it was "all Sir Garnet." But in 1884 his fortunes were sagging as his political enemies out-manoeuvred him. He looked back longingly at one of his greatest successes, the Red River expedition of 1870, when *voyageurs* and Canadian boatmen had ferried his expeditionary force through the wastes of northern Ontario to crush the Métis rebellion in the present-day province of Manitoba. "Water is water, and rock is rock," argued Wolseley's supporters, most of whom had served with the Red River expedition. If it had worked in Canada's northwest, it would work in Egypt. All he had to do was find some Canadian boatmen to work their magic on the river, and Gordon was as good as saved.

If only it had been that easy. Above the second cataract of the Nile, the long and treacherous rapids began, and above the third cataract, the waters had not even been charted. Soldiers who knew the Nile better than Wolseley tried to point out that all water and rock was not created equal, but the government was blinded by the economy of the plan. To Wolseley, it was simply a problem of recruiting the right men. To Prime Minister John A. Macdonald, it was a sticky political problem. Ever the canny politician, he had to balance the pro-imperial sentiment of English Canada with the dangers of appearing to act as a puppet of Britain. "The time has not yet arrived, nor the occasion, for our volunteering military aid to the Mother Country," he said. "The Suez Canal is nothing to us. . . . Why should we waste men and money in this wretched business? England is not at war, but merely helping the Khedive to put down an insurrection. . . . Our men and money would therefore be sacrificed to get Gladstone and Co. out of the hole they have plunged themselves into by their own imbecility."[10] In the end, there was a classic Canadian compromise. The Governor General's office and any interested private individuals were free to recruit and pay the boatmen, but the government would do nothing beyond giving permission for some Canadian militia officers to command the contingent.

That, at least, would be simple. There were already Canadians in Egypt with the British Army, and lots of officers were keen to follow. For them, Britain's empire was Canada's empire, Britain's army, Canada's army. The Mahdi's actions were an affront to Britons everywhere, and they were determined to avenge the wrong that had been done to them. The real problem was that there were far more volunteers than there were spaces. Finding the boatmen turned out to be just as easy. As a group, the *voyageurs* who had taken Wolseley to the Red River in 1870 were all but extinct, but they had been replaced in the popular imagination by the shantymen. Soon to be immortalized in Ralph Connor's novel *The Man from Glengarry* (and, a century later, by Great Big Sea's song "The River Driver"), the shantymen worked the rivers of eastern Canada, driving logs downstream to the mills. It was hard, dangerous work, and the shantymen were the toughest of the tough. Wolseley had asked for 500 of them, and 386 were engaged, almost half of them from the Ottawa area and the rest from elsewhere in Ontario and Quebec; plenty more were available, but the relief expedition couldn't afford to wait for them.

Unlike their officers, these men were not fired with the love of empire. Of the politics of Egypt, they knew little and cared less; Gordon probably meant no more to them than the Mahdi. They were drawn by the relatively good wage over the slow winter season (when there was no work on their home rivers), and the chance to see part of the ancient world. Contemporary accounts portray Canada's first overseas expeditionary force as a wild, harum-scarum lot, as Frederick Denison, the Toronto militia officer and veteran of the Red River expedition who commanded them, was to find out. He led a worship service on board,

The shantymen arrive at the Nile.

and ended with *God Save the Queen*. "I am trying to inoculate them with a good loyal spirit," Denison wrote in his diary. "They certainly take to it very kindly and are all good subjects of Her Gracious Majesty."[11] But their real allegiance was to their stomachs. One night, the ship's cook burned the men's rice, so the captain gave each of them an extra half gill (i.e., a quarter of a pint) of liquor. At the next meal, and at almost every other, someone claimed noisily that the soup or the stew was burned, and the legion of shantymen nodded their heads vigorously in the hopes that the captain could be fooled into reopening the grog jar.

As soon as they reached the Nile, the shantymen were all business. The first half of the journey, from Alexandria to Wadi Halfa, was more like a pleasure cruise, but when they reached the cataracts, the going got tough. Wolseley's relief force would be carried in 800 specially built whalers, each weighing 1,100 pounds and able to carry three-and-a-half tons of supplies. After much trial and error, small parties of boatmen were stationed at each rapids, so they could get to know their own stretch of water. They would board each boat in turn below the cataract and, with soldiers providing the oar-power, guide it upstream to the next stretch of calm water; then, they would return downstream and pick up the next boat. The shantymen were the first to admit that it was an enormous challenge; as Wolseley had been warned, water was not necessarily water. Their skill made a deep impression on the British officer who commanded the river column:

> I watched this triumph of skill over a difficulty that to any one unaccustomed to such work would have seemed insuperable. Boat after boat came down at lightning-speed, the men giving way with might and main to give steering power; the bowmen standing cool and collected watching the water, and only using the oar should the steersman seem to need help; the steersman bringing round the boat with marvellous judgement at the right moment.[12]

But Khartoum had still not been reached (the relief force would not arrive until after Gordon was dead at the hands of the Mahdists) by the time the army of shantymen reached the end of their contract. They had been engaged for six months from 9 September 1884, which meant that their employers were committed to returning them to Canada by 9 March 1885, so they could reach their beloved rivers for the spring season of work. Even a wage hike from $40 to $60—more than twice what they earned logging—could not tempt most of them, and only eighty-nine of the boatmen decided to re-engage. The rest were back in Halifax on 4 March 1885. In contrast to the Canadian contingents that would come home from future wars, this lot hardly excited patriotic pride and fervour: "weather-beaten stalwart heroes of the Soudan," the *Globe* called them, "with white helmets, coarse and dirty clothing, Turkish, Soudanese and Egyptian turbans of every possible colour and shape, blue, white and grey blouses, deep-dyed, sun-burnt cheeks, and shaggy hair, and unshaven faces."

Once the souvenirs had outlived their usefulness as sources of celebrity, most of the boatmen probably put aside their service in the Sudan and said no more about it. But for the militia officers, the expedition remained a shining moment of imperial solidarity. Fighting the Fenians or the Métis was amusing, but ambitious Canadian soldiers craved the kind of opportunity that only a global empire could provide. So, when Britain mounted another foray towards the Upper Nile in 1896,

Canadians were ready and willing to assist. James Domville, colonel of the 8th Hussars of New Brunswick, offered to build and operate steamboat, rail, and telegraph lines for the British Army advancing into Sudan. Instead, the job of building the railway lines went to Canadian Édouard Girouard, a graduate of the Royal Military College in Kingston and more recently the railway traffic manager at the Royal Arsenal, Woolwich. Sam Hughes, the unstable newspaper owner and politician who would go on to become the Minister of Militia and Defence, urged the new prime minister Wilfrid Laurier to send a Permanent Force infantry battalion, or at the very least a unit of Canadian volunteers, for service in Africa. But Laurier was even more wary of being drawn into imperial wars than Macdonald had been and easily turned aside the suggestion. When war began in South Africa in 1899, he would not find it so easy.

South Africa had always been a key piece in the imperial mosaic because of its strategic location, but the discovery of gold in the Boer republic of the Transvaal in 1886 (just twenty years after the world's richest diamond deposits had been discovered in a nearby British possession, the Cape Colony) complicated the issue. Fortune-seekers from around the world flocked to the region, and within a decade the Transvaal was the biggest gold producer in the world and the economic engine of southern Africa. Suddenly, Britain's decision in 1884 to give up territorial claims to the Transvaal seemed misguided, and imperialist hawks in Britain began to explore ways to reassert control over the goldfields. But on what pretext? Here, the Transvaal government obliged. Alarmed by the influx of foreign prospectors (known as *uitlanders*), the Boers began to restrict their political and economic rights in order to maintain the Afrikaaner ascendancy. For Britain, to bully the Boers simply for gold was out of the question. But to protect the rights of the *uitlanders*, the majority of whom were British subjects—that was a *casus belli*. The Boers had violated the fundamental rights of Britons—they were no better than the Mahdists, and they had to be stopped. South Africa had to be made safe for everyone, even if it meant war.

At first, few Canadians saw it that way. Outright opposition to intervention in South Africa was scattered and ill-organized, and easily drowned out by the noisy imperialists in press and pulpit. But most Canadians simply didn't care that much. As Presbyterian minister and fervent imperialist George M. Grant pointed out, they believed that "Canada was directly concerned little more than if war had broken out on Saturn." And so it was easy for Laurier to argue that the situation was irrelevant to Canada—Britain could "do the fighting, at her own cost and change, while we did the singing of 'God Save the Queen.'"[13] But as the summer of 1899 wore on, events played into the hands of interventionists. Gradually, they began to sway the neutrals and the simply disinterested, and Laurier's fragile coalition of isolationists began to crumble. Then on 11 October 1899 came news that the Transvaal government (supported by its neighbour and ally, the Orange Free State) had delivered to Britain an ultimatum that could not possibly be conceded; days later, Boer commandos moved into the British colony of Natal, and then into the Cape Colony. Saturn was suddenly a whole lot closer.

The response in Canada to the news was dramatic, and unexpected. "An electric current flashed across the Continent, from Halifax to Victoria," wrote Grant, "and a cry went up that the war was Canada's as well as England's." Observers commented time and time again that Canadians surprised even themselves with the fervour of their response. "We did not know that what some consciously valued," wrote Grant, "was unconsciously cherished, with all the force of a native instinct or elemental passions, in the hearts of millions." The clamour was almost reflexive. Canada would send troops—*must* send troops—and militia units across the country scrambled to get ready for the mobilization order that they assumed would be only hours away. But Laurier was desperately searching for a compromise. He knew that rushing to war in South Africa would outrage French Canada, but to stand aside would create a firestorm in English Canada. In the end, he opted for the lesser of two evils, as he saw it. Canada would provide a thousand men, infantry, cavalry, and artillery; Ottawa would pay to equip them but once they left Canada all costs would be borne by the British government. There were just two weeks to assemble and equip the 2nd (Special Service) Battalion, Royal Canadian Regiment of Infantry (RCR), and move the men to Quebec City for embarkation.

There were more than enough volunteers to fill two or even three contingents; Toronto and Montreal alone could have provided a thousand eager young militiamen with ease. But the Department of

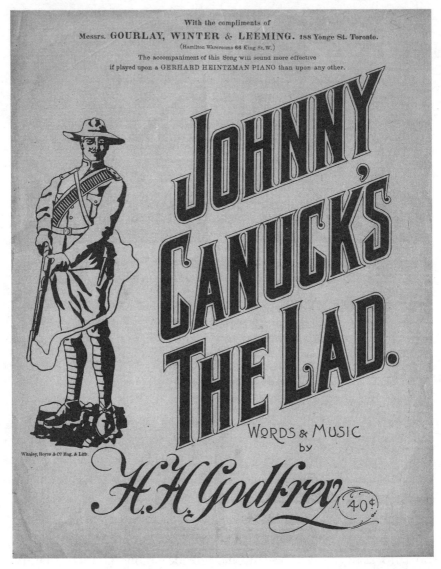

This 1900 song celebrated the willingness of Canadian men to fight for the British Empire in South Africa.

Militia and Defence was determined that this would be a national effort. The force would be divided into eight companies, each of 120 men and each representing a different region. It could be no other way, for this was more than just an expeditionary force going overseas, more than just some young roisterers out to see the world. Canada's volunteers, wrote one journalist,

> symbolized the far-reaching strength of Victoria's arm. They typified the all-pervading influence of Victoria's power. They told of an Empire newly aroused to a realization of its true greatness. They signified the result of centuries of colonizing effort, of generations of a colonizing policy whose aim had been to bind ever closer in one high destiny the new and growing nations of the earth.[14]

Few volunteers would have expressed things so floridly, but many would have agreed with the sentiment. One of them was Walter Moodie, a surveyor's assistant in Kaslo, British Columbia. Moodie also dabbled in journalism and sent the occasional dispatch home to be published in his local newspaper.[15] In his first letter, written on 16 November 1899, not long before the contingent reached South Africa, he gave an account of the soldiers' triumphal procession from the west coast. It began with a telegram from Militia headquarters in Ottawa: "'Kaslo Contingent two men enlist at once' were the words that flashed over the wires and set the pulses of Kaslo's volunteers for service in the Transvaal tingling," he wrote. But who was to be chosen? There would be no fitness test or skills assessment; the matter was settled "on the occasion of the very pleasant and successful dance given by the company." Moodie was one of the lucky ones and on the morning of 22 October 1899 he was "accorded the heartiest send-off a man could ever ask for." The other fortunate volunteer, George Wilkins, was in nearby Sandon, so a special train full of Kaslo soldiers and other enthusiastic locals was dispatched to collect him. "Right heartily did the Kaslo boys show the people of Sandon their feelings towards their comrades for the front," wrote Moodie, and "after a last song, handgrip and cheers for our Queen the train pulled out for Kaslo." The two volunteers, or as Moodie preferred to say "the would be Boer-hunters," spent the night in Kaslo before travelling on to Revelstoke, to join a contingent from the BC coast. They had a rousing send-off from "the Revelstoke Rifle Coy, the Citizens and a parade of the school children who presented us with a large number of portable editions of our country's flag," and then it was back on the train to Calgary. They spent just twenty minutes there—a few of the men received permission to visit friends and relatives, and "one sturdy young gunner from New Westminster came on board again smiling and said quickly 'well the mother took it better than I expected.'" To the strains of *Rule Britannia* and *The Maple Leaf Forever*, hundreds of well-wishers saw the train off for the east. At Medicine Hat, they were greeted by glorious prairie sunshine, frosty air, the town's band, and contingents of volunteers from Rossland and Nelson, in the BC interior. All through the prairie provinces, the reception was the same—cheering crowds and "a band to greet us is the order whether we pass by day or night." At Winnipeg, a horde of civilians and a deputation from the Royal Canadian Dragoons escorted them to the barracks, "where we were entertained at a very welcome lunch, the bracing air of the prairies proving a great appetizer. After lunch we were addressed by the Mayor of the City and . . . each [man] being presented with a tin of Tobacco by one of Winnipeg's merchant princes we returned to the station and resumed our journey." Despite being four hours late reaching Fort William, "we were indeed royally entertained . . . The ladies of the town were at the station at 6 a.m. with most delicious sandwiches and excellent coffee and they kept it hot till we arrived about 10 a.m." There was the obligatory speech by the mayor, then "cheers all round and we were off again taking with us to eat on the train a bushel basket each of delicious Ontario pears and apples." Upon reaching Quebec City, the volunteers were given leave while final preparations were made.

> At 10.30 Monday morning we paraded in full marching order at 11.30 we were inspected by Maj. Genl. Hutton [the GOC] in the old Esplanade which has witnessed so many like scenes. At noon we were inspected by his Excellency the Governor General and staff accompanied by the Rt. Hn. Sir Wilfrid Laurier. After an hour's march through the old city through streets thronged with thousands we arrived at the Allan Line wharf and boarded the good old "Sardinian." From the Citadel boomed the farewell guns, from the stern of our vessel were fired rockets and from steamers on the river and piers along the shore our national airs were wafted to us by the many regimental and city bands. Away on top of the King's Bastion on the citadel figures stood out

silhouetted against the evening sky, the famous Dufferin Terrace was thronged, all the wharves down the river from the Cove to the Custom house were black with crowds of people and several steamers decorated with evergreens and flags and thronged with people accompanied us a couple miles down the river.

Moodie's wide-eyed optimism is just what his readers in Kaslo would have expected, and it is strikingly similar to accounts from other volunteers. What made the greatest impression on them, or at least what they chose to record in letters and diaries, were the national and imperial symbols that were everywhere in evidence—cheers for the Queen, flags, patriotic songs. Thanks to the Militia department's mobilization strategy, the first contingent that left Canada for South Africa in 1899 could easily be portrayed as representative of the nation as a whole. Moodie's cross-Canada train trip, picking up volunteers along the way, was an ideal metaphor in that regard, better, because it was less purple, than Gaston Labat's use of the rainbow, whose seven colours represented "our seven Provinces, all of which have been cemented in a perfect, a fraternal, an indissoluble and indivisible bond, by the blood which our heroes shed under the torrid sun of South Africa."[16] At the same time, it offered proof of the young dominion's attachment to Mother Britain. The Empire was a family, with Britain as the doting but firm mother and the dominions as the rambunctious children, scattered around the globe but always ready to spring into action if called. The fact that Canada had been so swift to offer aid was a sure sign that "the unselfish loyalty of a child for a parent filled people of all creeds and nationalities living under the flag of the Dominion with joy at the great opportunity given to them to prove that their loyalty was of the kind which is glad to make sacrifices." Just what the Boer War meant for Britain and the Dominions was obvious, at least to teacher and historian Thomas Guthrie Marquis: "The children of England from the ends of the earth had flocked to prove that Imperial Union was already a fact."[17]

The rhetoric of imperial unity was stirring, but news from the front was anything but. The fighting ability of the Boers surprised everyone, as did the ineptitude of certain British generals, and by December 1899 the forces of the Empire had been embarrassed by the shaggy Afrikaaner farmers on their equally shaggy horses. The cities of Ladysmith, Kimberley, and Mafeking were under siege; a string of defeats culminated in Black Week, when three more times British armies were routed; the British commander in South Africa was sacked by a desperate government— this was not how the script was supposed to play out. Soon, the British government decided it could use more Canadian troops, and Laurier, seeing a growing political advantage in coming to Britain's aid, obliged. The second contingent, which left Canada in early 1900, consisted of two battalions of mounted infantry and three batteries of the Royal Canadian Field Artillery (RCFA), or the Rebel Chasers From America, as they became known. In March, a third contingent left Canada. This was Lord Strathcona's Horse, a mounted unit organized and paid for by the financier who, as Donald Smith, had been a driving force behind the Canadian Pacific Railway. The fact that they lost so many of their horses to disease en route led one wit to call them Lord Strathcona's Foot. Others would follow—recruits for the South African Constabulary, postal clerks, nurses, artificers, more mounted riflemen. In all, over 7,300 Canadians volunteered to serve in South Africa, and 270 died there. They acquitted themselves well in what was, for soldiers of the old school, a frustrating war. Canada's troops were involved in few pitched battles, the most famous being the victory at Paardeberg on 27 February 1900. Nineteen years to the day after Britain suffered a humiliating defeat at Majuba in the first Boer War, two companies of the RCR fought with a tenacity that belied their inexperience. When the firing stopped that morning, the Canadians had captured over 4,000 Boer soldiers, including one of their most senior and respected generals, and opened the road to Bloemfontein, the capital of the Orange Free State. Suddenly they were the darlings of the imperial contingents, "the flower of the British Army"—more than that, Canada's "sons had become men in the eyes of the world."[18] But after the besieged towns were relieved and the Boer capitals captured, the rest of the war was spent chasing Boer commandos back and forth across the veld. They proved to be maddeningly difficult to catch, for they seemed able to vanish into a cloud of dust. Gradually, however, the imperial forces penned them into a smaller and smaller area until even the wiliest of the Boer generals had to admit that the game was up.

Because of the nature of the war, the Canadians came home in dribs and drabs, rather than all at once. The first volunteers had enlisted for a six-month term and, despite the encouragement of their senior officers, most had no interest in extending their engagement, even for the sake of the Empire. They felt that they had done all that could be asked of them. "The Colonel paraded us yesterday and asked us in the name of the Imperial authorities to enlist for 3 months longer," wrote William Green, a carpenter from St Thomas, Ontario, in his diary. "But we don't see it that way. Every man is of the opinion that we have done all that should be asked of us volunteers by staying this extra month, and that no honour can come to Canada or to the Regiment by staying longer."[19] The fact that there was little prospect of action (they did not consider pursuing Afrikaaner horsemen across the veld to be "action") hardly helped the situation. Some of the Canadians decided to take their discharge in South Africa—the irrepressible Walter Moodie got a job with the Central South African Railways in Johannesburg—but most returned home to pick up their lives. Green came back to St Thomas to find that the city had proclaimed a half-day holiday in honour of returning soldiers. After a marathon of banquets and speech-making and with a silver medal and over $50 in gifts from a grateful city, he quietly went back to building a successful contracting and lumber business in St Thomas.[20]

The Boer War had an enormous, if mixed, impact on Canada's young military. On the one hand, it strengthened tendencies towards autonomy. In the popular imagination, Canada was no longer a child in the Empire but had proven its maturity in battle. In fact, the more politicians and journalists talked about the war, the more they elevated Canada's achievement, often at the expense of Britain's. The stereotype of the Canadian militiaman—strong, healthy, a fine shot, a natural rider, a creative tactician, self-reliant, no-nonsense—emerged as the antithesis of the British Tommy, who was over-trained to the point that he couldn't think for himself, had his creativity stifled by iron discipline, and was under-nourished and so underdeveloped physically. Britain's professional standing army had not been very impressive. Too many commanders had failed the test of battle and too many units had crumbled into disorganized rabbles in the face of the enemy. All too often the British Army proved unable to supply its troops with even the most basic necessities of food and water, and sanitary and medical arrangements were so poor that more British soldiers died from disease than enemy action. In comparison, the performance of Canada's amateur soldiers and tiny Permanent Force looked pretty good.

The Department of Militia and Defence knew that this popular view hid more than it revealed; even at Paardeberg, four companies of the Royal Canadian Regiment retreated in disarray at the height of the battle, leaving just two to carry on the fight. More than anything else, the South African experience demonstrated that there was a lot of work to do and that it was not enough merely to train men to shoot rifles, load cannons, and ride horses. Large citizen armies had to be supplied (so the Ordnance Stores Corps was created in 1903), they needed things like bridges, latrines, and bivouacs (so the Canadian Engineer Corps was created in 1903); they needed medical care (so the Army Medical Corps was created in 1904); and they needed to be paid (so the Canadian Army Pay Corps was created in 1907). All of these innovations, and others, meant that a modern army was much more complicated to control, so the Canadian government replaced the increasingly cumbersome and anachronistic GOC system with a Militia Council and a Chief of the General Staff in 1904. It was important to cultivate a cadre of trained officers who could respond when needed, so the first Canadian Officer Training Corps units were founded at McGill and Laval universities in 1913. To ensure that the raw materials for filling the ranks were as ready as they could be, the Department of Militia and Defence encouraged the formation of rifle clubs and school cadet corps. Even the Boy Scouts found favour for inculcating the kind of martial values that would be useful in wartime.

One of the greatest beneficiaries of this drive for autonomy in military preparedness was the Royal Canadian Navy. Although it was not founded until 1910 (and the Royal Naval Canadian Volunteer Reserve in May 1914), the first steps were taken in the wake of the Boer War, when Britain and Canada found it mutually beneficial to withdraw the last Royal Navy personnel from the imperial stations at Halifax and Esquimalt. Britain was interested in concentrating its strength in home waters, while Canada found the ongoing British presence to be incompatible with its new nationalist aspirations. In November 1905, some 800 men, women, and children of the Halifax garrison left for England to begin the process of transferring the station to Canadian control. The following year, both the Esquimalt and Halifax naval stations were formally turned over to Canada. To garrison the stations, the Permanent Force was doubled, from 2,000 to 4,000 men, although recruiting was slow, even with a 25 percent pay hike. Ironically, the Canadian government had to ask Britain for permission to enlist hundreds of recently discharged British soldiers, simply to meet manpower needs.

Here was the paradox. Even as Canada was edging towards autonomy and distinctiveness, the Canadian and British militaries were, both intentionally and by happenstance, moving closer together. The Earl of Dundonald, who was appointed GOC in 1902, began the practice of linking Canadian militia units to British regiments as a way to formalize ties and create opportunities for Canadian soldiers. The first was Toronto's 48th Highlanders, which affiliated with the Gordon Highlanders; by 1914, fifteen infantry and one cavalry unit were linked. The new Canadian formations were all based on British models; the Militia Council was patterned after Britain's Army Council; and even the first Chief of the General Staff, Percy Lake, was a British officer, albeit one with long service in Canada. And despite attempts to give Canadian soldiers distinctive uniforms and Canadian-made weapons, standardization across the Empire was in full swing. In 1909 an imperial defence conference used the soft-sell approach to convince the dominions to agree to standards in unit formation, transportation, weapons, and equipment and clothing patterns. The process continued at the next conference, in 1911, when the Dominions Section of the Imperial General Staff was created. By this time, a system of imperial defence, something the Canadian government had resisted for so long, was firmly in place and, as historian George Stanley put it, the Canadian militiaman was "a replica of the British Territorial Tommy in arms, training, equipment, and habits of thought."[21]

The two apparently divergent trends were in fact easily reconciled. Canada was maturing, yes, but within the British Empire; there was little indication that the process would in any way weaken the ties of affection to Mother Britain. "Canada has thrown off her swaddling clothes, and stands forth as a full grown member of the family which makes up the Empire," wrote one journalist.[22] The character of the new relationship is nowhere clearer than in the activities of the Canadian militia in the late Victorian and Edwardian era. As more units were established, a militia culture emerged that stressed friendly competition between regiments; when units became more accomplished, they began to look for new challenges. They competed in everything, including drill, music, and athletics, but took particular pride in shooting, where the friendly rivalry went beyond Canada's borders. In 1872, Canada sent its first entry to the Wimbledon shooting meet, organized by Britain's National Rifle Association—the first time that a colonial unit had entered. The competition moved to Bisley (where it remains to this day) in 1890, and Canadian militiamen were very successful over the years. In 1892, Private T.H. Hayhurst of Hamilton's 13th Regiment defeated a soldier from the 3rd Lanark Rifle Volunteers in Scotland to win the Queen's Prize for the best marksman in the Empire, and came home to a hero's welcome in Montreal, Toronto, and Hamilton. In 1904, Private S.J. Perry of the Duke of Cornwall's Own Regiment in Vancouver became the first native-born Canadian to win the King's Prize. By 1914, the annual Bisley meet was front-page news in Canada, with readers eagerly following the counts of outers, inners, and bull's eyes on a daily basis. Regimental and national pride was at stake, but such events were about much more than sport. As Thomas Marquis put it at the time of the Boer War, "It will be a sorry day when England and her Colonies cease to play ... Wimbledon and Bisley, the cricket and football contests, have long been paving the way for this sudden springing to arms on behalf of the Empire."[23]

Ceremonials were just as important in expressing the new imperial relationship. The late Victorian and early Edwardian era was the high-water mark of the British Empire, when grand festivals such as the Quebec Tercentenary celebrations in 1908, the Coronation of King Edward VII in 1902, and the funeral of Queen Victoria in 1901 showcased and celebrated imperial military co-operation. But no event was bigger than Victoria's Diamond Jubilee of 1897. She had come to the throne in 1837 as a precocious teenager; sixty years later, Victoria was Britain's longest reigning monarch, the "grandmother of Europe," and ruler of the largest empire the world had ever seen. It was only right that she be honoured with the most elaborate celebration the Empire could mount. The centrepiece would be a grand procession through London to St Paul's Cathedral for a special Thanksgiving service. As befitting her imperial status, military representatives from every British colony and possession would take part, and as soon as the plans were made public, militiamen across Canada vied for one of the coveted spots in Canada's official contingent (192 men were selected, but another 10 paid their own way to England and managed to be part of the festivities). The procession took place on 22 June 1897, with the colonial troops leading the way. The Royal Canadian Dragoons were near the front, with the Canadian artillery and infantry following later, and they were joined by a display of imperial military exoticism: the New Zealand Mounted Rifles, the Cyprus Military Police, the Trinidad Field Artillery, the Mauritius Royal Engineers, the Gold Coast Hausa Constabulary, the British North Borneo Dyak Police, and many other units. At St Paul's Cathedral, Victoria remained in her carriage, for the service was held on the front steps, against a backdrop of imperial colour: clerics in surplices of rich purple and red, a boys' choir flanked by the band of Her Majesty's cavalry on one side and scarlet-coated infantry on the other, the Honourable Corps of Gentlemen at Arms and the Yeomen of the Guard. The procession stretched for six hours, but was only one of many such events. On 2 July 1897, Victoria reviewed the colonial contingents at Windsor Home Park; they were arrayed in long lines, with the Canadian infantry standing proudly between the men of the Hong Kong Regiment and the British Guiana Constabulary. It was a stirring sight, wrote Scottish novelist and politician Sir Herbert Maxwell:

> [T]hese men came to us, not in gratitude for any priceless advantages we have bestowed upon them—for we have done nothing of the kind—but simply because their blood is the same as ours, their traditions the same, and their sympathies. We are still well able to take care of ourselves; but who shall say that the Old Country may not one day need the strong right arms of her children across the seas?[24]

Seeing Canada's troops lined up with soldiers from around the Empire provided a sense of power—one could experience a rush of pride at Canada's contingent, and be equally proud of the Empire at the same time. But even something like the Quebec Tercentenary celebrations,

Canadian mounted troops in Queen Victoria's Diamond Jubilee procession, from a
contemporary stereographic slide

which drew hundreds of thousands of spectators, only reached a small
proportion of Canadians. Before the First World War, Canada was
overwhelmingly rural, and most people never got a glimpse of the kind of
imperial military ceremony that was on display in the big cities. They were
able to see the militia at work, in the sham battles that occasionally took
over rural townships in the years before 1914 and never failed to draw
interested spectators. One such exercise took place in Dundas, Ontario,
in 1911. Grey Force, comprised of militia units from London, Guelph,
St Catharines, Chatham, Woodstock, Wentworth County, and Hamilton,
was assigned to capture the town of Dundas, which was being defended
by Red Force, made up of units from Toronto. Grey Force set up its base

at Copetown, and sent out its main attacking column at 11 AM (no battle could be fought without a decent breakfast), the 30th Wellington Rifles in the vanguard and the 7th Regiment of Fusiliers from London bringing up the rear. They pushed east towards Inksetter's Lane, then northeast to the Waterloo Road, before having their first brush with the enemy, a troop of the Royal Canadian Dragoons from Toronto, at Christie's Corners. But the city slickers were forced to retreat, allowing Grey Force to continue the advance, now with the support force marching up from Ancaster as well. And then, just as a mighty clash between the two forces was to occur,

> the umpires called a 20 minute respite in the hostilities, and this gave the men of the Grey army time to take a rest . . . and to partake of a haversack lunch . . . farmers and their wives were out at the roadside with baskets of fruit and pails of water, and in return for this kindness the men were particular to do no damage as they crossed fields and barnyards.

Suitably refreshed, the men returned to the advance on Dundas. At Bullock's Corners, they came upon another strong enemy force, but soon drove them across a nearby creek, despite the defenders having destroyed the only bridge in the area, or rather having placed on the road a modest sign that said "Bridge Blown." By this time, all of Grey Force was in motion, and soon Red Force was pushed back to its main base in Dundas. Everything was about to come to a head in one final titanic battle when the umpire blew his whistle and announced a cease fire—the battle was called on account of darkness. Everyone in Grey Force knew they had won but the umpires declined to declare a victor—why spoil a lovely day of battle by sending one side home with hurt feelings?

In small-town Canada, the sense of power was experienced through these sham battles, but in many other ways as well. Children grew up with it, by gazing at the wall map that showed Canada the same colour as a quarter of the globe and by reading passages in their texts that told of imperial glories. It was implicit in the meetings of community groups—the Sons of England, the Daughters of the King, the Imperial Order Daughters of the Empire—where topics for discussion ranged from the Indian Mutiny to varieties of Canadian apples. It was expressed when they named their streets, their schools, and their towns after the heroes of the British empire. But in places like Kitchener, BC; Wolseley, Saskatchewan; and Raglan, Ontario, few people would have stopped to wonder if a strong Canadian nationalism could co-exist with a passionate pride in the British Empire. Those who did would probably have concluded that the two were in no way contradictory, or even separate; one could glory in being Canadian without it being any less glorious to be part of the British Empire. But only politicians, newspaper editors, and the idle *literati* were inclined to consider such abstractions.

How many people in Canada paid attention to the disquieting news reports coming from Europe in 1914? "War was the last thing its people thought of," wrote John Castell Hopkins in 1919. "No preliminaries of international negotiation, or far-away verbal conflict, or military and naval preparations abroad had really brought the issue home to the minds and hearts of the masses."[25] The Europeans always seemed to be arguing about something, and most people could recall more than one war scare that came to nothing—why should the summer of 1914 be any different? The Austrian archduke Franz Ferdinand and his wife had been assassinated in Sarajevo at the end of June, but there was no reason to think it should lead to anything beyond a Balkan war, if that. There was certainly nothing to indicate that the great powers need be involved. In mid-July, the *Globe* assured readers that there was no cause for alarm: "The relations between Great Britain and Germany are most satisfactory, and so far from the two Germanic Nations going to war, all their immediate interests are bound up with the maintenance of peace." But a couple of weeks later, European relations deteriorated. The Austrian government, in response to the assassination, sent an ultimatum to Serbia that was carefully written to be unacceptable. With this, the net of alliances began to tighten. Germany would stand by Austro-Hungary, its only real ally, for better or for worse. Russia would defend Serbia in the event of an attack, and France was pledged to support Russia if it came to war. Britain was allied to France and Russia, and proposed a conference to avoid war, but peace did the Austrians no good; they looked to a short, sharp war to reinvigorate the Austro-Hungarian empire. Fearing that a conference might actually succeed, they abruptly declared war on Serbia and bombarded Belgrade. It had come to war . . . but would it spread?

In Canada, every day brought a new crop of rumours—German cruisers in the Pacific were steaming towards British Columbia to seize gold and coal stores in Vancouver, Victoria, and Prince Rupert; King George V had been assassinated; Austrian reservists in Canada, at least 150,000 of them, would soon be getting their call-up papers and leaving for the front in specially chartered steamers. Then, on 29 July, the British government advised Canada to move to the Precautionary Stage, which meant that a surprise attack was possible. Militia units on the coasts were called out, the Royal Canadian Garrison Artillery and the Royal Canadian Regiment were put on active duty at Esquimalt, Quebec City, and Halifax, and guards were posted at wireless stations and cable landings. But any other preparations could wait. It was a long weekend coming up— Monday was a civic holiday, and there were other things to worry about. In Saskatoon, baseball pitcher Sammy Beer was going for his thirteenth consecutive win in the Western Canada League. Perhaps there would be a break in the shocking case of an Ontario doctor wanted for questioning in the death of a young woman during a botched abortion. Albertans were in the midst of one of the earliest harvests in the province's history. Many Canadians headed for the beach, lake, cottage, or resort. Prime Minister Robert Borden would spend the weekend golfing in Muskoka. Any crisis would surely keep.

TWO

THE FIRST COLONIES

Historian A.J.P. Taylor referred to the First World War as war by timetable: the great powers had drawn up detailed and complicated mobilization plans to bring millions of soldiers to a war footing and then launch complex military operations against their enemies. But everything depended on keeping to a schedule, particularly for Germany: with enemies on both sides, its success in war depended on being able to defeat France quickly, then turn to the east, to knock out Russia before the Czar's armies could mobilize fully. The quick defeat of France was the object of the Schlieffen Plan, an offensive that would sweep through Belgium and northern France to envelope Paris. But Belgium was neutral, its borders guaranteed by Britain according to the Treaty of Utrecht of 1839. On the 3rd of August, German cavalry units crossed the frontier; the following day, Berlin declared war on neutral Belgium. Would Britain live up to its obligations to defend Belgium, and support France? People who were enjoying a holiday weekend remained blissfully unaware that the crisis was almost upon them.

The Colonial Office in London was a hive of activity on 4 August but by the evening it was all but deserted. After a weekend of almost continuous meetings, the British cabinet had drafted and dispatched an ultimatum to Germany: withdraw all invading troops from Belgian soil by midnight (Berlin time), or a state of war would exist between Britain and Germany. The ministers had departed, leaving the office in the hands of a few equally exhausted senior clerks, unshaven and bleary-eyed, who had instructions to wait for a German response to the ultimatum. The hours dragged by. Finally, a few minutes after 11 PM and with no reply from Germany, the clerks gathered up a handful of telegrams addressed to the dominions and colonies. Each was just ten words long: "See Preface

Defence Scheme, war has broken out with Germany." Leaving the calm of Downing Street, the clerks fought through the crowds in Whitehall and eventually battled their way to a post office in the Strand. They handed the telegrams to the woman at the counter, who merely flicked through the forms, paying no more attention than if they were birthday wishes.[1] With that simple act, news went out to His Majesty's representatives around the world that the British Empire was at war.

The telegram for Canada was addressed to the Governor General, Prince Arthur, the Duke of Connaught. He was the favourite son of Queen Victoria, appointed in 1911 but with a longer history in Canada. As a young officer in the Royal Engineers, he had spent a year with the Montreal garrison, and also served with Garnet Wolseley's expedition to the Red River in 1870. Beloved by Canadians in part because he and his family travelled widely across the country, Connaught was in Banff, Alberta, on the last weekend of July. With the deepening crisis, he decided to return to Ottawa but it would be three days of almost non-stop train travel before he arrived. Until he did, Rideau Hall was just as deserted as the Colonial Office. Francis Farquhar, an experienced soldier who was Connaught's military secretary, was also out of town, leaving the office in the hands of Arthur Sladen, who had been private secretary to every Governor General for nearly a quarter of a century. As a cool summer evening settled on Ottawa, he waited for instructions from London.

Elsewhere in the city, a sense of nervous anticipation grew, especially in official circles—at least amongst those who were in the capital. A few of the senior cabinet ministers had remained, but most of them were still on their summer holidays. On the last day of July, Prime Minister Robert Borden arrived in Ottawa, having cut short his Muskoka golfing holiday. Late on the evening of Monday, 3 August, Liberal leader Wilfrid Laurier arrived from his summer retreat at Arthabaska, Quebec. With Laurier out of town, responsibility for the Liberal Party had fallen to a young William Lyon Mackenzie King, former MP and secretary in the party's information office. He spent the day monitoring the situation in Europe and drafting a Liberal response, and a little after 7 PM learned from a contact that the ultimatum deadline had passed and that Britain and Germany were at war. Arthur Sladen at Rideau Hall reported that there had been no official notice yet, but a quick call to the *Ottawa*

Free Press confirmed the rumour. By the time King reached the Rideau Club to have dinner, crowds had gathered along Sparks Street and in front of the Parliament buildings. The band of the Governor General's Foot Guard marched along Wellington Street playing patriotic tunes against a backdrop of waving flags and banners. It was a real carnival atmosphere.[2]

That weekend was the beginning of a mass migration that would see as many as 400,000 Canadians journey to Britain to join the war effort, either as soldiers or to work behind the scenes. In a reversal of history, they became colonists of a sort, establishing outposts in Britain that became bastions of a Canadian empire in the Mother Country. Many were returning to the country of their birth; for others it was their first glimpse of a place that had existed only in books, school lessons, or the tales of relatives. It was a land, and a cause, that would awaken both their imperialism and their nationalism.

In most cities, the scene on that August weekend was the same as in Ottawa. Crowds gathered around newspaper and telegraph offices, where bulletins were printed and posted in the windows, projected on the sides of buildings using enormous lantern-slide machines, or read out by a staffer with a megaphone. The Red Ensign, the Union Jack, and the *Tricolore* were out in full force (not many towns could manage a Belgian flag), and striped bunting trailed from upper windows. Firecrackers danced and snapped on the pavements, and fire department pumper trucks shot jets of water high into the sky. *God Save the Queen* and *Rule Britannia* mingled with *O Canada* and *The Maple Leaf Forever* as voices competed with bands. For people living in Canada's cities, there was little sleep that night.

But Canada in 1914 was overwhelmingly rural. The vast majority of Canadians lived not in large cities, but in small towns and villages and on farms. In such places, there were no telegraph offices and the newspaper, if there was one, was only a weekly. There were few bands, and often scarcely enough people to make a crowd. In any case, farmers didn't have the luxury of being able to stand around waiting on news, especially in August when there were crops to get in. The war certainly came to rural Canada, but it came as country folk liked things to happen—slowly, deliberately, in their own time.

That Canada would accompany Britain to war was never in question. In strictly legal terms, Britain's declaration applied to the entire Empire, and earlier in the weekend the Canadian government had pledged its support. "The Canadian people will be united in a common resolve to put forth every effort," read a message to the British government on 1 August, "and to make every sacrifice necessary to ensure the integrity and maintenance of the honor of our Empire."[3] But for most Canadians the legal niceties were irrelevant—only a lunatic or a scoundrel would doubt that when Britain was at war, Canada was at war. That one phrase echoed and re-echoed through the Dominion. One expected to hear it from the English-Canadian establishment, but it was repeated by French-Canadian nationalists, immigrants, militant labourers, socialists—it would have been hard to find a dissenting opinion. "If it means war for Britain it also means war for Canada," wrote the *Globe*. "If it means war for Canada, it means also the union of all Canadians for the defence of Canada, for the maintenance of Empire integrity, and for the preservation in the world of Britain's ideas of Democratic Government. Before the world Canadians are not divided." *La Presse* agreed: "All Canadians understand today that when Great Britain is at war, our Dominion is likewise. . . . The manifestations of loyalty and devotion to the British Empire which have broken out all over our territory . . . show without a doubt that all Canadians, regardless of race, have but one heart and one soul in this hour of danger." Two newspapers, two languages, two solitudes, but they spoke with the same voice, the voice of imperial unity. Britain and Canada were not separate entities but a single body.

Just like in the Boer War, the parent/child relationship became a powerful symbol for the situation. Canada's poets bombarded the public with patriotic verse, carrying titles such as "We Are Coming, Mother Britain," "The Love of the Sons," and "The Call of the Motherland." Picture postcards, rapidly becoming the most popular means of communication, turned the Empire into a pride of lions, with the cubs coming from afar to join Britain the lioness in the fight against the Hun. Songwriters adapted the metaphor into jingles that sold by the thousands, no matter how painfully naive they may seem to modern ears: "Sons of a greater Empire, / Rally from farthest shore. / Ready aye for the battle, / Boys, fight

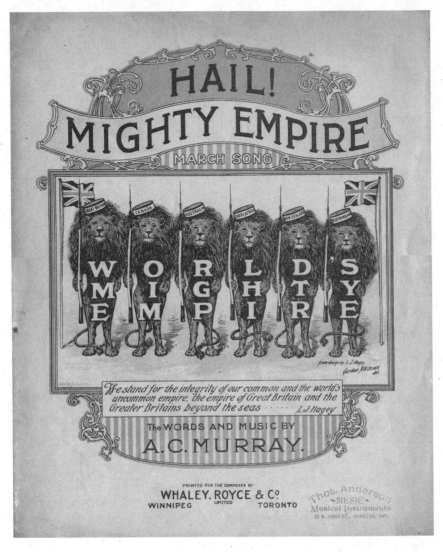

Lions were the most common animal to symbolize the imperial relationship—this sheet music is from 1913.

as your sires of yore . . . / Oh, list the war notes pealing, / Come gird you for the fight, / Whelps of the British Lion / Keep Britain's honor bright."[4]

It was not *if* Canada would join the fight, but *how*. Pledges of foodstuffs for Britain poured in from the provinces—100,000 bushels of potatoes from New Brunswick, four million pounds of cheese from Quebec, 100,000 bushels of oats from Prince Edward Island, 25,000 cases of canned salmon from British Columbia—and the able-bodied offered themselves for service. The Imperial South African Veterans of Canada told the government that it could enlist up to 4,000 men with at least two years' military experience. The 6th Regiment (Duke of Connaught's Own Rifles) of Vancouver—including Sam Perry, Canada's 1904 Bisley winner—volunteered en masse, while the little town of Strathmore, Alberta, offered 100 mounted riflemen. The city of Calgary and the provinces of Manitoba and New Brunswick also promised contingents of a thousand men each. Those who only *wished* they were able-bodied found other ways to serve, some of them by forming Home Guard units connected with clubs, companies, or community groups. As one historian put it drily, "the personnel, largely over military age, drilled enthusiastically after business hours, with no well defined purpose."[5]

The Home Guards had no official military standing, but thousands of other Canadians had already been called to duty. The Non-Permanent Active Militia had moved to a wartime footing with a speed that surprised those who had chuckled at the amateurish manoeuvres held before the war. The few militia units mobilized at the end of July were joined by the rest of Canada's peace-time, part-time army, and by the end of the first week of August there were guards at armouries, military storage facilities, harbours, dry-docks, bridges, grain elevators, locks and canals, hydro stations, waterworks, wireless stations, and railway terminals. And if there was no real threat to property, there were certainly plenty of imagined threats. Two men, feared to be German spies, were arrested while skulking around Camp Petawawa in eastern Ontario; rumour had it that they came by airplane, but a search of the woods turned up nothing. There were reports that a German cruiser had shelled the cable station at Canso, Nova Scotia, and that Austrian ships were about to carry out an attack on the wireless station at Glace Bay. A cache of dynamite was reportedly found under a grain elevator in Windsor, Ontario, and a few hours east, in Brantford, local police raided what the press described as a "foreigners' boarding-house . . . where a large numbers of Austrians and Hungarians have their headquarters," and confiscated guns and ammunition.

There was much more than simple anti-immigrant prejudice at work here. Most European armies used a system in which one's term as a

"Doing their bit: The BC salmon canning himself in order to release labour"

full-time soldier was followed by a term as a reservist, when one could be called for duty at any time, from anywhere in the world. Canada's pre-war immigration boom had brought in hundreds of thousands of European immigrants, including tens of thousands of military reservists. Just because they lived in Canada did not excuse them from fulfilling their obligations. The Austro-Hungarian army had been among the first to mobilize, and its reservists in Canada were called to duty as early as 26 July 1914. The order went out to Austro-Hungarian diplomatic officials in Montreal, Winnipeg, Saint John, and Sydney, who used local agents and ethnic labour bureaus to inform reservists of their obligation to return home and join the colours. Every day, Canadian newspapers carried reports of Austro-Hungarian reservists preparing to leave for the battle front, and other reservists too—French, Belgian, Russian, German, Swiss, and British. On 1 August 1914, reservists of the Royal Navy were summoned (British Army reservists were called on 10 August) and they left farm and factory to return to duty. As many as 15,000 British reservists went from Canada over the course of the war.

Even before the first week of war was ended, the first Canadian had died in uniform and the first Canadian homes were in mourning. Early on the morning of 6 August, the war not even two days old, the light cruiser HMS *Amphion* was steaming towards its base at Harwich. It had already been a good war for its flotilla; the day before, *Amphion* and two destroyers had tracked and sunk a German vessel laying mines in international waters off the north German coast. The cruiser was returning to England with some German survivors as prisoners, but as dawn broke over the North Sea a blast shook the *Amphion* as it struck a mine planted by its erstwhile opponent. She drifted helplessly back into the minefield, another explosion lit up the dawn sky, and within fifteen minutes she had disappeared beneath the North Sea. Over a hundred British seamen died, including Stanley Wilson of Toronto. A fifteen-year veteran of the Royal Navy, he was probably the first Canadian to die in the war.

As the *Amphion* settled beneath the waves, Canadians were learning what their military contribution would be. In 1913, Canada had developed a mobilization plan that made the most of its tiny army. The militia was supposed to be 60,000 strong, although there were only about 43,000 men on the books, and the Permanent Force hovered around 3,100 all ranks. According to the plan, eastern Canada would recruit volunteers for one infantry division while the west would provide men for one mounted brigade; each area of the country, and each militia unit within each area, had a quota to raise. No one expected there to be any difficulty finding the necessary volunteers, such was the enthusiasm sweeping the country. As Connaught informed the Colonial Office on 4 August,

> Great exhibition of genuine patriotism here. When inevitable fact transpires that considerable period of training will be necessary before Canadian troops will be fit for European war, this ardour is bound to be dampened somewhat. In order to minimize this, I would suggest that any proposal from you should be accompanied by the assurance that Canadian troops will go to the front as soon as they have reached a sufficient standard of training.[6]

On 6 August 1914, the British government gratefully accepted Canada's offer to send an expeditionary force; one division was requested, and the finely tuned mobilization apparatus should then have swung into motion. But for Sam Hughes, now the Minister of Militia and Defence, that plan was far too bureaucratic. He would not have appreciated A.J.P. Taylor's notion of war by timetable. Going to war should not be about schedules and quotas; it should be about zeal, ardour, and élan. He had in mind something very different, something that would stir the soul and quicken the blood— "a call to arms, like the fiery cross passing through the Highlands of Scotland or the mountains of Ireland in former days."[7] Sadly, a fiery cross was not really an option. The next best thing was night letter telegram to the commanding officers of 226 militia units, even though electrical pulses along a wire were a poor substitute for a blaze of light on the horizon.

Within a few hours, the mess that Hughes had created was evident. Militia commanders were well aware of the quotas set out in the pre-war mobilization plan, and naively assumed that they should begin recruiting according to the terms of that plan. Not until the telegrams reached them early in the morning on 7 August did they learn that everything had changed. The old quota numbers had disappeared; instead, they were told to make themselves ready to provide either a double company of 250 men or a single company of 110 men, to be formed into battalions at some future time and place. The order provoked consternation in armouries across Canada. Any decent city unit could raise a thousand men over a weekend, and most were already halfway there—were they really to be limited to 250? And there were orders that regiments from rural areas and small cities would be limited to 125 men—but there was no indication of what constituted a "small city."

There were second thoughts elsewhere, too. The British government had gratefully accepted four other Canadian offers of battalions, but most of those offers had been made without paying much attention to the cost—around $100,000 to equip and maintain an infantry battalion of a thousand men, nearly $2 million in current values. Calgary and Manitoba swallowed their pride and admitted bluntly that they couldn't afford it; New Brunswick took a different tack and claimed it had never even made an offer. But where two provinces and one of the Dominion's fastest growing cities had to admit defeat, Montreal millionaire Hamilton Gault was unfazed.

Gault had come by his fortune the old-fashioned way—he had inherited it. His father had owned cotton mills, among them the biggest in North America, and on his death had bequeathed to Hamilton the family's place at the top of Montreal society. The younger Gault was very good at the social side of things, but in business he was something of a disappointment. Soldiering, however, was very much to his taste. He had served with the 2nd Canadian Mounted Rifles during the Boer War and was a fixture in the Montreal militia; Gault saw August 1914 as a heaven-sent opportunity for a man who had never quite gotten the hang of the cotton industry. He assumed, like most people, that the war would be short and despaired that it might be over before Canadian militia officers got to the front. So, he decided to buy his way into action. He would establish and pay for his own unit, formed largely from British ex-soldiers in Canada, and offer it to the British government. To command it, he turned to Francis Farquhar, the Duke of Connaught's military secretary. Connaught's daughter consented to lend her name to the new unit, which became Princess Patricia's Canadian Light Infantry (PPCLI). In ten days, Farquhar had interviewed some 3,000 applicants and chosen 1,098. All but forty-nine of them claimed to have previous military experience, and more than 90 percent of them were British-born.

Across Canada, the crush was the same. Militia units bore the brunt of the enthusiasm for war, and turned away hundreds and sometimes thousands of eager volunteers who failed to meet the requirements. Most units had the same experience as the PPCLI: within a week or ten days, all of the spots had been filled and the lucky ones began leaving for war. In her poem "The Departure," Katherine Hale captured a scene that must have been repeated countless times in cities across the country:

> There was mirth and music, kisses, hopes and fears,
> Cigarettes and banners, chocolates, socks and tears . . .
> Every woman cheered you, some few women wept,
> Graybeards longed to join you, peaceful babies slept . . .
> Here's our love and greeting from the old home town;
> Here's to speedy meeting, and to your renown;
> Here's to every gallant heart in the khaki brown![8]

The men mugged for the cameras, as they might have done on leaving for summer camp. "For Britain from St Stephen NB," read a sign brandished by departing volunteers in southwestern New Brunswick.[9] They were on their way to what picture postcards would call Canada's Mobilization Camp.

In 1912, Hughes had ordered the purchase of a parcel of land at Valcartier, about twenty miles north of Quebec City, to use as a training ground for the province's militia units. It had many practical advantages—centrally located, good rail access, close to Quebec's port facilities—and some symbolic ones. Beside it ran the Jacques Cartier River, named for the founder of Quebec, and it lay amongst lots that had originally been granted to British soldiers demobilized after the fall of Quebec. But Valcartier Camp had been laid out to train 5,000 militiamen, not the 32,665 men who would be there by 8 September. What followed was every bit as impressive as the speed with which Canadian men offered themselves for service. The extra land was acquired, and on 10 August 1914 workers began clearing the site. Within twelve days they had built a camp: 2.5 miles of rifle ranges with 1,500 targets; twelve miles of water mains; fifteen miles of drains; railway sidings; 200 baths; buildings; electric light; telephones; and tents for over 30,000 men.

When the first volunteers arrived on 18 August, the labour gangs were still hard at it. The sweet smell of fresh-sawn pine hung in the air as the

Wearing civilian clothes or pieces of militia uniform, men from Montreal arrive at Valcartier in September 1914 to begin training.

clang of hammer strikes and the snorting of draft horses echoed over the parade ground. It was clean and new and exciting, and brought back memories of the field-trip-cum-summer-camp atmosphere of pre-war militia exercises. When artillery officer James Ross arrived at Valcartier from Toronto, it was nearly midnight with a steady drizzle falling, and the men still had a good two hours' work ahead of them to unload and feed the horses. By the time they finished, everyone was drenched to the skin but there was little complaining: "the men collected huge piles of bushes and built several gigantic bon-fires. Around these, their spirits revived and amid songs and merry jests, the clothing and accoutrements of most of us began to dry out."[10] A soldier from New Liskeard, Ontario, also recognized the milieu of pre-war militia camps, but with a few differences: "The men are a great deal better physically and in other ways than those who usually attend camp and more eager to learn and there is less grousing."[11]

It was difficult to get down to any comprehensive training—new drafts of men were arriving every day and administrative details like issuing kit and weapons, inoculations, and completing paperwork took precedence over rifle practice and parade ground drill. And then there was the frequent reorganization. Because of Hughes' call to arms, militia regiments sent men to Valcartier in groups from a few dozen to over a thousand. They had to be assembled into fighting formations, but that was more complicated than it sounded. New infantry arrivals were first divided into twelve battalions, some representing as many as seventeen different militia units, and then the contingent was reorganized into sixteen battalions, each of about 1,100 men. Some of them were provided by one militia regiment—the 8th Battalion, for example, was assembled almost entirely from Winnipeg's 90th Rifles—while others were polyglots. The 16th Battalion (Canadian Scottish) was drawn from militia units from across Canada that shared a common character as Highland regiments: the 50th Gordon Highlanders of Victoria, the 72nd Seaforth Highlanders of Vancouver, the 79th Cameron Highlanders of Winnipeg, and the 91st Argyll and Sutherland Highlanders of Hamilton. The twelve artillery batteries were formed from pre-war militia units, but volunteers from the eleven engineer units of the Non-Permanent Active Militia were cobbled together into three field companies. Other supporting units—signals, medical corps, service corps—were thrown together the same way. Such practical issues took time to resolve and not until the reorganization— not to mention the issue of clothing and equipment—was complete could the move overseas begin.

On 20 September 1914 there was a final review by the Duke and Duchess of Connaught, Princess Patricia, Prime Minister Robert Borden, and a host of dignitaries, with as many as 20,000 spectators in attendance. The parade of 25,000 soldiers, 2,000 horses, artillery pieces, field ambulances, and all of the engines of war took hours to pass the reviewing stand and moved one journalist to marvel that so many men were "prepared to have a post in the life and death grapple on the fields of Europe." They made a stirring sight, and although the writer commended them for their "general bearing and all-round smartness," he could not resist giving special mention to the kilted battalions "which made the blood of more than Scotsmen tingle." There was a huge open-air church service preached by Canon Frederick George Scott of Quebec City, who had preached the farewell service for the contingent that went to South Africa in 1899. Lest anyone doubt the devotion of the assembled soldiers,

The Seaforth Highlanders of Vancouver, about to be reviewed by the Duke of Connaught at Valcartier, 20 September 1914

the *Globe* hastened to point out that "not one man was compelled to go"—but they turned out all the same.

Over the next few days, the units marched to Quebec City to board the converted passenger liners that would take them to England. Like the departure of the first contingent for South Africa, it was a scene full of imperialism and nationalism, all jumbled together. William Howe of Toronto's 3rd Battalion gazed up "at the cliffs & fortress on the St. Lawrence where Wolfe fought . . . it is some Height," he wrote, tortuously and ungrammatically, "& it look as if it must of been some fight to get it."[12] For Reverend William Beattie of Cobourg, Ontario, the real historical import of the event lay in its truly imperial nature, which was revealed a few days later, when the convoy was joined by the *Florizel*, carrying the Newfoundland contingent, and two British battleships:

> One of the latter, The Princess Royal, which is of the very latest type, steamed in close yesterday and went up through our lines just to give us a chance to see her and to make us feel how well

GREAT EUROPEAN WAR, 1914—1st Canadian Expeditionary Force

Numbering 33,000 Officers and Men.
Assembled at Valcartier, Quebec, August, 1914
Embarked for England at Quebec, Sept. 26th, 1914.
Landed at Plymouth, October 16th, 1914.

SHIPS OF CONVOY.
H.M.S. "MAGNIFICENT."

.H.M.S. "ECLIPSE," G.R.H.U   H.M.S. "DIANA," G.R.D.H.   H M S. "CHARYBDIS,"
G.Q.R.M. (flagship)

1. Megantic	HPCF	12 Carribean	LVCN	22 Tunisian	RNLC
2. Ruthenia	RPQM	13 Athenia	VQRT	23 Arcadian	RJQT
3. Bermudian	HBPK	14 Royal Edward	HMDQ	24 Zealand	HJLD
4. Alaunia	JDKM	15 Franconia	HSDC	25 Corinthian	RQBH
5. Ivernia	RNJD	16 Canada	PLMX	26 Virginian	HCJG
6. Scandinavian	QDST	17 Monmouth	RTBF	27 Andania	JCPL
7. Sicilian	RKBG	18 Manitou	PWJL	28 Saxonia	RPNQ
8. Montreal	RSKQ	19 Tyrolia	RLVM	29 Grampian	HLKW
9. Lapland	LQSN	20 Scotian	HSKG	30 Lakonia	RGMC
10. Cassandra	HJBG	21 Laurentic	HNML	31 Montezuma	RHKW
11. Florizel	HNLT			32 Royal George	HLTW

H.M.S. "AARON."   H.M.S. "GLORY." G.R.P.T.

Rear Cruiser: H.M.S. "TALBOT," G.V.C.L.

Soon after the 1st Contingent arrived in Britain in 1914, enterprising printers began selling souvenir postcards to mark the voyage.

we are guarded. It was a thrilling moment when she came abeam of us and her band struck up "The Maple Leaf" and the thousand jolly tars gave three rousing cheers for the Canadian Contingent, while we responded with "Rule Britannia" and round after round of cheering.[13]

With 25,000 men packed into thirty steamers with all of their gear and horses for a twelve-day journey across the north Atlantic, there were bound to be problems. First there was the waiting as the convoy formed up off the Gaspé. The combination of excited young men, close quarters, and enforced inactivity is a bad one, and those who could get into trouble took full advantage of the opportunity. Once they reached the open ocean, seasickness was almost epidemic for the first few days, and men with strong stomachs had all the food they could eat. But by the end of the trip food stocks had dwindled and the men were making do on bread and cheese. Conditions in the storage holds were appalling and by common consent the men who cared for the horses were the real heroes. Only fifteen animals died en route, their carcasses hoisted out of the holds and dropped over the side.

Still, spirits were high on board the vessels and the atmosphere was much like it had been at Valcartier—like schoolboys going on a field trip. Without proper bathing facilities, the men splashed and played in huge canvas tanks set up on deck, or sprayed each other with hoses. There were drills and calisthenics, even more challenging on the rolling decks of steamers, and concerts and singalongs. And whenever the swells weren't too heavy, the officers organized sports. William Howe wrote proudly to his wife and children in Toronto that he had competed in his company's boxing tournament. Better yet, he had won the potato sack race, finished second in the wheelbarrow race, and reached the final in the egg and spoon race. For Howe, the war was starting well.

The convoy's port of destination kept changing, but at 7 AM on Wednesday, 14 October 1914, the *Alaunia*, a Cunard liner whose maiden voyage came at Christmas 1913, and the *Montreal*, a Canadian Pacific steamer launched in 1900, led the contingent into Plymouth Sound. The estuary was a showcase of British naval might, with everything from battleships to little torpedo boats that buzzed around the harbour, and the men could hear cheering crowds on shore. But they were not allowed to disembark. Inadequate port and rail facilities, and the fact that the steamers had been loaded haphazardly at Quebec, complicated things enormously, and units had to wait on board until arrangements were completed. "The strain told on the men," recalled Alfred Andrews, born in Qu'Appelle, Saskatchewan, and so in the minority in the predominantly British-born contingent. "There was trouble over meals and the men got into fights over little things. Everyone's nerves were on edge. Boat loads of sightseers passed us. They threw up fruit etc. We felt like the monkeys at the zoo."[14] Annoyed at having to stay on board with the city of Plymouth—and its pubs and young women—so tantalizingly close, they took matters into their own hands. As James Ross wrote,

> Several of the men including about seven from the 9th Battery lowered one of the ship's boats and went ashore just as the officers were finishing lunch. They landed and turned the boat adrift. We notified the police ashore and sent a piquet with Capt. Crerar to round them up again. This occurrence

was a distinct breach of discipline as orders were that no men were to go ashore. They have since been located and dealt with.[15]

With such breaches becoming frequent, commanders did what they could to accelerate the process, but some units still had to live on board for almost ten days before disembarking.

Their next destination was the Salisbury Plain. For millennia, the plain had been home to the peoples of ancient Britain. They came first in the Stone Age, leaving barrows, earthworks, and Stonehenge as their legacy on the landscape. The people of the Bronze Age farmed there, and Iron Age villagers left hill forts and tumuli dotting the landscape. The Romans laid out their long, straight roads across the plain, and then the Anglo-Saxons came to found the settlements that, more than a thousand years later, were still thriving. Now, after thousands of years of human occupation, the Salisbury Plain was about to become the first colony in the new Canadian empire in Britain. As Rudyard Kipling put it, "the camp is Canada on the scale of 1 to 240—an entire nation unrolled across a few square miles of turf and tents and huts."[16]

The War Office had acquired the site during the Boer War as a militia training ground, but its facilities were totally inadequate for the 30,000 Canadians who would soon be arriving. British militiamen and some New Zealand soldiers in England put up thousands of tents in encampments that would become so familiar to Canadians—Pond Farm, West Down North and South, Bustard, Larkhill, Bulford, Sling Plantation. As Canada's official historian described it, the Salisbury Plain was an idyllic place:

> The upland area of deep bottoms and rolling downs, rising to over six hundred feet, was bare but for scattered clumps of trees and a few lonely farms. . . . A thin turf cropped by grazing sheep grew in the few inches of poor soil overlying impervious chalk. In the narrow sheltered river valleys, embedded in the underlying green sand levels at three hundred feet, rambling thatched villages clustered among deciduous trees by the clear waters.[17]

Not many men from the 1st Contingent would remember the Salisbury Plain in language taken from a tourist brochure. It was lovely for the first few days, but on 21 October 1914 it started to rain. It rained the next day, and the day after that. Out of the next 123 days, it rained on 89, more than double the normal level of precipitation. The subsurface clay of the plain held the water, and soon the lush fields had been transformed into acres of gluey mud. "Last night was one of the wettest that I have ever seen," Eric Hearle, a British-born student who enlisted from Guelph, Ontario, wrote to his mother.

> Talk about monsoons and cloud bursts we sure get them, and as it has rained persistently since we got here you can imagine the condition of the plains, they were literally flooded and in the grey morning we could see nothing but water. Many of the tents had to be left as they got flooded out, by vigorous good torrents running through them. And imagine the clammy sensation of some of the peaceful sleeping tommies when the canvas broke through the pole at the top and covered them up, a struggling mass in the blankets who had to do some hard struggling to free themselves from the folds of the tent which seemed to draw together the more they struggled. Just after one of the worst downpours a fellow asked me to lend him a knife to cut a hole in the side of his tent to let the water out.[18]

Windstorms periodically blew over the upland, flattening tents large and small, and enormous bonfires were the only way to dry out the men's blankets. There were plans to replace the tents with huts, but the labour shortage was so severe that even with turning hundreds of Canadian soldiers back to their peacetime occupations as carpenters—a popular assignment, as it meant two shillings extra pay a day—there were still 11,000 men of the 1st Contingent living under canvas by Christmas 1914. The temperature at night sometimes dropped below the freezing mark, and even the huts provided little defence against it. "It was a very sharp frost that night," Jack Davey, a Somerset native who had emigrated to Canada just a couple of years before the war began, wrote to his beloved Kate, "& the floor of the huts are about 2 feet from the ground & its

Winter on the Salisbury Plain, 1914–15

hollow underneath so the wind blows in under & keeps it cold as we have to sleep right on the floor & that night they hadn't got enough coal to keep the fire going."[19] Meningitis struck the camp, killing twenty-eight men, and hospital admissions skyrocketed—although if VD cases are discounted, the rate of hospitalization dropped by 30 percent.

Fortunately, the men were not restricted to camp. At first, up to 20 percent of the contingent could be on a six-day leave pass at any time (each man was also given a free rail ticket to anywhere in the British Isles), but the numbers were soon reduced because of reports of drunk and disorderly behaviour amongst Canadian soldiers in London and elsewhere. Still, they had considerable freedom to travel. A reorganization of the contingent meant that dozens of junior officers lost their jobs, creating a pool of surplus officers who were effectively on indefinite leave. The combination of high rates of sickness and limited hospital space forced commanders to announce that men on sick leave who had family in Britain could recuperate at home. Any soldier who could afford it, no matter what his rank, was free to bring his wife and children from Canada to set up a home away from home. This was especially popular with recent immigrants, and the Canadian Patriotic Fund, a charity established to support soldiers' dependants, encouraged women to follow their husbands to Europe—after all, a needy family that moved to Britain was one fewer charge on the Fund's resources. And they came by the shipload—literally. One liner alone brought nearly a thousand in 1915, "to add," said the *Manchester Guardian*, "to the already large Canadian colony which the war has settled in our midst."[20] All of this meant that the men of the 1st Contingent had plenty of opportunity to mingle with British society.

The vast majority of the contingent was British-born, and for those who had come to Canada as adults with families of their own, this was very much a homecoming, and a triumphal one at that. In their impressions of those first few months in England, there is a vague sense of superiority, an underlying assumption that the best of Britain had emigrated to Canada, and were now coming back to help pull Mother Britain's chestnuts out of the fire. On one level they felt at home in Britain. After all, there were parents to visit, and perhaps brothers and sisters— the cost of trans-Atlantic travel being what it was, the war gave these men a chance to see relatives whom they probably wouldn't otherwise see again. Harold Sands, who had emigrated with his new wife to Kelowna, British Columbia, in 1912, went back to Britain with the 1st Contingent and spent his early leaves with his parents and aunts in Sussex (he often mused to his wife about bringing her and their children to live in Britain for the duration, but they remained in Kelowna), doing all the things he had done with them when he was a boy. For Eric Hearle, leave from the Salisbury Plain made possible an extended family reunion:

> Beat it down to Salisbury in a motor lorry going that way, caught the next train to Cornwall and surprised Granny early in the morning. . . . I saw the Love's, had a long talk with Mrs Boose, & went for a dandy drive with Mr Signors. Everybody seems very well and practically unchanged. . . . I had telegraphed Uncle Paul to meet me at the station, I stayed in the train, and reached Yelverton in the afternoon. Betty was at Looe with Aunt Bess but came back yesterday I've had dandy fine weather on leave & had a nice quiet time with nice walks and long evenings around the fire and believe me a fire, good grub & comfortable bed, are comforts not to be sneezed at. . . . I still had a swell time

at Exmouth. The solid enjoyment one gets in sitting in a cozy arm chair by a blazing fire in a really artistic well lighted room & read a book or drowsily listen to Mrs Love, Dorothy & Violet playing a trio or while away the time pleasantly playing cards is only to be appreciated by living in a mud hole. I was able to get around some on Friday & on Saturday we had a swell time. In the afternoon we went to Exmouth moving picture show & saw some dandy pictures then we beat it home for tea & caught the train to Eaton in time to see the Pantomime did I enjoy it—I should smile![21]

Harold Markham, who had left his home at Morecambe in Lancashire to settle in New Brunswick, spent time with his relatives but also visited a school near his father's hometown. He was the first soldier from the colonies to visit, and the fact that he had a local connection made him something of a celebrity. "The teacher took the opportunity to make an object lesson of me," he wrote, "on things Canadian and the fine part Canada is taking in the present Imperial and world crisis." Markham gave a little talk to each class, and one group of students treated him to a rousing chorus of *The Maple Leaf Forever*, which they had memorized for the occasion. To end the day on a high note, he escorted home three young women who taught at the school. "It is not entirely an unpleasant thing to be a soldier on active service," he noted. "The girls over here won't look at a man unless he is 'dressed to kill' in the present appropriate sense of that term."[22]

At the same time, the sense of comfortable familiarity was accompanied by a realization that they could not go back, nor did they want to. They had become Canadianized to the extent that Britain's flaws were now clear to them, just as Canada's advantages were. "Of course it's nice to be here & able to see my relations," Jack Davey wrote to Kate, "but Victoria is home to me now, I don't think I shall ever want to come to England again once I get in Victoria. The five months I have been away from there seems much longer than the three & half years I was away from England & it seems a much longer distance from this side too."[23] Harold Sands was just as emphatic, and the mud was only part of the reason for his sour mood:

I shall not stay in England. I have not got any interest at all
here now I don't think I could ever settle down here any more
it's allright to come & have a look at the old place once more
but I bet if you were here for a little while you would soon get
tired of it I know I am sick of it it's always raining every day
& everything's wet & muddy I think this is one of the most
godforesaken places in the world.[24]

Winnipeg bank clerk George Lewis, a native Channel Islander, agreed:
"believe me, I can say for myself, and I am sure the rest of the boys agree
with me, that Canada is by far the best place."[25]

Of course, nothing stoked national pride better than criticism, real
or implied. Even with all the adoring crowds and enthusiastic welcomes,
many soldiers sensed a vague feeling of disapproval directed at them, an
opinion that could be captured in a single word: colonials. The soldiers
themselves may have been convinced of Canada's superiority but some
Britons seemed to take an opposite view. It was not the best of Britain
who had emigrated to Canada; rather, it was the men who could not
quite make it in the old country. Manitoba novelist and poet Douglas
Durkin captured the type in his poem "Colonials":

> We filled your nights with terrible frights, we troubled your
>   days with fears,
> For the youngest sons are the cussedest ones in dignified
>   families;
> You took us aside in your wounded pride and covered our
>   heads with tears,
> Then gave us a tip on taking a trip—and bundled us overseas!
>   It was, "Poor young beggar, Colonial!"
>   And, "Oh, you worried us so!
>   You know we couldn't put up at 'ome
>   With stuff like you, so we let you roam."[26]

The move had not helped them any. They might have been toughened by
the frontier, but they had become uncivilized, uncouth, and even a little
bumptious. Certainly they were jolly keen, but there was no denying that

Harry Sands with his family, before he left for Valcartier in 1914

the British race had slipped a bit in Canada—their notorious discipline problems were proof of that. The first job was to bring them back up to British standards.

Few things annoyed a Canadian more than this suggestion. Perhaps they were being over-sensitive or defensive, but they eagerly grasped every opportunity to argue the superiority of the Canadian way over the British. "The Canadians are far ahead of Kitchener's men in marksmanship," wrote Howard Curtis, a Peterborough, Ontario, native who joined up in Edmonton in August 1914, to his sister. "No doubt we will make good when we get into the firing line"[27]—and they bristled at anyone who suggested otherwise. Jack Davey wrote to Kate about discontent amongst the men in his unit: "a lot of them were sore when they read in the papers that Kitchener said that the Canadians weren't fit for foreign service & that they weren't included in the first six armies that were to be sent to the front immediately."[28] So, while the return home allowed them to re-connect with their British roots, it had an equally powerful effect on their sense of nationalism.

Still, there was no denying that the men of the 1st Contingent were celebrities. "The first thing an Englishman asks when he sees a Canadian soldier is, 'Are you a REAL Canadian?'" wrote Kenneth Haig, who was working as an accountant in British Columbia when the war began, to his hometown newspaper back in Cobourg, Ontario. "Canada is certainly the most popular colony now in the Empire. Every English paper you pick up has announcement of something else Canada is donating to the Empire."[29] As the senior dominion and the largest empire contingent in Britain, Canada took pride of place in the kind of ceremonial events that had brightened militia life before the war. Ceremony was still the lifeblood of the imperial connection, and it was even more important when the very survival of the Empire hung in the balance. On 9 November 1914, a picked detachment of 350 men, led by Colonel Victor Williams, a Port Hope, Ontario, native who had served in the Boer War and commanded the Canadian contingent at the coronation of King George V in 1911, represented Canada at the Lord Mayor's Show in London and marched in the annual procession, the "big, bronzed men" of the CEF sharing the accolades with the New Zealanders in their slouch hats and the Newfoundlanders, "strong, well-set-up men of the

The Canadian in peace and war, as envisioned by an English artist—a play on the stereotypical Canadian character

open-air life."[30] Ten days later, a delegation of soldiers attended the burial of Field-Marshal Earl Roberts, VC, at St Paul's Cathedral, while over 400 officers and men attended the memorial service in Salisbury Cathedral, where the Royal Canadian Horse Artillery fired a nineteen-gun salute. At such events, it was often impossible to separate imperialism from nationalism. On 11 November 1914, a group of Canadian soldiers was specially selected to represent Canada at the ceremonial opening of the parliamentary session. This was a celebration of British democracy and its spread throughout the Empire, so it was only fitting that Canada's delegation be restricted to men who had been born in Canada.

Such events were impressive and it was certainly fun to enjoy a degree of celebrity status, but the men of the 1st Contingent had not enlisted for ceremonials. Every last one of them probably hoped to get to the front lines quickly, but Christmas 1914 passed and January 1915 dawned hard and sharp on the Salisbury Plain, and still they waited. At least the war wasn't over yet. Germany's opening master-stroke, the Schlieffen Plan, had failed. Instead of enveloping Paris and knocking France out of the war in a matter of weeks, the German armies had been stalled in a number of pitched battles with the French and the British Expeditionary Force (BEF). The advance had been stopped along the Marne River, and over the next few months both sides tried to regain the advantage by mounting a series of out-flanking attacks. This only succeeded in pushing the war towards Switzerland in one direction and the English Channel in the other. In one of the last such attacks, the Germans tried to drive the BEF out of Ypres, an ancient cloth city that anchored the last piece of Belgium still in Allied hands. Ypres was a jewel of Gothic architecture, its stately Cloth Hall looming over the market square as an homage to the source of the city's prosperity, St Martin's Cathedral symbolizing the piety and devotion of its people, its approaches guarded by medieval fortifications like the Menin Gate. A tactician might have advised the Allies to abandon Ypres and straighten their defensive lines, but such a retreat was unthinkable. As the 1914 campaigning season came to a close, Ypres remained stubbornly in Allied hands, a symbol of British resolve and Belgian resistance.

But the first months of the war had hit the Allies hard. French losses had been grievous, far heavier than they would be at almost any other time in the long struggle to come. The BEF, too, had been hit hard, the superbly trained force losing over 80,000 casualties. They would need to be replaced in the line before the campaigning season began in the spring of 1915, and preferably sooner than that. Britain's New Armies that began recruiting in December 1914 were far too raw to go to the front but the Canadian battalions—full of men with military experience—would do admirably. The British preferred them to join British units in the field as needed, but the Borden government was firm: the Canadian contingent would go into the lines as a division, not piecemeal. Beginning on 17 February 1915, the units of the 1st Division were temporarily attached to British formations in the front lines near Armentières; by 3 March, they had taken over their own section of the front, 6,400 yards of trenches near Fleurbaix. They took part in the war's next big bloodletting, providing covering fire for the BEF's failed attack on Neuve Chapelle and Aubers Ridge. The 1st Division took 100 casualties; British divisions lost nearly 13,000. A month later, the 1st Division was moved north, to take over from the French a section of the line defending Ypres, along the southern slope of the Stroombeek ridge. Through the Canadian sector, the main road ran northwest in the shape of an elongated Y. It began in Ypres and passed through the Menin Gate and the village of St Jean before dividing at Wieltje. To the left lay little Keerselaere and eventually Poelcapelle, behind German lines; to the right, over the shallow Gravenstafel Ridge, was the hamlet of Gravenstafel and Berlin Wood, which anchored the eastern end of the Canadian line. Southeast of Berlin Wood, the trenches were held by the British 29th Division. On the other side, past Keerselaere, the line was in the hands of the 45th Algerian Division.

No one was really sure if this was a quiet sector or not. There were casualties every day, mostly to enemy shelling, but such losses were part of life at the front—normal wastage, the army called it, without a hint of irony. There was certainly no indication that the 22nd of April would see anything unusual. The sudden outbreak of small arms fire to their northwest, beyond Keerselaere, that broke the relative quiet of late afternoon wasn't necessarily anything to be concerned about, but the ugly yellow-green cloud that stained the horizon over the French lines certainly was. In an instant, the rifle fire seemed to increase tenfold as enemy artillery shells began to slam into Ypres. Soon, men of the Algerian division were streaming south, panic-stricken and gasping for breath as chlorine gas tore at their lungs. The Senegalese division to their left had also retreated in disarray and German troops were pushing deep into Allied lines, nearly three miles in some places. The Algerian and Senegalese divisions had virtually ceased to exist and the Canadian contingent now found itself with its entire left flank, a distance perhaps twice as long as its frontage, exposed. Their commander would later write that it was one of the worst tactical positions he had ever seen, or even read about. The Germans seemed to hold all the cards. If they could exploit the initial success and drive to the south, they could cut off three entire divisions, maybe more, force the Allies to yield Ypres, and perhaps complete their conquest of Belgium. All that stood in their way was a newly arrived and almost completely untested Canadian division.

What followed was one of the most confused, and confusing, battles of the war. The three Canadian brigades, supported by nearby British battalions and the remnants of the French colonial divisions, fought desperately to hold their lines, rushing platoons and companies here or there to plug gaps. Canadian battalions were attacked, surrounded, and wiped out as German assaults slowly pushed towards Ypres. Keerselaere was lost, and then Gravenstafel, and then St Julien. But a mile or so south on the St Julien-Ypres road, the line finally held. The German advance, worn out by the fierce resistance of Canadian and British battalions, slowed and then ground to a halt. For the Germans, it had been a battle of missed opportunities; not for the last time, the chance for a major breakthrough went begging because of timidity and delays in exploiting success. For the Canadians, it was a brutal baptism. Faced with a dire tactical scenario like the one facing the 1st Division of 22 April, a more experienced formation might have recognized the impossibility of the situation and pulled back. Perhaps because they did not know any better, the Canadians stuck in and fought. When they gave ground, it was only when there was no one left who could hold a rifle or no more bullets left to fire.

They certainly saved the sector, but the men of the 1st Division suffered horrific casualties in the process. Some 18,000 strong when the battle began, the division lost about 6,000 men among the dead, wounded, and missing. "We have had some warm times but I am quite unharmed," James Ross wrote home in the midst of the battle, "but I am afraid there will be many sore hearts in Canada by the time this reaches you."[31] Eric Hearle came through unscathed, but Reverend Beattie was out of commission with a broken rib. Jack Davey was taken prisoner; he was eventually returned to England in a prisoner exchange, having had his leg amputated while in captivity. On 22 April, William Howe had written to his family in Toronto: "Dear Wife we hear all kinds of rummers hear but I must tell you this that those who gets through is going to be very lucky & I hope I shall be one of them but what is to be will but I do hope shall have the chance to see all my children once more."[32] Two days after writing the letter, Howe was dead. Eight months later, his eldest son John followed his father into the army, and in August 1917 he too was killed in action.

After Ypres, the Canadians were lionized as heroes of the first order. Any dismissals of them as soldiers in need of a good dose of British stiffening were forgotten. The word "colonial," which until recently had carried with it some implied criticism, was now a mark of distinction—they were now "hardy colonials" instead of merely "colonials." After the Second Battle of Ypres, British journalist Austin Harrison could refer to "that grand colonial type of manhood that we now recognize as the cream of the race."[33] The language of the Boer War was revived to distinguish Canadian soldiers from their British comrades. Now, life on the frontier was presumed to have given Canadians the very characteristics that made them superlative warriors—the ability to overcome obstacles, resourcefulness, enterprise, "an individuality not yet crushed by tradition," and what Lord Baden-Powell summed up as the skills of "scouts naturally engrained in them by force of the life they live in the woods and plains."[34] Douglas Durkin's poem "Colonials" ends with a recognition that things had changed:

> We've given you men and striven again—and Tommy knows
>   how we stood!
> 'Twas a blitherin' Hun that started the fun, but we'll make the
>   bounder pay—
> So here's to the Land of the Helpin' Hand—and here's to the
>   Lion's Brood!
>   And it's "Oh, you fightin' Colonial!"
>   And, "Blime, you've grown a lot!
>   We ain't got nothin' at all on you—

> But you're goin' to stay till the fightin's through,
> Ain't you, old top, eh, what!"

Now the Canadians were the backbone of the British army—they had saved the last corner of Belgium, and the entire war. "There is a notable and romantic sound in Canadian names," wrote *The Times*, "and never can the names of Ontario and Toronto have sounded with a more splendid roll in British ears" since they had stemmed the German onslaught at Ypres. Even the fact that the majority of men in the 1st Division were British-born was irrelevant: "whether born here or elsewhere, the men from the Dominion are essentially Canadian in temper and outlook, organized by Canada, inspired by Canada, and of the very warp and woof of Canada."[35]

For Canadians, Ypres became the focus of intense national pride. But even as others were beginning to recognize Canada's distinctiveness, that pride remained within the context of the Empire. At a Thanksgiving service held in London just after the battle, an officer of the 1st Division read a verse that captured the mix of Canadianness and Britishness, of nationalism and imperialism, that still held sway:

> Mother, perchance thou hadst a tender doubt,
> Not of our love, or strength, or will,
> But of our gift for battle and our skill
> To stay the foeman's desperate fury out.
> If so, against this doubt, let Ypres plead;
> We gained, yea, inch by inch, our little glory, too,
> Helping the store of pride we share with you,
> Proving us also of the Island breed.
> And, happy portent! what we then did forge
> For Empire's chain was done upon that day
> To our race sacred, when were wrought for aye
> Those golden links of Shakespeare and St. George.[36]

At home, although nationalist symbols started to appear more and more in popular culture, in the press, and in the schools, it was not at the expense of imperial symbols. On 21 October 1915, on Trafalgar Day, an empire-wide, one-day appeal was held for the British Red Cross Society. It was observed, among other places, at Toronto's Harbord Collegiate Institute:

> A patriotic programme had been prepared, and the meeting was opening with the singing of "Rule, Britannia" by the school, led by Mr. Young. It was moved and seconded that the minutes of the first meeting be taken as read; and after an opening address from the President, Mr. Davidson, stating the reason for our meeting on that day, and the meaning of the day we were celebrating, and welcoming the Junior Literary Society to our meeting, he called on Miss Pearl Russell of Form IVB for a recitation. She favoured us with an encore, and then Mr. Lavelle Norris of Form IVA rendered "The Death of Nelson" on the euphonium, and played the "Marsellaise" as an encore. Then came the "pièce de resistance" of the meeting—the Trafalgar Day Oration by Mr. Garfield Weston of Form IVB, who had been chosen as Trafalgar Day orator. The choice of his form and the staff was justified by the splendidly vivid portrayal he gave of the Battle of Trafalgar. He explained the day, and why we celebrate it, and his handling of the subject was masterful. Mr. Weston's speech was fittingly following by a piano duet by Miss Fraser and Miss Richardson—"We'll never let the old flag fall." They were enthusiastically encored and re-encored, and willingly replied to both. Miss Edna White of IIIA was the next artiste, and she also favoured us with a patriotic recitation, entitled "Go Silently England," and was encored. The last number of the program was a short address from our Principal on the Battle of Trafalgar, illustrated by very interesting views of Nelson and his flagship, the "Victory." The meeting was closed by the singing of the National Anthem.[37]

In the midst of a world war in which Canada was emerging as a nation in every sense of the word, it was still entirely appropriate for schoolchildren to celebrate the great victories of the imperial past.

Ypres left huge holes to be filled in the 1st Division, and elsewhere as well. Canada's first infantry battalion, Princess Patricia's Canadian Light Infantry, had also suffered grievously in the salient. Although it had sailed with the 1st Contingent, the Princess Pats were not part of it. The unit had gone to France to join a British division in December 1914, when Hamilton Gault became the first member of the CEF to face the enemy in the trenches. The PPCLI entered the Ypres salient in January 1915 and, although it escaped the worst of the gas attacks of April 1915, in May it grimly held on against German attacks on its trenches near Frezenberg. When it was stood down after the battle, the battalion had been carved down to barely a company. Its founder, Hamilton Gault, was on his way back to England with terrible shrapnel wounds. The commanding officer, the Duke of Connaught's military secretary Francis Farquhar, was dead, and nearly 700 Princess Pats had been killed, wounded, or were missing.

But more Canadians were already on their way to fill the gaps. On 6 October 1914 the Borden government had offered a second contingent of 20,000 men and recruiting got underway almost immediately. By the summer of 1915, the 2nd Division's three brigades of infantry, accompanied by artillery, cavalry, and all the lines of communication units, were on their way to France. It had already been decided that Canada's divisions should be brought together to create an army corps; as soon as the 2nd Division was ready to move to the front, the Canadian Corps would come into being. As part of that reorganization, the PPCLI and the Royal Canadian Regiment (which had spent a year on garrison duty in Bermuda) were brought back into the Canadian fold. On 13 September 1915, the former commander of the 1st Division, Edwin Alderson, opened the headquarters of the new Canadian Corps, nearly 38,000 men strong. At the same time, the CEF got a new home in Britain. The government in Ottawa had no desire to revisit the shambles of that first winter on the Salisbury Plain, and insisted that its troops be centralized in a more suitable training area. After 1915, the Canadian empire took root in a different part of Britain.

THREE

GROWING UP AT WAR

Anchoring the end of a crescent-shaped piece of coastline on the English Channel, the town of Folkestone has seen more than its share of invaders over the millennia. The Iron Age Brythonics were probably the first, followed by the Romans, the Angles, the Saxons, and the Jutes. In 1066 the Normans landed some thirty miles west of the town to launch their conquest of England. The Vikings sacked Folkestone, and in the late eighteenth century the French might have too, had Napoleon unleashed the army that he was mustering in France for the purpose. A tourist invasion began in the 1840s, when the South Eastern Railway bought the harbour and began running cheap excursions from London, bringing restaurants, cafés, and large seaside hotels in their wake. Beginning in 1915, another invader appeared at the gates: the Canadian Expeditionary Force. Folkestone and the surrounding countryside would become the largest Canadian colony in Britain during the First World War. Tens of thousands of Canadians would come to its training camps, making very familiar the place names that now only exist on an ordinance survey map: St Martin's Plain, Sandling, Westenhanger, Dibgate, Otterpool, Shorncliffe.

"The site was a few hundred acres in extent," wrote Calgary doctor Captain Harold McGill of the plain around Folkestone,

> almost perfectly level and devoid of trees, with a northern boundary where the field merged gradually with the Kentish uplands. The other three sides sloped abruptly down. On the south the plain was separated from the sea beach several hundreds of feet below by a steep slope that was almost a precipice. The Folkestone-Hythe road ran along between the

foot of the hill and the sea. On the east and west sides the plain
was marked off by deep narrow valleys, or ravines, as we would
call them in Canada. Across the valley to the east was another
small tableland similar to our campsite. . . . . A golf course
occupied the high ground across the valley to the west. Officers'
quarters were at the south end of Dibgate Plain overlooking
the sea of which we could view a wide expanse in fine weather.
Every night we could see the Dungeness lighthouse blinking out
its signal to ships in the English Channel, while in clear evenings
we could clearly discern the coast of France across the Straits of
Dover to the southeast, and even make out houses with the aid
of our field glasses.[1]

Soon, another major Canadian enclave sprang up to the west, in
Hampshire, around Bramshott, Witley, and Bordon. Not far from
Aldershot, since the 1850s the home of the British Army, these camps
were on the South Downs, a chalky upland not unlike the Salisbury
Plain. From the high spots on the Downs, on a clear day the men could
see Portsmouth, where the troopships gathered to take them to France.

With the creation of Canadian Corps and the move away from the
Salisbury Plain, the late summer of 1915 marked a turning point in the
nation's war effort. Thoughts of a quick victory had faded to a distant
memory, and the nation was reconciled to a long, bitter struggle. More
men would be needed, and more commitment from those who could
not enlist. After Ypres, the war became more of a national struggle; the
notion of fighting for Britain and the Empire persisted, but more and
more it had to share space with the idea that the war was being fought for
Canada. As Canada's High Commissioner in Britain Sir George Perley
told an audience in Stepney in east London, "I object when anyone says
that we have sent soldiers to help Britain. We have sent them to help
ourselves, and to see that the country handed down by our fathers shall be
preserved for those who followed."[2] The Canadian Expeditionary Force
itself was also changing. After the raising of the 1st and 2nd Contingents,
the majority of new volunteers were Canadian-born. From mid-1915 on,
most of the soldiers crossing the Atlantic for Europe would be visiting
England for the first time.

But in May 1915, the old sweats of the 1st Division were still carrying Canada's colours at the front. It seemed desperately unfair to send them into the line again, so soon after their initiation to gas warfare. The reinforcements were only just getting used to their new units, while the veterans of Ypres had barely had time for a rest. But there was little grumbling. They gathered their kit and marched south, across the border into France, past Armentières, where the division had been introduced to life on the Western Front just a few months earlier. They were about to get a taste of the pitfalls of alliance warfare. The British and French were determined to find a weak spot in German lines and punch through to gain a strategic advantage, often a piece of high ground that offered a good vantage point over the low-lying landscape. But they could not always agree on where the weak spot might be. Alliance warfare meant having to launch an offensive at a time and place not necessarily of your own choosing, to support an ally's campaign or to relieve pressure on an ally's lines. In the spring of 1915, the French had planned a major offensive in Artois to capture a feature called Vimy Ridge; this, they imagined, would give them control of the Douai Plain to the east, and the major German transportation networks that ran through it. To support the French by pinning down German reinforcements, the BEF agreed to launch a smaller attack, between Festubert and Neuve Chapelle, despite a severe shortage of artillery shells and the fact that many divisions were still rebuilding after the Ypres battle. The first attack, at Aubers Ridge on 9 May, went badly but the French continued to press for help and the BEF agreed to try again, on 15 May. This time, there were early and rather surprising signs of success. Advancing at night, British battalions pushed hard on German lines, which wavered and then gave way. It looked like the beginning of a rout, but in fact the Germans were only doing what they frequently did, to such good effect: giving up useless ground to retire to better defensive positions.

But the BEF command sensed a big breakthrough and sent in the Canadians to press the advantage. It was a disastrous decision, for the lack of proper preparation was shocking. There was insufficient artillery to provide covering fire, and what was available lacked the experience to lay down an effective barrage. Officers were unclear of their objectives and battle plans were kept secret from all but the most senior commanders. Maps had been misprinted, and the same symbol had been used to denote all physical features—but it hardly mattered because the landscape no longer bore the slightest resemblance to any map. One key objective, a German strongpoint known as K5, did not appear on any map and was invisible to the attacking Canadians in the trenches. But they attacked anyways—on five separate days they attacked, clambering across No Man's Land, a spider web of water-filled ditches and shell holes, towards objectives they could not locate in a landscape that gave them no way to maintain their direction. After sustaining 2,500 casualties and advancing a scant few hundred yards, the exhausted Canadians were relieved, having achieved little of substance. The strongpoint K5, which had cost so many lives, was now in the middle of No Man's Land, denied to both sides. But the French were still trying to make headway in Artois, so the BEF's supporting operations had to continue. The Canadians' next assignment, a few weeks later and a few miles farther south, near Givenchy, was depressingly similar. The key feature of the sector was the Duck's Bill, a forward position in Canadian lines, exposed to German fire on three sides and offering virtually no protection to the infantrymen as they prepared to attack. Three Canadian battalions hurled themselves forward, and all three were smashed, to no apparent end. By this time, the French had given up trying to capture Vimy Ridge, leaving the BEF free to stand down, rest, and reinforce.

After Givenchy, the Canadians went to a quiet sector and were out of major operations for nearly a year. During that time, battalions were brought back up to strength and the new units of the 2nd Division acclimatized to life at the front. They began to experiment with large-scale trench raids, the operation for which Canadians would become justly famous, and pioneered the technique of sending heavily armed parties across No Man's Land at night to collect information, take prisoners, and destroy emplacements. The trench raid seemed like the kind of free-for-all that would appeal to ill-trained and ill-disciplined colonials, and that was how the propaganda portrayed it. "The art of woodcraft, the inherited instinct of men whose fathers and grandfathers had been mighty hunters before the Lord," read one account, "gave the corps supremacy almost at once over their adversaries in these contests of small groups in the dark."[3] But the success of a trench raid had little to do with the arts of the forest, and everything to do with careful planning, tight coordination, and down-to-the-minute timing. It was also an excellent way to keep the enemy off balance during the generally quiet winter months.

That second winter of the war was a time for the Allies to evaluate their strategy. The only priority for the French was the Western Front, but opinion in the British government and military was divided between the Westerners, who agreed with the French and saw any diversion of resources to other places as a waste, and the Easterners, who believed that the quickest path to victory was to attack the enemy away from the Western Front. But their biggest and best hope, an offensive in the Dardanelles to knock Turkey out of the war, went disastrously wrong and by late 1915, the British government had conceded that the Western Front must be the main theatre of operations. Other parts of the world were stripped of troops for Flanders, with nine divisions being removed from Egypt alone. To take their place, the British government asked if Canada would provide twelve battalions of infantry for duty in Egypt, in addition to the 3rd Division that was then being organized for the Western Front. Anxious to keep Canadian units together, Ottawa suggested instead that it would complete the 3rd Division and then add a fourth to the Canadian Corps in Flanders. The British accepted, and the 3rd Division was assembled in December 1915, mostly of unallotted units already in England, along with eighteen reserve battalions to reinforce the Canadian Corps; the 4th Division was created in the spring of 1916. By that time, there were more than 50,000 Canadian troops in the field, holding a six-mile front in the Ypres salient, between Ploegsteert and Kemmel.

The 1916 campaigning season opened with limited German attacks against British lines near Ypres. In retaliation, the BEF determined to capture German positions at St Eloi, where the enemy held a slight bulge into Allied lines. But rather than go back to the standard bombard-and-advance tactics, the plan called for enormous mines to be detonated under German lines. They were large enough to obliterate the trenches and their defenders, allowing Allied soldiers to stroll forward unopposed and occupy the positions. At least that was the theory. It didn't quite work out that way. The mines did indeed demolish large sections of the front line, but they left a barren moonscape devoid of any identifying features except the craters, the largest of which was 55 metres across and 20 metres deep—you did not cross the battlefield so much as climb up and down it. One crater looked much like the next, and Canadian soldiers were often not entirely sure which of the seven large and seventeen smaller craters they were occupying. After two weeks of bitter, close-quarters fighting with bayonet and grenade, the torment ended with the four largest craters still in German hands. The cost for fourteen days of pointless bloodshed was nearly 1,400 Canadian casualties.

In the wake of St Eloi, the Canadian Corps was given a new commander. General Edwin Alderson, who had seen the Corps through its first battles but whose performance under fire had not inspired total confidence, was shifted to a largely meaningless job as inspector of Canadian forces in Britain. In his place came Julian Byng. To an upwardly mobile British general, the Canadian Corps was not a plum assignment—Byng is said to have wondered whom he had offended to get stuck with the command. After all, he had apparently done everything right so far, with a fine career in the Sudan and the Boer War, and a creditable performance commanding a cavalry division at the First Battle of Ypres in 1914. More recently he was responsible for virtually the only successful episode of the Dardanelles campaign—the withdrawal. Despite his protests, he was clearly the right man at the right time. Casual in dress and manner, he was a stern disciplinarian who believed in hard work, and was a tireless worker himself. Byng was deeply impressed by the fighting spirit the Canadian divisions had already shown, and was confident that he knew how to make them better—by improving discipline without flattening the spirit of innovation and improvisation that made them so good, by channelling unit rivalries into a more productive unit cohesiveness, and by purging the corps of officers who owed their commands to political influence rather than ability. When Byng arrived at Canadian headquarters in May 1916, it was immediately clear that the days of the genial Edwin Alderson were over.

But Byng had very little time to get started when another blow fell, this time on the newly created 3rd Division. Looking at the maps of the division's sector nearly a century later, one could be forgiven for imagining an idyllic landscape—Sanctuary Wood, Maple Copse, Observatory Ridge, Armagh Wood, Mount Sorrel. But Armagh Wood was an abattoir described by the 2nd Battalion historian as a "forbidding area of stinking shell-holes and fire-blasted tree stumps,"[4] and Mount Sorrel was a scarred lump of earth that glowered sullenly over the battlefield. Sanctuary Wood, the most easterly projection of the Ypres salient into German-held territory and the last piece of high ground in the salient in Allied hands, was anything but a sanctuary. It was terribly vulnerable, for if the Germans took it, they could overlook the entire salient and perhaps force a general Allied withdrawal. On 2 June 1916, what the 14th Battalion historian called a "tornado of high explosive" was unleashed on Canadian positions near Mount Sorrel, south of Sanctuary Wood.[5] In six hours of thunderous bombardment, the 4th Canadian Mounted Rifles lost nearly 90 percent of its men, while the PPCLI took 400 casualties. And as proof against the myth that all senior officers fought from a safe distance, the Princess Pats and the 5th CMR both lost their commanding officers—for the Patricias it was their second commander killed in action, while Colonel G.H. Baker of the CMR became the only Canadian Member of Parliament to be killed in action. General Victor Williams, commander of the 8th Brigade and Commandant of Valcartier when the 1st Contingent was there in 1914, was badly wounded and captured, and General Malcolm Mercer, a Toronto lawyer and art patron who had formed the 3rd Division and was taking it into action for the first time, was killed by German shellfire—despite the title of the later novel, generals did not always die in bed. For the next twelve days, the two sides waged one of those back-and-forth battles for which the Western Front has become notorious. There was no front line worth the name—"shell-holes and ditches, with here and there a short knee-deep excavation extending for only a few yards, constituted the 'front line,'" recalled the 2nd Battalion chronicler.[6] Finally the fighting petered out and the adversaries began to dig in, in roughly the same positions they had held before the battle started. The main difference was that another 8,000 Canadians had been added to the casualty rolls.

A month after Mount Sorrel, the massive British offensive on the Somme began, another product of alliance warfare. Haig did not particularly want to attack on the Somme—there was very little of tactical value to be gained there—but he grudgingly acceded to French requests. After all, gaining ground was only one objective of many. The main goal was relieving pressure on other sectors by drawing enemy reinforcements. Put in the most brutal terms, the plan was about killing Germans on the Somme so they couldn't kill Frenchmen elsewhere. But it went wrong from the start. After losing 60,000 men on the first day, 1 July 1916, Haig grew more determined than ever to make something of the offensive. And so the attacks ground on. The Somme has become shorthand for the futility and idiocy of the First World War—hundreds of thousands of lives thrown away over a few miles of artillery-shredded countryside. The Canadian Corps was in reserve for the first months of the campaign, so it was almost inevitable that it would be brought in at the end, to finish things up. The ANZACs had fought to exhaustion at the ruined hamlet of Pozières and in September 1916 Canadian divisions replaced them, to capture the village of Courcelette and then take the major German defensive position in the sector, Regina Trench. For two months, Canadian soldiers pushed northwest towards their eventual objective, paying dearly for every yard of trench ahead of them. All too often, under-strength battalions were asked to do jobs that would have challenged a full-strength unit. Sometimes they beat the odds and got the job done; when they failed, their officers held painstaking autopsies of the attacks to look for ways to do it right the next time. On 18 November 1916 soldiers from seven battalions of the 4th Division swept across No Man's Land to capture the last part of the inaptly named Desire Trench. The following day a drenching rain consumed the Somme, as if trying to cleanse the corrupted ground. Haig decided to shut down his once promising offensive which, like so many others, had yielded little but enormous casualty rolls. For the Canadian Corps, the cost topped 24,000. Among them were Harold Sands, who had written so often about wanting to bring his wife and children from Kelowna to Britain for the duration, and Howard Curtis, the Peterborough native who a few months earlier had written forcefully to his sister about the quality of Canadian soldiers.

The horrific losses of 1915 and 1916 shocked the country, and sharpened the issues. Now with four divisions in the field, the Canadian Corps' need for reinforcements was greater than ever. In January 1916 Prime Minister Borden pledged that Canada would put a half million men in uniform and the recruiting apparatus moved into high gear.

It continued to be about defending Britain and the Empire, but the new message was to keep faith with the fallen. Poets, songwriters, and graphic artists adopted a new image: the soldier himself calling for help. A jingle called "There's a Fight Going On, Are You In It?" claimed to bring "a message from the trenches from the lads in khaki true / Boys we're waiting here for you." Another song, entitled "The Call," carried a similar plea: "Some boyhood chum has fallen / And as he stricken lies / He appeals to you to take his place in the glorious enterprise." In one recruiting poster, a wounded soldier pointed directly at passersby. "You are needed to take my place" read the caption.

As the calls to volunteer became more strident, recruiters became more innovative. Many units trumpeted promises that recruits would start receiving pay and allowances as soon as they signed their attestation forms. In cities, they used streetcars as mobile recruiting stations—if men were too busy to come to the army, the army would come to the men—and decorated the trolleys with bracing slogans: "Join in the March of the Empire's Victorious Troops," "Join with Britain's Best—Don't LAG Behind," "We Go Overseas Quickly," "Free Trip to Europe." The public recruiting meeting, long a staple of the voluntary system, was now widely regarded as useless, for the able-bodied male rarely turned up to be publicly harangued. Major J.M. Bell was very successful in raising men for the 73rd Battalion near his hometown of Almonte, Ontario, but beyond his old stomping grounds, his oratory was less successful. One impassioned speech drew only a single volunteer from the crowd, a man whom locals knew as the village idiot.

When voluntarism slowed, local committees turned increasingly to shaming young men into volunteering. Although militia officials had long condemned the practice as unproductive, citizens and local recruiters continued to use it with a vengeance. A leaflet distributed by the 123rd Battalion in Toronto asked men if they were happy to be in civilian clothes while other men were in uniform. "Do you realize that you have to live with yourself for the rest of your life?" it inquired pointedly. Other recruiters asked women to "make your son, your husband, your lover, your brother, join now . . . get the apologist, the weakling, the mother's pet into service." Women who refused to send their men to war, predicted one advertisement, would have to shoulder part of the blame afterwards.

A mobile recruiting station, used by the 176th Battalion in St Catharines, Ontario

More and more, poets directed their pens at men who had declined to answer the call. Horrific images began to appear in recruiting posters, which increasingly emphasized the duty of Canadian men to avenge the atrocities committed in the occupied areas. The good-natured chiding of earlier recruiting songs gave way to alarmist songs like "Arm Canadians! March to Glory!" which painted nightmarish pictures of atrocities in order to shame men into doing their duty: "Wailing babies and weeping mothers / Tortured by the fiendish Hun, / Call to you and me—my brothers: / Can we our duty shun?"

Schools had long championed the virtues of patriotism and civic duty, using pageants to teach imperialism and nationalism. Other plays let schoolboys mimic battles or invited schoolgirls to practice thrift by planting gardens while wearing banners that read "Lettuce Beat the Kaiser," "We Will Squash Him Flat," or "We'll Turnip and Plant Him."[7] Nova Scotia schoolgirl Violet Black carefully recorded in a notebook the songs she sang in school during the war, including "Soldiers of Canada" ("Wars cruel fangs had reached the Motherland / Canadian boys must help repay"), "When We Meet the Kaiser," "Good Luck to the Boys of the Allies," and "Britain Calls" ("Future years will tell our story / How the empire stood / Firm, united, crowned with glory / Purchased with our blood").[8] But with the need for men becoming desperate, schools also became de facto recruiting offices. The Nova Scotia Council of

Public Instruction agreed to proclaim 25 February 1916 as Nova Scotia Schools Recruiting Day, to "bring the need of recruiting to the attention of everyone in the homes of all the people." For the day, schoolchildren were instructed to use "their influence in this very urgent and important work for the empire and civilization." They were to take home to their fathers, brothers, and cousins a letter pleading for volunteers—"Perhaps you may touch the heart of some grown-up boy in your village and be the cause of his joining the Nova Scotia Highlanders," pupils were told. Teachers were permitted to observe the day any way they saw fit, so long as they distributed the letter to pupils from all families having men between the ages of eighteen and forty-five.[9] At Harbord Collegiate Institute in Toronto, Principal E.W. Hagarty had more personal reasons for becoming a recruiting sergeant. Long a leading light in the city's high school cadet movement and the founder and first commanding officer of the 201st Battalion, Hagarty was mourning the loss of his son Daniel, who was killed in action with the PPCLI at Mount Sorrel. Thrown out of a job when the 201st failed to reach full strength and suffering as a grieving parent, he turned his energies towards his students. Whenever there was important war news, he assembled the student body in the auditorium for a lecture on the situation, and he was known to stop senior boys in the halls and ask them why they were not yet in uniform.

With so much more to play for and so much energy going into recruiting, the response was dramatic. In August 1914, nearly 22,000 men had enlisted in Canada but the numbers had dropped to barely a third of that by April 1915. Then they started to climb again until December 1915, when they topped 23,000. For the next four months, the response was even better, peaking at almost 35,000 men in March 1916. Lines at recruitment offices, so common in August 1914, were again a fixture in Canadian cities.

But it was a different kind of man coming forward. Now, and for the rest of the war, the majority of volunteers were Canadian-born, men with a slightly different relationship to the Mother Country. They were raised and educated in an environment that valued the British connection and everything that went along with it. Although they had never been there, Britain was not a strange land to them; they knew of its people, places, and history from school books, local rituals, and family stories.

"In years that are long since passed when first I read about the Strand, Piccadilly, Leicester Square, etc.," wrote a Prince Edward Islander upon arriving in Britain in 1915, "I little thought that I would travel through them."[10] This made for a comforting sense of familiarity. "We gazed at it all as in a dream, yet we felt no sense of strangeness," wrote Donald Macpherson, a Toronto schoolteacher. "It seemed quite a familiar country and not a land that we had never seen before."[11] But their familiarity was only second-hand. When they came to Britain as part of the CEF, they came as tourists.

Many of them would make trips to ancestral homes, to meet distant relatives and see places they had only heard of. When Muriel McGregor came to Britain as a nursing sister in 1916, she looked forward to seeing the Highlands of Scotland, the birthplace of her mother, a proud Scotswoman whose home in Waterdown, Ontario, was called Clunes, after the town where she was born. When Muriel finally got the chance to travel north in November 1917, her trip became a kind of family reunion, beginning with a visit to an elderly minister who knew her mother as a child:

> . . . went out to see Rev. Allan Cameron, he was in bed, his wife who is a charming little woman, entertained us for awhile, then when she heard we were going out on the afternoon boat, she insisted on going and waking the old man, who came down. They wanted us to wait until Monday, so we could meet their family . . . we went back to the hotel, where John McIntyre [another family friend] was waiting for us, he took us out to tea and then came down the boat with us to Fort Augustus, where we had to stay over Sunday as John's guests . . . [John] decided to come the rest of the way with us, we were very glad to have him with us as he pointed out all the places of interest all noted battlefields, noted roads, etc. Showed us a road built by great great grandfather . . . then we changed at Spean Bridge where we met Rev. Mr Walker McIntyre, he remembered you and dad calling to see him, remembered Uncle Archie . . . then we hired a car from Ft William called on Camerons, took Miss Cameron to Clunes with us. . . .[12]

For most Canadian soldiers, leave meant sightseeing and experiencing things that were entirely new to them. Nova Scotian Percy McClare had never been to a museum until he got to Folkestone. "It was quite a place and had a lot of things," he wrote home to Mount Uniacke. "I was never in one in my life, and I enjoyed it. It was worth looking at."[13] A typical leave became something like a modern package tour, the days filled with rushing from one landmark to another. Austin Tudor, a young clerk from Hamilton, Ontario, described one such leave in a letter home:

Dear Mother,

Just a few lines to let you know that I have just come back to camp from a leave to London, and it sure is some place and I enjoyed my stay there very much.

I was staying at the Union Jack Club. It is a fine place, good beds and plenty to eat. It was at this club that I met sailors and soldiers from all parts of the world. New Zealanders, Australians, South Africans, American, English and Canadians, and they are very fine fellows. . . .

I was down Piccadilly and Leicester Square. The traffic on these streets is very heavy and all the street cars are double deckers and run on underground electric wires. . . . And then they have what they call the Tube, it is an underground railway. It is run by electricity and I think it is the quickest way to get around London, as the cars can travel about 35 miles an hour. And then the motor busses they are double deckers also, and if a person wants to go sight-seeing, I think they are the best.

I went up to Madame Tussaud's Wax Works and believe me, I never thought that they could ever make such life-like figures with wax, but it is wonderful what they can do, and if a person ever goes into the "Chamber of Horrors" they never will forget it. I know I never will. I also saw Buckingham Palace, Parliament Buildings, Crystal Palace, Westminster Abbey, St. Paul's Cathedral, and they sure are old buildings, but the

PLATE 1. The imperial family, from a postcard of the Boer War era.

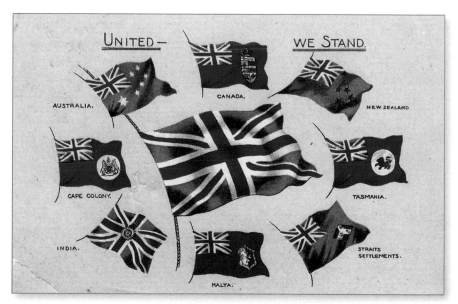

PLATE 2. At the end of the nineteenth century, the Union Jack flew at every corner of the globe.

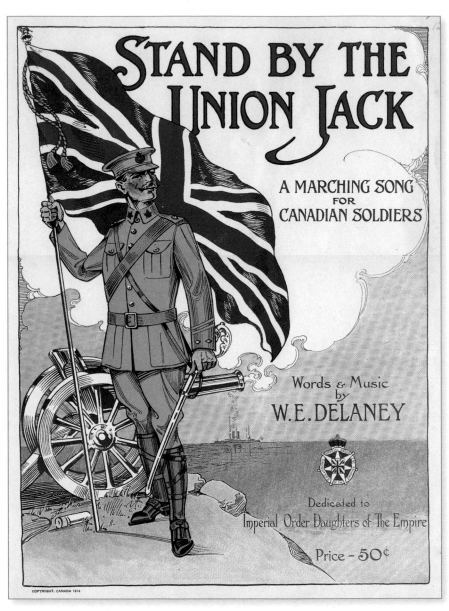

PLATE 3. Canada prepares to come to the aid of the British Empire, 1914.

PLATES 4–5. The bonds of Empire, brought to life by a graphic artist.

PLATE 6. John McCrae's poem "In Flanders Fields" became a powerful weapon in mobilizing support for the war.

PLATE 7. "Be yours the torch to hold it high"—one could also carry the torch by purchasing Victory Bonds.

PLATE 8. The immense ocean liner affirmed that the ultimate beneficiary of Canadian Victory Bond contributions was Britain, an ocean away.

PLATE 9. The mixing of national and imperial symbols—loyalty to King and Country, 1915.

PLATE 10. First World War Britain needed Canada's agricultural products as much as it needed her young men and women in uniform.

PLATE 11. For recruiting purposes, the Irish Rangers of Canada took advantage of the tendency to conflate the notions of fighting for Mother Britain and fighting for one's own mother.

PLATE 12. The bonds of Empire, brought to life by a graphic artist.

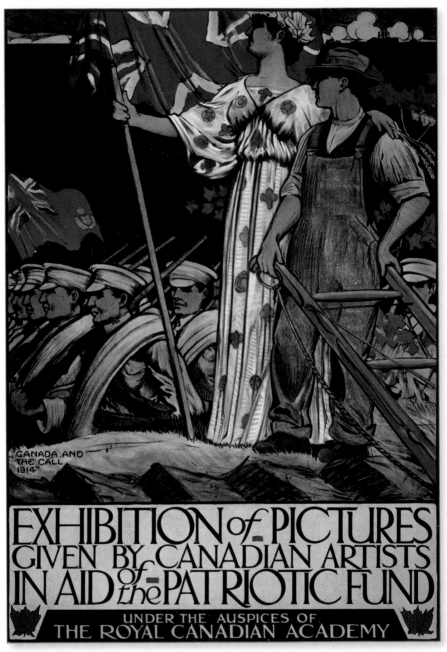

PLATE 13. The merging of civilian and military might in support of the Empire's war effort.

stone work on them is magnificent and then I saw the Horse Guards of Whitehall, which I think is grand . . .[14]

Perhaps because they knew only Canada, these soldiers were much more likely than men of the 1st Contingent to draw comparisons between their

Sergeant Thomas Ronaldson of the 8th Battalion seeing the sites—Stonehenge, 1915

homeland and the Mother Country. Men who had been farmers before
the war cast a discerning eye over British agriculture. Percy McClare was
impressed that the farmers in Britain enjoyed much better housing, their
brick or stone farmhouses being far superior to the clapboard variety that
prevailed in rural Canada.[15] John McKendrick Hughes, a New Brunswick–
born farmer in Alberta who found himself a surplus officer in Britain,
pronounced British grass much greener and more lush than Canadian,
and Angus Martin, who had worked as a compositor in Toronto before
enlisting, appreciated the hedgerows as "works of art . . . far more
picturesque than the Page wire fences separating Canadian fields."[16]
Harry Rumney of Simcoe County, Ontario, recorded a veritable laundry
list of contrasts. British farms produced better sheep than Canadian, but
inferior cattle. Canadians grew better hay and harvested their crops more
efficiently, but the British farmer was better at using his land, allowing no
acreage to go to waste. More than one soldier remarked that the country
lanes were far better built and maintained than roads in Canada.[17] And,
not inconsequential to a farmer, Canada had smaller weeds.

British cities revealed different contrasts. Percy McClare was horrified
by what he imagined were the loose morals of Londoners. "The
Strand . . . is, in my eyes, one of the worst places in the city," he wrote
home, but it was the women of the city that most distressed him. "They
will come up to you, that is, after nine oclock, and they will take you by
the arm and want you to go home with you [sic] and stay all night with
them."[18] Queen's University undergraduate and gunner Robert Brown
found the Thames "a very disappointing river being at this place very
muddy and little wider than the Rideau Canal," and told his mother
that "I don't like the appearance of the cities nearly as much as ours.
The houses are of brick and at some of the places I could see rows and
rows of long tenement houses all alike and crowded close together."[19]
William Calder, a British Columbia artilleryman, also found Britain too
urban: "over here you cannot go 100 yds without passing a house why
the whole damn country is a Town."[20] Another soldier joked that the
streets were so narrow that people had to flip a coin to see who would
get to pass first.[21] Garfield Weston, who left Harbord Collegiate in part
because of Principal Hagarty's badgering, only to enlist of his own accord
a year later, had his eye firmly on post-war business opportunities for

the family bakery business. He spent some of his leave time inspecting British factories, particularly ones that specialized in baked goods, to understand their shortcomings, but also to collect ideas for the Westons' Toronto operation.[22] Arriving in England in 1915, Helen Fowlds, a nurse from Peterborough, longed for the efficient Canadian system of handling passengers' luggage: "we hunted expert baggage smashers and paid six pence to see our trunks shamefully banged around," she wrote to her mother. And she was disheartened by the English cities she saw: "dirty and smoky and composed of rows and rows of little houses. No

Garfield Weston, taken shortly after his enlistment in March 1917

wonder the lower class English people lack personality—their existence is so ordered—and so 'much of a muchness.'"[23]

But it was the trains that most surprised the Canadians. At first they chuckled at their size—they were over-sized wheelbarrows, watch-chain charms, vest-pocket editions of real trains, or cigar boxes on wheels. Their engine whistles sounded "feeble and futile," and the men marvelled that they could actually pull carriages. The teasing stopped once the trains got going. The road beds made for a smoother ride than anything they were used to, the third-class carriages were as comfortable as most first-class carriages in Canada, and the speed—"they have some dinky little engines here," wrote a soldier from Wallaceburg, Ontario, "but they go like h–l."[24] So while things were different in Britain, they were not necessarily inferior to the Canadian way. John Hughes recorded his men watching labourers carry bags of wheat from a ship and laughed because such an old-fashioned way of unloading had long since been replaced by mechanization in Canada. The big, strong Canadian soldiers immediately decided that they should help the older, smaller men with the unloading only to discover that they were no match for the wiry British stevedores.[25]

For the most part, the hospitality of the British people knew no bounds. One Canadian chaplain had been in Britain for only a few weeks in 1914 when he received this letter:

Dear Major Piper,

I want three soldiers for Christmas—for three days in fact. Good bath, grate fire in bedroom, smoking-room with cigarettes found—every expense paid for sightseeing. I am sure many Canadians have no friends in England. Be sure and send [at least] two. Will forward money when I hear from you. Will be greatly disappointed if you don't send anyone. I know that you are a total abstainer, and I would prefer total abstainers if possible.[26]

Such invitations were quite common and before too long there was an office in London to coordinate them; potential hosts could register

Canadian soldiers enjoying themselves at the Duke of Portland's estate, one of many British mansions that gave hospitality to the visitors

their location, accommodation, and preferred dates, and would be matched with a Canadian soldier who was looking for somewhere to spend his leave. Although their general impressions of the British were overwhelmingly favourable, one frequent and consistent complaint was that they sometimes felt taken advantage of. Word quickly got out that the Canadian soldier was better paid than his British counterpart, and unscrupulous merchants took this as licence to overcharge. "The people around the camp seemed to think that the Canadians are millionaires," wrote Bert Cooke, a Toronto delicatessen owner who had been in Canada only a year when the war broke out, after being charged the astronomical sum of two shillings and sixpence for a meal. "I got over the shock only to be gypped again."[27] There were stories of prices being doubled or trebled whenever Canadians were near, to the point where many soldiers asked for supplies to be bought in Canada and mailed over, rather than purchasing them locally. "If you happen to run across a couple of good warm combination suits of underwear I would also appreciate them," Garfield Weston wrote home. "I could get them here but in these small towns they soak us Canadians about three times their actual value."[28]

Reports of gouging spread as the number of Canadians in Britain grew. Once it was clear the war would be long, Canada's colonization of Britain became even more extensive. By the end of 1916, there were some 160,000 Canadian soldiers in Britain. The majority of them were there to be trained for the front, but tens of thousands of soldiers were in Britain for the duration, as headquarters staff, forestry or railway troops, ordnance stores men, or with the pay, veterinary, or service corps. And then there were the civilians. Travel between Britain and North America was never restricted, as it would be during the Second World War, and throughout the war railways and steamship companies continued to advertise aggressively, offering one-way fares or package tours to trans-Atlantic passengers in all price ranges. Aside from holiday-makers, there was a constant stream of people embarking on fact-finding missions—clergymen, journalists, trade unionists, academics, politicians, civil servants—and businessmen kept up a steady migration across the Atlantic to monitor their financial interests, just as they had done before the war. But it was the ongoing movement of women that was most remarkable. In May 1916, there were in Britain some 3,000 Canadian wives alone, and thousands more would follow that summer, to the dismay of the authorities: "too many Canadian women have been coming to England, in an irresponsible way, merely to be near relatives whom they might not see once in a year. Some of them lived extravagantly and aroused surprise or comment, while some were stranded or in difficulties." By early 1917, the number had swelled to over 30,000. Some were following relatives but many were little more than tourists "who had drifted to England, in one of the curious contrasts of wartime, for social reasons, for pleasure, for curiosity or similar motives."[29] They came in such numbers that a special club was opened for them in London. The more Canadians came to Britain, the more parts of Britain became Canadianized. In 1914, Canada's empire in Britain was largely confined to the Salisbury Plain; from 1915, there were outposts all over the British Isles.

This was not new, for there had long been Canadian offices and clubs in Britain. As early as the 1760s, the New York Coffee House in London had been a meeting place for businessmen with interests in the Canada trade, and in 1810 the Canadian Club was founded "for persons who had resided for some time in Canada." By 1909 trade offices and commercial agents were open in Birmingham, Manchester, Leeds, Hull, Bristol, Glasgow, Belfast, and London, in addition to the office of the High Commissioner, Canada's diplomatic representative in Britain. Many provinces had an agent-general's office in London, to act as a trade commission and immigration bureau. The major banks—the Royal Bank, the Bank of Montreal, and the Canadian Bank of Commerce—established branches in London before the war, as did the railways and other corporations, and there were countless immigration agents and travel bureaus serving the Canadian market. Such offices became even busier during the war. Canadians could cash cheques or pick up mail at one of the banks, which usually kept a supply of Canadian newspapers on hand as well. There was strong demand for steamship passage across the Atlantic, and railway offices and travel agents were kept busy booking passage for soldiers on leave or civilians who could afford the trip. The federal and provincial governments were still very interested in encouraging immigration, and kept their agents busy looking for people who might want to make a new life in Canada after the war.

The Grand Trunk Railway was one of the many companies that opened the doors of their London offices to members of the CEF.

But the average soldier was not about to spend his precious leave time in a bank branch or an immigration office. As the British-born were out-numbered by men with no close relatives in Britain, pressure grew to keep them out of trouble while on leave. There was a nightmare scenario that must have kept the philanthropic awake at night. A young Canadian soldier, fresh-faced and clean-limbed, arrives in London from his unit in France for some leave. Because he was born on the wide prairie (or maybe it was the deep forest), he has no near relatives in Britain who can keep an eye on him, give him a bed and meals, and see that he gets the right kind of entertainment. He has money in his pocket and wants to enjoy himself, but has no clear idea of what to do; unschooled in the ways of the big city, he has been assured that it is easy to get a meal and a room. But on his first day he falls into the clutches of the unscrupu-lous —perhaps a prostitute or a fellow full of vague promises to act as his personal tour guide. Naive and trusting, he falls in with any suggestions and disappears into the crowd with his new friend. A few days later he re-emerges, his money gone and now a drunk or a syphilitic, or both.

Imagine the same scenario after a number of expatriates in Britain had established the Overseas Forces Reception Committee. Our soldier arrives from the front well after midnight, the mud of Flanders still clinging to his uniform. It is long past the time when decent people would be found at a railway station, and he certainly would never consider entering the lobby of a respectable hotel looking as he does. Then he spots the committee's sign, and beside it stands a kindly old gentle-man—his own father's age, perhaps—who beckons him over. A couple of other Canadian soldiers are already with him, and soon the gentleman has their kitbags safely stored in a special facility so they needn't haul them around London. He hails a cab and in no time at all, the soldiers are safely on their way to a special hostel run just for them.

One of the more popular destinations was 11 Charles Street, the Maple Leaf Club, a London mansion that had been donated by Hon. Mrs Ronald Greville, a society matron of the wealthy McEwan brewing family. For three shillings a day a soldier got room and board, a bath, fresh underwear, and a dressing gown and slippers. There was a billiard table and a library stocked with Canadian newspapers and magazines, a tea canteen that never closed, and concerts and other recreations. There

Peel House in London, a welcome stop for Dominion soldiers far from home

was such a heavy demand for accommodation for Canadian soldiers on leave that a second Maple Leaf Club was opened, at 5 Connaught Place near Marble Arch, and then another, in a home in Grosvenor Gardens, that was supported by the IODE, the provinces of British Columbia and Ontario, and the Canadian War Contingent Association. By war's end, an umbrella organization called the Victoria League (which took care of soldiers from all parts of the British Empire and oversaw most of these facilities) had fourteen houses and two huts that provided over 560,000 nights' worth of accommodation and served over a million meals. With that, journalist Gertrude Arnold could tell a very different story from the tale of a naive Canadian soldier who fell prey to the vices of the city:

> Travelling up from Bramshott a week or two ago, four of our youngest soldiers were in a compartment, on their way to London to enjoy the first holiday for three months. It happened that none of them had ever been there before, and as we were drawing in to the great dark city, which seemed buried in shadows, their excitement subsided a little, and they became rather quiet. Night, in these Zeppelin days, is not an exhilarating time to arrive in London. We had chatted about Brockville, and

Sherbrooke, and Charlottetown, their various home towns, and I asked them where they meant to stay in London. "Don't know." "Why not try the Maple Leaf Club?" "So we will." And so they did. It was very satisfying to think of these young boys, out of four nice Canadian homes and many hundreds of other boys like them, comfortable and cared for by their own people in the Maple Leaf Club, instead of aimlessly taking the first lodging that turned up.[30]

In its first year of operation, the committee met and assisted nearly 190,000 soldiers, including 33,000 from other parts of the British Empire.

The other pressing need was for hospital and convalescent space. In the age before antibiotics and other wonder drugs, effective treatments often demanded long periods of rest; for things like exhaustion or battle stress, the only treatment *was* rest, and even relatively straightforward surgical procedures required a prolonged convalescence. In the early stages of the war, there were only two Canadian hospitals in Britain, the Queen's Canadian Military Hospital near Folkestone, and the Duchess of Connaught Canadian Red Cross Hospital at Taplow, which the fabulously wealthy Astor family had donated for the duration of the war. Because the facilities had such a limited capacity, the Canadian wounded were spread out in hospitals around Great Britain, including some in the remote parts of Scotland. There were no worries about the standard of care, but critics were concerned that a wounded soldier facing a long convalescence could be cut off for weeks and even months from the company of other Canadians. Treated by Canadian doctors and nurses and sharing ward space with other Canadian wounded, however, the soldier would find his convalescence eased by contact with welcome reminders of home.

So the push was on to open more Canadian hospitals in Britain. The government of Ontario paid for the 1,040-bed Ontario Military Hospital at Orpington, which opened on 29 February 1916 (a later addition brought it up to 2,000 beds). "It is a glorious institution," declared Bishop Francis Fallon, the legendary Mitred Warrior from London, Ontario, "well worthy of all the money and all the time and all the effort

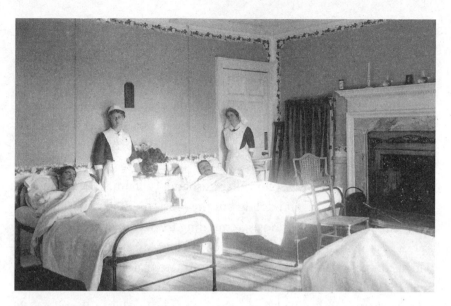

Beachborough Park Military Hospital at Shorncliffe, run by the Canadian War
Contingent Association

which have been spent upon it in order to bring it to this wonderful state
of perfection."[31] It was also, noted a British medical journal, "splendid
evidence of the Empire's unity. There were those who had thought that
the curious loosely connected links would not bear any great strain,
but the war had given the answer."[32] King George V donated a building
on one of his estates, which became the King's Canadian Red Cross
Hospital Bushey Park; it too was expanded over the course of the war
from its original 406-bed capacity. Special hospitals were established for
orthopaedic treatment, tubercular cases, and eye and ear wounds. Two
hospitals were set up for the treatment of venereal diseases and another
for intensive physiotherapy. By the end of the war, there were over forty
separate Canadian hospitals operating in Britain.

There was even more variety in convalescent homes, for there was
nothing to prevent someone from acquiring a house and opening a rest
home for soldiers. The Canadian government would pay a couple of
shillings a day for their maintenance, but because that hardly came close
to covering the actual costs, it was a role that was only open to wealthy
benefactors. Margaret Perkins Bull, the wife of a Toronto lawyer and

financier who had moved to Britain in 1912, invited recuperating soldiers
to her home in Heathview Gardens. The demand for space was so great
that the Bulls soon rented the nearby home of Ernest Shackleton—at
the time busily exploring the Antarctic—and opened it in June 1916 as a
thirty-two-bed convalescent hospital staffed largely by volunteer nursing
aides from Toronto. Residents of the hospital could stroll across Putney
Heath to the Bulls' home, where almost every night forty or more officers
joined them for dinner. It was a lively atmosphere: Margaret as the
gracious mother to every soldier, her husband, William, brandishing the
carving set with relish and doling out the roast, the Bull children (there
were five) ever the perfect hosts, reminding their guests what it was like
to live in a normal house with children.[33] The Massey-Harris Company,
which compensated for the downturn in tractor sales by manufacturing
artillery shells, opened a convalescent home for Canadian soldiers in
a Dulwich mansion called Kingswood, known locally as Bovril Castle
because its owner had invented the hot beef drink. One of the helpers
there was Anna Raynolds, the mother of artist Lawren Harris. Mrs
Sandford Fleming, whose father-in-law had given standard time to the
world, was the driving force behind a Canadian convalescent hospital
that opened in October 1916 at Lympne Castle, near Hythe, to replace
a much smaller facility near Canterbury. It was fitting that Lord Milner,
one of the strongest advocates of imperial federation before the war,
loaned his mansion to the Canadian Red Cross Society for an officers'
convalescent home. "This hospitality," wrote the society newsletter,
"is doing a great Imperial work and knitting strong ties of friendship
between the men of the Dominion and the people of the Motherland."[34]

By war's end, dozens of organizations had administrative offices in
London and the southeast to manage this aid effort, but the largest was
the Canadian Red Cross Society, headquartered in Cockspur Street. It
began operations in Britain at the same time as the 1st Contingent was
settling in on the Salisbury Plain, and in those early days confined itself
to providing comforts to Canadian soldiers. Especially appreciated were
local newspapers (as many as 100 sacks of them arrived at Cockspur Street
each week, to be sorted by province and kept in bins until requested) and
things like maple sugar or canned fruit that offered a taste of home. As
one soldier wrote to the Red Cross, "to see a glass jar filled with your

The Canadian Convalescent Hospital at Bearwood

cherries or peaches is like a glimpse of the homeland."[35] But as the war dragged on, the Red Cross expanded its work. Lady Julia Drummond, whose son Guy was killed at the Second Battle of Ypres, opened an information bureau in February 1915 so that frantic Canadians would have somewhere to contact for news of loved ones. By 1917, the bureau had 200 clerical workers on staff; in a busy week, the women would send out 1,500 personal letters with the latest information on soldiers in hospital or convalescing. The office kept a large roster of women (most of them the wives, mothers, or sisters of Canadian soldiers) who would visit Canadian wounded in hospital and ensure they had everything they needed. By 1918, there were over 1,300 women on call for hospital visits. There were also cars and drivers available to chauffeur soldiers wishing to see something of England while they were convalescing; some weeks, as many as 500 men were taken on driving tours to relieve the monotony of a long recuperation. There was a Prisoner of War Branch that supplied parcels to Canadians in captivity; it was run by Evelyn Rivers Bulkeley, who had come to Canada in 1911 as a lady in waiting to the Duchess of Connaught and whose husband had been killed in action in 1914. Every wounded Canadian received a comfort bag, often known as a Wonder Bag, upon arrival in hospital; full of necessities like toiletries, cigarettes, and writing paper, it was intended to provide an emergency supply of essentials for the first day or two. The Red Cross supplied thousands of Christmas stockings, put together by community groups across Canada and shipped to Britain in bulk. At the encouragement of Colonel Hagarty, the students of Harbord Collegiate assembled 500 stockings in 1917, all artfully decorated in the school colours. Of all the Red Cross's supplies, the stockings were the only gifts not distributed to soldiers from other parts of the Empire; made with the express purpose of providing a few reminders of home, they always contained trinkets that would mean nothing to an Australian or a South African. The size and scope of these efforts was manifest in the growth of the Canadian Red Cross in Britain; by the end of the war, it had become an immense organization of some 2,000 staffers and volunteers with forty rooms and six warehouses in various parts of London to run its operations.

But even that was dwarfed by the government's mechanism for running Canada's war. By 1915, the absence of a central authority in Britain was creating grave problems, as various cabinet ministers and officers travelled to Britain periodically and tried to run things on an ad hoc basis (the chief offender being the militia minister, Sir Sam Hughes). By the fall of 1916, Prime Minister Borden had had enough. In October he created a new ministry in cabinet, the Overseas Military Forces of Canada, to be responsible for all aspects of the war effort outside of Canada. Hughes, when he saw the job he coveted go to Sir George Perley, complained testily to Borden and was promptly asked for his resignation. Eventually, the new ministry came to be responsible for Canadian troops on the Western Front (through the Canadian Section of General Headquarters in France), Canadian units serving in other theatres of war, and Canada's military presence in Britain. Its most important task was paperwork—pay and records, estates, purchasing, audit department, stores—all of the administrative functions that kept a modern army running. It was responsible for all military hospitals and convalescent homes in Britain and oversaw the activities of various auxiliary groups, including the Red Cross, the YMCA, and the IODE. Most of its work was done by soldiers but the various departments of the ministry employed a small army of British civilians, over a thousand of them, primarily as clerks. As the Canadian empire in Britain grew,

The Catholic Women's League hut in the Canadian camp at Bramshott

the OMFC Ministry filled out and filed the forms that kept everything moving.

With the offices, hospitals, convalescent homes, and aid organizations, there were little bits of Canada scattered throughout the British Isles but nowhere did Canadians take over the Mother Country as they did around Folkestone. Aside from the military training establishments, there were more than a dozen hospitals and convalescent homes in the area, not to mention all the other hospitality centres that were established—Maple Leaf Club, Canadian Women's Union, Canadian Club for Women, Canadian Khaki Club, Canadian Club for Officers, and a handful of others. Units deposited their colours in the parish churches, and local schoolchildren laid flowers on the graves of Canadians in cemeteries. Festivities in honour of Dominion Day and Empire Day brought the townspeople out in force, and future Governor General Georges Vanier wrote to his family that officers of the 22nd Battalion "turned East Sandling camp into a suburb of Quebec" when they celebrated St Jean Baptiste Day.[36] Restaurants, shops, and hotels came to rely heavily on the CEF, and their prices tended to reflect the fact that Canadian soldiers were paid more than British. As Helen Fowlds wrote, "We are billetted here so aren't paying the bills, thank goodness, for it would be rather expensive." But it was a small price to pay for the chance to rub shoulders again with people from home. "The place is full of Canadians," Fowlds went on. "At lunch I saw hundreds and so many of their wives, etc. are here too. The whole town is filled with Canadians and such splendid big men as they are. I was far too busy watching their faces as they went by to pay attention to shopping. I met Reg Runnels, looking so big and brown and manly."[37] Going to Folkestone was as close as you could get in Britain to going home to Canada. You could be sure to meet any number of friends, relatives, and acquaintances there, or just enjoy being, in a sense, back in Canada. A Nova Scotian soldier described the area as

> a big Canadian city. There are soldiers everywhere you go, all with the Maple Leaf on their caps, and the good word Canada on their shoulders. If you go into Folkestone in the evening, it is almost beyond description. The mass of khaki is bewildering. But everybody is so good natured. Every now and then you meet some one whom you knew years ago. They are in other Battalions, but what difference? Everyone is a Canadian and everyone is on the same mission.[38]

The Canadian enclaves, whether in London or the southeast, were very much like nineteenth-century garrisons, with an impact that went far beyond the military. In Canada, British garrisons had provided defence, but had also given to their host communities music, sport, art, business. It was the same in First World War Britain. Most camps had a Tin Town, where locals operated shops and cafés in corrugated iron huts. Some of them were accused of over-charging in an essentially captive market, but even the scrupulously honest could make a decent living from the custom of Canadian soldiers. Unit sporting events, especially soccer, baseball, and track and field, were open to villagers who were starved for entertainment because the war had shut down many amateur and professional leagues. The local social scene was brightened by festivities to mark Dominion Day or Empire Day, the departure of a unit for France, or the visit of a dignitary. Most units that went overseas took with them either a brass band or a pipe band, and the large training camps held regular concerts for troops and locals alike. The Canadian

The colours of Canadian units hanging in the parish church at Witley

Pay and Record Office had a male voice choir that performed at military hospitals and charity concerts around London, and there was also a Canadian Military Choir, organized in late 1915 with six members. By the following summer it had over fifty vocalists, most of whom had seen active service. One of them had been awarded the DCM for gallantry at St Eloi, and nearly a dozen would die in active service.

All of this gave plenty of opportunity for the "colonizers" to mingle with their hosts, although not always on the best of terms. Any group contains a certain number of troublemakers, and the CEF was no exception. Local police constables had to deal with rowdy outbursts by drunken Canadians, petty theft, vandalism, and occasionally more serious crimes of fraud, assault, or murder. The memory of the 1st Contingent's escapades in British pubs had not faded entirely, and more than one British magistrate lamented that if Canadians had not been so well paid, they would have had fewer resources for getting into trouble.

But given the size of the Canadian community, there was probably less crime centred on the training bases than in society as a whole. What endured amongst locals was not the memory of drunken binges and property damage, but of kindness, generosity, and warmth. Locals opened their homes to Canadians for dinner or afternoon tea, or even turned over rooms to convalescent soldiers. Joe Leggett was just a child when a Canadian medical officer came to stay with his family while recovering from battle exhaustion. The children adored the doctor for

The pipe band of the 3rd Canadian Convalescent Depot stands ready to entertain the locals.

all sorts of reasons, not least for the knowing smile he flashed when they asked him for a medical note so they could play truant from school for a day. Leggett also had fond memories of the Canadian forestry units that were stationed near his home at Griggs Green—"those big hearted men who came to our part of Hampshire to lighten our darkness," he called them nearly seventy years later. They would give the local lads cast-off wood to take home so their families would never be short of fuel, and let them ride on the horse-drawn trolleys that moved logs around. They taught the secrets of operating a cross-cut saw properly, and would sharpen their tools whenever they dulled. Charlie Edwards' mother ran a small café in Bramshott's Tin Town, and the lad loved having the run of the camp, proudly carrying a military pass identifying him as the Chief Butterfly Catcher, Canadian Army. He haunted the dispatch riders' hut and idolized Sandy Bennett, who claimed to be Canada's fastest motorcyclist, and watched baseball, boxing, and the Dominion Day celebrations. Romances between Canadian soldiers and young local women were inevitable. In Liphook, there was a deeply discounted rate for marriage licences for Canadians (ten shillings instead of forty-eight) and a Folkestone historian estimated that there were some 1,100 marriages between townswomen and Canadian soldiers.[39]

Such close relations fostered feelings of imperial connectedness even as they enhanced Canadian nationalism. On the one hand, they deepened in the context of a united empire pulling together for a common cause—soldiers' letters reflect a strong interest in the British, as well as in the members of other military contingents in Britain. But at the same time, Canadians' self-image within that empire was becoming stronger and more confident. They still rankled at any suggestion that Canadian soldiers, as mere colonials, were not quite up to snuff and could be easily offended by the superior airs of ill-informed Britons. BC artilleryman William Calder vented his spleen in a letter to his mother in October 1916:

> One pup I was talking to in London had the audacity to ask me "what we ate out there and if we liked the good things we get here." Well I looked at him & said "You damn fool you have not started to live here in England yet" & walked off. . . . The

Englishmen . . . are always throwing it up to us Canadians that we are not enlisting in Canada & that the Canadian Contingents are only about 10% Canadian born—Why there is something for them to look forward to in getting to England while us poor devils are in a foreign country without any friends & 6000 m. from home among a bunch of thieves who are allways trying for our money—I wonder how many of them would volunteer to come & fight for Canada if we were in trouble.[40]

Lindsay, Ontario, native Cecil Frost, who would go on to become a lawyer and mayor of the city, was no gentler: "I am in favour of the Canadian Expeditionary Force being run by Canadians. Imperial officers do not understand us and it will cause perpetual friction to have it go on."[41]

But more often they were willing to take such comments in stride, success on the battlefield having given them the confidence to brush off their critics. As Garfield Weston wrote to his father,

The officers that train us here are much more severe in the way of discipline and for a while its [sic] going to be a little hard but we will soon get accustomed to it. We are practically beginning all over again in the way of training in fact yesterday we were doing the squad drill etc. This we took up at High School. They don't seem to have much of an opinion of our Canadian officers & trainers. Yesterday we were inspected by the commanding officer and after a long review he lined us up and made a few sarcastic remarks among which were, "You Canadians don't need to think that you know it all because you don't and have an awful lot to learn." Rather nice reception eh? However we were told to expect this so we weren't so greatly surprised.[42]

One of George Perley's responsibilities as minister was to be a cheerleader for Canada, and in one speech he embraced what had become an article of faith amongst Canadians in Britain: that life in Canada had turned Britons into better people who could teach the Mother Country a thing or two:

It will, we think, be generally conceded that the troops from the Overseas Dominions have shown rather more individual initiative, both among men and officers, than the regiments raised in the Mother Country. This can be partly accounted for by the fact that they are less trammelled by precedent, but it is also due to the greater stimulus to individual initiative obtained by Colonial experience. A very large percentage of the first units from Overseas were British born. Many had spent but a few years in the land of their adoption, but the freer life in these wide Dominions had already had its effect on their character. Life in these new countries does unquestionably stimulate initiative, and a clear proof of this fact has been given wherever Overseas units have been engaged.[43]

The last eighteen months of the war would offer even more proof of that. After closing out the Somme campaign in November 1916, the Canadian Corps had gone into winter quarters in Artois. It was a time for resting and refitting, but also for trench raiding, as they launched ever more ambitious night operations, some involving as many as 1,700 men. Again, the object was to keep the enemy off balance during the quieter winter months, and to keep troops sharp while preparations went ahead for the major Anglo-French offensive for the spring of 1917, which was to be in the Somme region once again. But in the meantime, the Germans had executed another strategic withdrawal. By surrendering a twenty-mile bulge into Allied lines, they were able to pull back to a carefully built defensive position (known as the Hindenburg Line) and free up fourteen divisions in the process. Unwittingly, they had surrendered the very territory that the Anglo-French offensive had targeted. This might seem like an incredible stroke of luck but instead it upset Allied planning badly. The Germans had laid waste to the ground as they withdrew, and it proved impossible to move troops up to the new front line in time for the planned offensive. In effect, it became two smaller offensives, a British one in the north and a French one in the south, with very little happening in the centre.

In the south, the French offensive got off to a bad start and never recovered. The German system of defence in depth meant that the front lines, those most vulnerable to a preliminary bombardment, were very lightly held. The French moved forward with relative ease and growing confidence until they encountered the second line of defence, its trenches virtually undamaged and its defenders waiting and full of fight. For a month the French hammered away until finally deciding that enough was enough. Their biggest gain was just a few miles; the cost was over a quarter of a million casualties on both sides. In the north, the picture was brighter. The ANZACs, with the longest frontage in the sector, achieved only modest gains but the British corps attacking eastwards from the edge of Arras advanced their lines as much as five miles. To their left, near the northernmost tip of the offensive, the Canadian Corps had been given the task of capturing Vimy Ridge, which had broken two French armies already. On a landscape in which the slightest knoll offered enormous tactical advantage, Vimy Ridge was of a different order entirely. From its highest point, referred to on military maps as Hill 145, one could see for miles across the Douai Plain to the east. Taking a few miles of ridge line could render something like a hundred square miles untenable for the Germans.

The original plan had envisioned just two Canadian divisions attacking part of Vimy Ridge, but when circumstances changed and the BEF took responsibility for more of the offensive, the Canadians were given the task of capturing virtually the entire ridge. It would be the first time the four divisions of the Canadian Corps would fight together in a single operation. Byng and his mostly British staff officers were determined to leave nothing to chance. To ensure that the attack was well supplied, labour battalions built tramways and plank roads that would carry to the front lines some 800 tons of ammunition, rations, and equipment a day. The advance relied on 50,000 horses to pull the trams, move artillery pieces, and shift stores, so reservoirs, pumphouses, and forty-five miles of pipe were constructed to ensure that the 600,000 gallons of water required for the animals every day was always available. Everything possible was done to ensure that the assaulting troops knew what they had to do, and were ready to do it. Byng ordered the preparation of a full-scale mock-up of the ridge behind the lines, so that officers and men could rehearse their movements—a radical idea at a time when all too many generals thought it unwise to trust the common soldier with too much information. And rather than using up all their energy slogging through the mud to the start lines, infantrymen in the first wave went forward through underground caves and tunnels, some large enough to shelter an entire battalion—and every man had a hot meal and a tot of rum in the hours before the attack.

The exhaustive preparations of Byng and his staff paid off. The barrage opened at 5:30 AM on 9 April 1917, with nearly a thousand guns pounding defences that had already felt the weight of a million artillery shells over the previous week. The Canadians swarmed forward, keeping perfect pace with the barrage as it crept ahead of them. Within an hour, the 1st, 2nd, and 3rd Divisions had all reached their first objective, the Black Line, and were preparing to move on. By 8 AM they had reached the Red Line, halfway to their ultimate goal, and by mid-afternoon all three divisions had swept past their third objective, the Blue Line, and taken their fourth, the Brown Line. Only the 4th Division, on the northern tip of the advance, encountered problems. It was responsible for taking and holding Hill 145, the highest and most important point on the ridge, and resistance in that sector was so stout that the 4th Division could not declare success until the middle of the afternoon on 10 April. The two-day cost was heavy—7,700 casualties, of whom 2,900 were dead—but that was a fraction of what the French and British had lost in failing to take the ridge earlier in the war.

The capture of Vimy Ridge was a stunning success, a triumph of organization, preparation, training, and raw courage. Its strategic importance was limited, thanks to the failure of the rest of the offensive, and it could not have succeeded without the superb British staff work and artillery support provided by British gunners. But this in no way minimizes the magnitude of the achievement. The Canadian Corps had demonstrated that a strong defensive position could be overcome at a relatively modest cost, and built an enduring legacy in the process. The conjunction of circumstances—the four divisions of the Canadian Corps operating together for the first time on Easter weekend, the Christian festival of the resurrection—transformed Vimy Ridge from a tactical triumph into the birth of a nation.

The Canadian Corps continued to draw tough assignments in subsequent weeks, and with success came a change. Julian Byng had shown too much ability to be left in command of a corps and in June he was promoted to command the 3rd Army. In his place, Arthur Currie was given charge of the Canadian Corps. Currie's star had been rising since the war began. A native of Strathroy, Ontario, he had moved to Victoria in 1894 to find his fortune, but his time in British Columbia is best remembered for failed real estate ventures and rumours that he misappropriated funds from his militia regiment. The war brought his chance for redemption. His handling of the 2nd Brigade at Ypres in 1915 had been capable, although not without fault, but since then his tenure at the helm of the 1st Division had rarely been less than impressive, and was sometimes brilliant. In demeanour, he was nothing like Byng— portly, fastidious, and particular about his appearance (in one famous photograph, Currie walks on dry duckboards while King George V and 1st Army commander Sir Henry Horne walk in the mud on either side of him), he lacked Byng's easy rapport with the common soldier. But he shared Byng's work ethic, commitment to preparation and organization, and willingness to innovate. He was thorough and dogged, and showed the flashes of flair and creativity that characterize the best commanders.

Still, his first offensive was a mixed success. Ordered to capture the city of Lens, in the heart of the coal-mining region of northern France, he concluded that the city could not be carried, let alone held, without first controlling Hill 70, a feature that overlooked Lens from the north. The attack went in on 15 August 1917 and made the most of superbly coordinated artillery support, both to take the hill in the first place and then to beat back the twenty-one separate counter-attacks the Germans mounted over the next three days. The push to capture Lens itself offered less to commend it. The ground, with its spoil heaps, pitheads, and workers' huts, was much less favourable to the attacker, and not even the Corps' fine artillery work was enough of an equalizer. Canadian tactics in certain elements of the plan left much to be desired, while the German defenders made the most of their advantages. When Currie suspended operations on 25 August, most of Lens was still in enemy hands.

Nevertheless, the Canadian Corps had contributed to the Allied goal of wearing down the enemy to prevent them from regaining the initiative. In the BEF's northern sector, there had been growing pressure to clear the Belgian coast, to make it more difficult for German submarines to attack

Allied merchant shipping. Sir John Jellicoe, Britain's First Sea Lord, even announced that unless the Allies took Zeebrugge, a key Belgian port for German submarines, the war would be lost. Haig's response was a two-stage offensive, first against Messines Ridge, south of Ypres, and then against German lines north of Ypres.

On 7 June 1917 British engineers detonated nineteen enormous mines under the Ridge. The blast, which could be felt as far away as the south of England, did not simply damage the ridge—it almost eliminated it, as well as most of the defenders, and within four days, virtually all of the offensive's objectives had been taken. Emboldened by this success, Haig pressed his political masters to sanction the second stage. Though they were dubious of his prediction that success might clear Belgium of German troops and draw neutral Holland into the war on the Allied side, Britain's war council gave Haig the necessary permission. On 31 July 1917 the big push went forward. In some ways, it was a carbon copy of any number of earlier offensives. There was great initial success as the attacking units quickly overran the lightly held German front lines, but as they reached the much stronger second line, the momentum petered out. After three days and 32,000 casualties, the British divisions had advanced 3,000 yards at best. From this point, the big push became a series of smaller, local attacks, some completely successful, some choked out by the soupy mud of the wettest summer in recent memory. By mid-October the advance had been carried to within 2,500 yards of the village of Passchendaele—an objective of the offensive's first day.

Just like on the Somme in 1916, the Canadian Corps was called in for the last act. The campaign was as good as over but there was real advantage to digging in to winter quarters on the high ground around Passchendaele rather than the low ground in front of it. The job of ejecting the Germans from that high ground fell to the Canadians. The start line they took over was virtually the same line they had defended more than two years earlier, before the gas attacks of April 1915. In a series of phased assaults that began on 26 October, the Canadian Corps put into practice the principles that had stood it in good stead at Vimy: thorough preparation, including building tramways to bring up sufficient supplies; a meticulous artillery fire plan; and clear and reasonable objectives. Canadian casualties were heavy—over 15,000 in three weeks of fighting—but the Corps did almost everything that was asked of it. Passchendaele village fell on 6 November 1917 and four days later, elements of the 1st and 2nd Divisions made a last push to consolidate the high ground. Then, Haig shut down the Third Battle of Ypres.

That winter saw the Allies' fortunes at their lowest point. The Passchendaele offensive might have worn down the enemy, but it also cost the BEF dearly and the immediate territorial gains were pathetically small. The French army, after another summer of punishing casualties, had been hobbled by widespread mutinies and was too fragile to engage in any significant offensive operations in the near future. Russia had finally succumbed to revolution and the new Bolshevik regime had pulled out of the war, allowing Germany to move all of its divisions to the Western Front. Although the United States had come into the war in April 1917, it was frustratingly slow to mobilize and it would be the summer of 1918 before the American Expeditionary Force could go on the offensive. And for the men holding the front lines, it was one of the coldest winters on record.

In Canada, the voluntary system had finally run out of steam and the Conservative government was forced to invoke conscription. Determined that the running of the war not fall victim to partisan politics, Prime Minister Robert Borden put together a coalition government and went to the people. The election was one of the bitterest in Canada's history, confirming English Canada's support of conscription and making plain French Canada's opposition to it. Then on 6 December a massive explosion, the largest in human history to that point, devastated the city of Halifax, killing some 2,000 people and flattening the north end. It was a shocking end to a difficult year.

The worst was yet to come. Beginning on 21 March 1918, the Germans launched a series of offensives along the Western Front. Bolstered by dozens of divisions brought from the east, they achieved breathtaking gains, pushing forty miles into Allied lines in places. In the Ypres and Somme sectors, the hard-won gains of three years were wiped out in a matter of weeks as Passchendaele, Kemmel, Festubert, Givenchy, Mount Sorrel, St Eloi, and Courcelette all fell to the advancing Germans. In hindsight, we know that Offensive Michael was the Germans' final throw of the dice and that it consumed their last manpower reserves. But at the time, it put everything in doubt. Planners who had spoken confidently about defeating Germany in 1918 now looked ahead to the campaigns of 1919 and 1920, although it was far from certain that the Allies could hang on that long. The possibility of losing the war was suddenly very real.

Throughout this period—it is not too much to call it a crisis—the Canadian Corps was in reserve. Individual divisions were detached occasionally, but for specific purposes and only temporarily, because Ottawa insisted that the Corps not be split up and that Canadians fight together. It proved to be the right decision, for time out of battle allowed the Corps to reorganize, rest, train, and become one of the strongest fighting formations in the entire Allied armies. But it was not all work. On 1 July 1918 the Canadian Corps marked Dominion Day with an enormous sports competition at Tincques. Nearly 50,000 Canadian soldiers and a host of dignitaries, including Prime Minister Borden, the Duke of Connaught, who had stepped down as Governor General in 1916, and American Expeditionary Force commander John Pershing, watched as the 1st Division won at track and field, the 44th Battalion from Winnipeg swept the soccer tournament, and the 7th Battalion Canadian Engineers prevailed in baseball. Two weeks later, the Canadian Corps left its reserve positions and returned to the line. The Allies were about to resume the offensive.

By June, the German attacks had run out of steam, but their commanders committed the fatal error of pressing the advance past the point of utility. The more they attacked, the less they achieved, and at a higher cost. Inexorably, almost imperceptibly, the initiative was swinging back to the Allies. Ferdinand Foch, the French general who became supreme Allied commander in March 1918, had decided that the first order of business should be to push the Germans back from three critical transportation hubs: St Mihiel, Soissons, and Amiens. Once this was achieved, and the reinforcement and supply network guaranteed, the Allies could move confidently to the offensive. In the south, St Mihiel was in the US sector, and American success there was helped by the fact that the Germans were in the process of withdrawing when the attack began. In the centre, east of Soissons, French, British, Italian, and US divisions co-operated to sweep the Germans from countryside that had been a battlefield since 1914. In the north, at Amiens, the attack was also a multi-national effort, with British, Australian, and Canadian divisions in the vanguard. Before dawn on 8 August 1918, the assault troops moved to the start line. There was no saturating artillery bombardment, just the normal harassing fire that characterized any night on the Western Front. Then, at 4:20 AM, some 900 Allied guns unleashed a savage barrage as the troops left the trenches—the Canadians in the centre, the Australians on their left, and the British on their right. Suspecting nothing, the Germans were caught off guard and defensive positions melted away under heavy pressure. In carefully timed movements, fresh battalions were brought up to replace spent ones so the advance could continue—it was a textbook operation. By day's end, the success had been stunning—an eight-mile advance in the Canadian sector, seven miles by the Australians, a little less by the British. Erich Ludendorff, the head of the German war effort since August 1916, would later call it his army's blackest day of the war: "Everything I had feared, and of which I had so often given warning had here, in one place, become a reality." Byng, always interested in the corps he had helped to shape, told Currie that Canada's attack at Amiens was "the finest operation of the war."[44]

After Amiens, it was really only a matter of time. Aware that the German armies were on the verge of collapse, Foch planned an enormous pincer movement to bring things to a conclusion. In the south, the French and Americans would push forward in the Meuse-Argonne, while in the north, the BEF would drive east from Arras. The centre would merely see a holding action, to keep the enemy diverted while the trap shut behind him. The offensive would see some of the highest casualty rates of the war—it is a great irony that the war of movement in 1914 and 1918 was far more lethal than the three years of trench warfare in between—but the troops were buoyed by their obvious successes. Journalists would later refer to the last three months of the war as Canada's Hundred Days, a nod to Napoleon's last desperate bid for power, and it saw the Canadian Corps overwhelm some of the toughest obstacles on the Western Front: the Drocourt-Quéant Line, a heavily defended network of deep trenches, concrete bunkers, and masses of barbed wire that sat astride the Arras-Cambrai road (Currie thought victory there was even more significant than at Amiens because it forced five German armies to

give up the territory they had won in the spring offensive); the Canal du
Nord, an unfinished canal some forty yards wide and twelve feet deep
that the Germans had heavily fortified; Cambrai, the first major city to
fall to the Canadian Corps; and Valenciennes, where superb planning
and execution prevented an attack from degenerating into a bitter
house-to-house battle. By the beginning of November 1918, the Corps
was pursuing the enemy towards Mons in Belgium, its reputation as the
shock army of the British Empire assured.

Canada's status as the senior dominion was also assured, for the
Borden government had used the power of the Canadian Corps to
leverage greater influence in the running of the war. This was partly
pragmatic—if Canadian soldiers were to continue to reinforce the
Western Front, the government in Ottawa demanded a say in how they
were used—but it also had a strong nationalist dimension. It emerged
from the assumption that Canada's new nationalism could be expressed
most effectively through the British Empire, not independently, and so it
was through imperial institutions that Canada should seek influence. Of
course, this was the only way that Canada *could* seek influence, in a legal
sense, because Ottawa lacked the legislative ability to conduct affairs
as an independent international actor. Nevertheless, few Canadians
questioned the Empire as the best forum through which Canada should
fulfill its nationalism. And so Canada took a leading role in new imperial
organizations such as the Imperial Munitions Board and the Imperial
War Graves Commission.

But more far-reaching was the creation of the Imperial War Cabinet.
The leaders of the Empire had been meeting regularly since 1887, but
the 1915 conference had been postponed because of the war. In 1917, it
could be put off no longer—Britain's need was too great to equivocate
on the argument of imperial leaders, first among them Robert Borden,
that the dominions would not keep the manpower taps open unless
they could help to shape imperial war policy. In May 1917 Lloyd George
invited the leaders of the Empire to Britain and constituted the Imperial
War Cabinet, to keep the various governments (Canada, Australia, New
Zealand, South Africa, and India) fully informed of the progress of the
war and to give them a voice in the formulation of imperial policy, on the
basis of full and equal participation. For Borden, it was a great victory.

At every opportunity he pointed out that the British prime minister was now only the first among equals and that each member nation, large and small, retained its full autonomy, self-government, and ministerial responsibility. The equality of status had long been conceded in practical matters, he said with more optimism than accuracy, but that relationship had been put on a formal footing with the creation, "or rather the natural coming into being" he added significantly, of the Imperial War Cabinet. A reorganization of the entire constitutional basis of the Empire would be necessary, but it could not be done while there was a war to win. Instead, the British government promised to call a special imperial conference as soon as possible after victory was secured, to build a new empire.

The establishment of the Imperial War Cabinet was just one indication of Canada's growing confidence within the new British Empire. Under Canada's guidance, the Empire was greater than it had ever been, as Newton Rowell, a cabinet minister in Borden's Union government, told an audience in Orono, Ontario, "a coalition of free, self-governing nations, all of equal status, all owing allegiance to a common Sovereign and bound together by common ideals and purposes."[45] Success on the battlefield had been an incredible tonic, but so too had success in the newspapers. Canada had one of the shrewdest and most effective propagandists of the war in Max Aitken, the New Brunswick native who had emigrated to Britain before the war and soon became a newspaper baron, financial tycoon, and Member of Parliament. More than one British leader complained of Aitken's inference that every Allied victory was really a Canadian triumph, with the British and French tagging along behind to tidy up afterward. The Australians, too, chafed at Aitken's skills as a promoter; they had their own gifted publicist in C.E.W. Bean but in the war of column inches, the Aussies were badly beaten by Aitken's publicity machine.

One of Aitken's pet themes was the Canadian nation as the new engine of the British Empire. In the last two years of the war, the imperialist-nationalist ideology reached its peak. Once dismissed as mere colonials, Canadians showed a bullish confidence that they had proven themselves as the senior dominion and could teach Mother Britain a thing or two about running the war. From this line of thinking, which was behind every private who chafed when a British officer looked down on him as a "comedian" as much as it was behind his prime minister's insistence that Canada help direct the war, it was no very great step to believe that Canada would show Britain how to run an empire, for in Canada an imperialism had emerged that was finer and more able to carry on the great British tradition.

The magazine *Canada* had long advanced this argument. The editor wrote the following in April 1916:

> Up to the present time, more vigorous policy and greater constructive statesmanship has been apparent Overseas than in the Mother Country. In Australia, Canada, New Zealand, and South Africa the leaders of the people and the people themselves have shown a bolder spirit and greater unanimity in their participation in this great war than has been shown at home. The old British spirit has renewed its youth in these younger lands, and the Mother Country would do well to use their vigour.

The magazine often observed that "the spirit of the Overseas Britisher is of a more vigorous quality than that of his brother in the Motherland," and others soon picked up the argument.[46] Sir George Perley told the Royal Colonial Institute that "the Imperial feeling is very much alive in Canada. We perhaps feel the Empire to be a more vital thing than does the ordinary citizen of England."[47] The soldiers themselves felt the same, although they tended to express themselves in more concrete terms. As Leslie Frost, an infantry officer who later became Ontario's premier, wrote home,

> Let Canada raise her own army, feed it, and officer it and it will be better than having Englishmen, who think we are backwoodsmen, run it. It's all right to talk Imperialism in Canada but come across and give England a great big dose of Imperialism and it would do more good. Then perhaps they would cease regarding us as 'colonials.'[48]

The 11th of November 1918 saw those "colonials" moving towards the outskirts of Mons where, four-and-a-half years earlier, the BEF had first clashed with the invading Germans. Now, the German armies were steadily being pushed to the east as the Allies liberated village after village from their occupiers. Retreating units mounted stout rear-guard actions, and as late as 10 PM on 10 November, Canadian Corps headquarters issued operational orders that the drive to encircle Mons should continue the next day. Then, at 6:30 AM that morning, word came up the lines that an armistice would take effect at 11 AM. Commanders were advised to use caution to avoid needless casualties but a few minutes before 11 AM, Private George Price, a conscript from Moose Jaw, Saskatchewan, stopped a German bullet to become the last fatal casualty of the Great War. Anyone who was prepared to look beyond the tragedy of being killed two minutes from peace might have found it entirely appropriate that, in St Symphorien Cemetery, the Empire's last soldier to die in the war would lie just a few feet from Private John Parr, its first soldier to die on the Western Front.

FOUR

CANADA: A BRITISH NATION

News of the Armistice brought Canadians out into the streets in scenes that called to mind that distant August holiday weekend in 1914. Kitchens were emptied of pots and pans to use as noisemakers, bundles of straw were turned into flaming torches, and church bells and factories, whistles sounded without cease. People poured out of their homes, many wearing only night clothes (for it was not yet dawn when most of Canada heard the news), but modesty took a back seat to celebration. People sang, cheered, prayed, wept—there was joy, exhilaration, exultation, and, perhaps more than anything else, relief.

But the dark clouds refused to lift right away. George Price was the last Canadian to be killed in action but in the months after the Armistice, thousands more died, of wounds, disease, accidents, foul play, and suicide. The first year of peace was not a happy time in Canada. The 19th of July 1919 was proclaimed Peace Day, in honour of the signing of the Treaty of Versailles that ended the war against Germany, but there was as much bad news as good. Canada's soldiers were too slow coming home, and all too often that journey proved to be their last. Many families suffered along with the Willmots of Cape Breton; they rejoiced in the knowledge that their son Percy had survived the war, only to watch him die of complications from minor battle wounds within six months of his Nova Scotia homecoming. The influenza epidemic that killed more people around the world than the war still had some fight left in it. Labour unrest, simmering since the middle of the war, had flared across the country, most seriously in Winnipeg, where a general strike shut down the city for days. Unemployment was creeping upwards along with the cost of living as the economic stimulus provided by the war ran out.

Political life was as fractious as ever—so much for the dream that the war would create a finer, gentler country.

And then he appeared, "the Sir Galahad of the Royal Household," as Mackenzie King called him, "the young knight, our future king, whose joy is in the service of others." On 15 August 1919, Edward, the Prince of Wales, arrived in Saint John, New Brunswick, to begin a three-month tour of the Dominion. After four years of war, a deadly epidemic, and a summer of discontent, Canadians let their emotions go. At every stop (even in Quebec, where he always began his speeches in his impeccable French), enormous crowds turned out to greet the prince. "Never before among the older people had so much enthusiasm been roused over one individual as has gone out to this Royal lad," noted the Edmonton *Bulletin*, "while the younger people are absolutely devoted to him." To the 100,000 people who came to see him speak on Warriors' Day at the Canadian National Exhibition, he preached the gospel of imperial unity: "besides being Canadian, we are all Britishers which, for lack of a better expression, means loyalty to the British flag and to British institutions. . . . I am a Britisher through and through, and I know of no place where I could feel prouder to say so than in Toronto."

Militia units in Hamilton, Ontario, parade to welcome the Prince of Wales in 1919.

"I hope every City and District will win my flag"

H.R.H. Prince of Wales

Let us win the

PRINCE OF WALES' FLAG

VICTORY LOAN, 1919

The community with the largest subscription to the 1919 Victory Loan drive won the Prince of Wales' flag, to be presented by His Majesty.

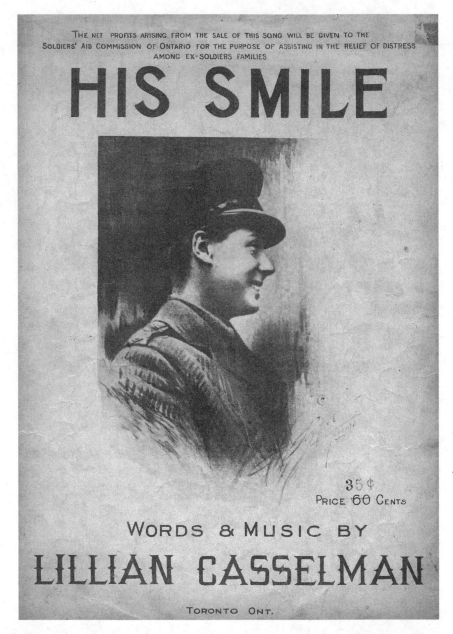

A typical manifestation of the enthusiasm generated by the visit of the Prince of Wales in 1919

All across the country, Canadians were proud to say so, too. The Royal Visit of 1919 provided a fitting epilogue to Canada's war story, as the future sovereign of the British Empire was received and acclaimed by the people of the senior dominion that had given so much to see the Empire through to victory. "It is largely due to his influence that there exists today a stronger bond of understanding and interest between all parts of the Empire, and a deeper and more sincere loyalty to the throne," wrote one school textbook.[1] In the twenty years after Edward's triumphant visit, Canada was reshaped. Its empire in Britain was dismantled, leaving only scattered remnants. It began to forge a new, independent path on the international stage, and a new sense of self along with it. But through the two decades of peace ran the British connection, a silken thread—or a golden chain, depending on one's politics.

It had taken more than four years to build Canada's wartime empire in Britain; it was taken apart in a matter of months. The biggest priority was bringing home the men of the Canadian Expeditionary Force. To be fairest to the individual soldier, the best system was first in, first out—the survivors of the 1st Contingent would return to Canada first, while the late war conscripts would get the lowest priority. But that meant taking apart units and sending men home piecemeal; it was quite conceivable that a battalion would lose all of its officers, or worse, all of its cooks, in the first movement. Besides, Canadian Corps commander Arthur Currie thought it was important for the men of the Corps to return home in their units, and be welcomed by their home communities as units. Such celebrations would provide a fitting ending to a great national experience, and would give civilians a chance to celebrate their soldiers in a very public way. "The men would arrive in Canada happier and feel more contented and with discipline better maintained," military authorities believed, "if the Unit organization were adhered to until the last possible moment."[2] These arrangements applied only to the roughly 100,000 men of the Canadian Corps; everyone else, including reserve units and headquarters staff in Britain, would go home piecemeal in drafts.

Because of their relative positions in the field, Currie decided that the 1st and 2nd Divisions would join the Allied occupation forces in Germany, while the 3rd and 4th Divisions stayed in Belgium until they could start moving back to England. Canadian units remained in

Germany over Christmas 1918, but in the New Year they started returning to Belgium. Although by rights the 1st Division should have gone home first, administrative and other factors made it much more sensible for the 3rd Division to be the first to cross back to Britain; it was followed by the 1st, 2nd, and 4th Divisions, with the last units crossing in mid-April. The men of the Canadian Corps were destined for demobilization camps at Bramshott and Witley, while troops already in England went to camps at Seaford, a coastal resort town not far from Folkestone, and Ripon, a cathedral city in central Yorkshire. Kinmel Park, an estate on the north coast of Wales, became the final staging point for drafts sailing from Liverpool.

Between 11 November 1918 and 2 April 1919, over 110,000 men returned to Canada, an impressive number to be sure, but for the men who were waiting to go home not nearly enough. Few questioned Currie's opinion that units should go home together, but no one could have predicted the delays that would plague the process. In the first place, there was a heavy demand on shipping space. The Canadian Expeditionary Force was the largest of the Empire's contingents to be returned home, but there were also hundreds of thousands of Australians, New Zealanders, South Africans, and Indians awaiting transport. The troops of the British Empire, however, were vastly outnumbered by the more than two million US soldiers in Europe, and the government in Washington was able to exert enormous pressure to ensure that the doughboys got home early. Then there were the endless forms to be completed. The Canadian government had decided that most of the discharge paperwork would be done in Britain, so that once the soldiers reached the Canadian cities where they would be demobilized, they could be released with few formalities. This sounded good in principle, but in practice it meant that Canadians waited for dozens of separate forms, covering everything from their teeth to the state of their kit, to be completed and filed for each of them.

In the anti-climax of the post-Armistice months, boredom turned to restlessness and restlessness to discontent. The vast majority of Canadian soldiers waited, if not patiently then with a degree of resignation, but it was the sort of atmosphere in which troublemakers found many outlets for their energies. It started with small-scale disturbances—some

Part of Witley camp's Tin Town

soldiers rioted near Kinmel Park when they were mistakenly barred from
a dance hall; a bunch of engineers and railway troops at Ripon decided to
fire off a load of surplus ammunition, terrifying the locals in an incident
that became known locally as the Ripon War. Canadians around Witley
looted a few shops in the Tin Town that they thought were guilty of
price-gouging, but in this case the rioters could hardly be blamed—in
Guildford police court, a canteen manager at Witley had been convicted
and fined for selling cigarettes to Canadian soldiers that were intended
to be distributed free to them.[3] But gradually, the excuses became less
convincing as discipline deteriorated. In January 1919, a group of soldiers
from Witley camp stormed the police station in the town of Godalming,
determined to liberate a pal whom they believed had been wrongly
arrested. A month later, soldiers raided a canteen at Witley and one man
was shot and killed by sentries. On the night of 14–15 June, they rose up
again, burning Witley's Tin Town. Soldiers were happy to see the huts
operated by the YMCA and the Navy and Army Canteen Board go up in
flames, for those organizations had bad reputations for taking advantage
of soldiers. The men went out of their way, however, to protect Mother
Edwards' café at Bramshott, because she had always done right by the
lads. The Salvation Army, too, was safeguarded because the Sally Anns

never turned away a soldier just because he didn't have the price of a cup of tea and a bun.

But the most serious disturbances took place at Kinmel Park and Epsom. At Kinmel Park, all of the problems with the demobilization process came together in one hundred-acre military encampment: over-crowding in poorly built huts that offered little protection against the cold winds blowing in from the Irish Sea, inexperienced officers who could not control the men, over-charging by local merchants, delays in issuing pay, bad food, and the knowledge that other soldiers were getting home ahead of them. On the evening of 4 March 1919, when news reached the camp that a ship designated for their return had been pulled from service (for good reason, but no one thought to tell the men that), the anger boiled over. "Many men were broke and couldn't buy cigarettes or soap, but were all looking forward to getting away home," said Toronto steamfitter Archie Wallace, a former prisoner of war who had enlisted in August 1914, at the inquest into the disturbances. "Then came the cancellation of sailings . . . this was the climax. On the day before the riot it was on everybody's lips—it was the general feeling—every man I met was talking the same thing."[4] As night settled over the camp, small groups of soldiers began looting canteens, warehouses, and parts of the Tin Town. The violence slowly spread to most of Kinmel Park's many compounds, and officers could do little as the rioters roamed back and forth, collecting supporters as they went. By morning the camp was in chaos, with the officers attempting to prevent rioters from taking over the administrative buildings. In a series of pitched battles, rifle fire broke out and five soldiers were killed before order could be restored. In the uneasy calm that settled over the camp, the authorities held an inquest into the riot. It was not, as the press reported, an attempted Bolshevik coup that aimed to overthrow the officers and take control of the camp. One brigadier-general reported that he had been treated with the utmost respect by the rioters as he toured the camp trying to restore order: "Some of them actually put down their loot in order to salute me, and then picked up their loot again."[5] Nor was it simply soldiers attacking the local community in its most visible form, the Tin Town; military authorities were surprised to find that amongst the rioters they arrested were at least a dozen local civilians who had taken advantage of the disorder to join the looting. The only conclusion to be drawn was that the five soldiers, so close to going home, would not have died if the camp had been better administered, if the soldiers had been treated with more dignity, if their officers had been more conscientious.

To the south, the town of Epsom was a favourite destination for soldiers in the giant camp at Witley, but their presence in one of the shrines of British horse racing was not always welcome. The Canadians were known as inveterate gamblers, and they did not appreciate it when a few soldiers were arrested during race week for running games of chance on the street. In fact, relations between the soldiers and the locals (including many recently demobilized British soldiers who lived in the area) had been worsening for some time. Canadian soldiers complained that they were taunted and roughed up by local men as they walked through town; things were worse after an evening of drinking. The police had made arrests on both sides, but also knew that Canadians did not take kindly to local constables enforcing the law and, as they had done at Godalming, were quite happy to launch a rescue mission in such circumstances. They often complained to Canadian military authorities that they needed help with policing, but nothing came of their requests.

The evening of 17 June 1919 was just like most other evenings in Epsom: local men and Canadian soldiers got into a brawl on the main street, and the constables arrested two Canadians and jailed them in the police station. As they had done in the past, a small group of Canadians marched on the station and demanded their release. The police naturally refused, but this time the Canadians returned to camp for reinforcements. Within an hour, as many as 400 soldiers had laid siege to the police station and were pelting it with bricks, rocks, chunks of wood, and iron railings torn from the ground. Local policemen, numbering fewer than a dozen, desperately tried to hold back the invaders but the soldiers were determined to get what they came for. The two prisoners were freed, but not before every policeman had been injured and one—a sergeant who had served in the Royal Horse Artillery—lay dying from a blow to the head.

Feelings in the Epsom area were never quite the same. A local police inspector warned that tension was high in the town and that, unless the situation was handled very carefully, more rioting would occur. Eight

Canadian soldiers were eventually tried for the rioting, but only two saw any prison time. Not until 1929 did ex-soldier Allan McMaster, while being held in Winnipeg on an unrelated charge, confess to killing Station Sergeant Green. Eventually, military authorities put Epsom out of bounds to Canadian soldiers, but not before Private Frederick Bruns, a Moose Jaw native, disappeared from the camp. His body was later found in a chalk pit near Epsom; no official cause of death was recorded, but a recent historian claims that he was the target of a revenge killing.

The response of Canadian authorities to the troubles in Epsom was subdued. The magazine *Canada* tried to put a brave face on things, insisting that "The esteem and admiration in which Canadians are held by their kinsfolk in the Mother Country is one of the few good things resulting from the Great War. The sturdy independence of the Overseas Britisher is thoroughly valued and appreciated in the Old Country."[6] It did not try to excuse the rioters but laid blame at the feet of a few troublemakers: "it is most unfortunate that an inaccurate, exaggerated, and highly sensational account should have appeared in the English Press, without the qualifying effect of an official statement."[7] There was some truth to this criticism, but more troubling was the notion that the British press had turned against the Canadians. On 9 March 1919, hundreds of US soldiers waged a three-hour battle with police outside the YMCA Eagle Hut in central London after constables tried to break up a sidewalk craps game. Much to the annoyance of Canadian officials, the riot went largely unreported and the few papers that did mention it put it down to over-exuberant spirits.

In contrast, the hooliganism of Canadian soldiers was excoriated in the press. A few journalists were willing to admit that the fault probably did not lie all on one side. The Canadians "suggest that some of their number were the subject of an unprovoked assault by civilians during race week, and that this assault was the origin of the almost nightly fights since with the youths of Epsom," wrote one local newspaper. "As regards the bellicose relationships with the youths of Epsom, the fault may not be all on the side of the Canadians; very possibly is not."[8] But the voices of moderation were very much in the minority. In a long editorial, the Epsom *Advertiser* traced the problems back to the character of colonial soldiers and the success of their propaganda machines:

it is possible that we Britishers have erred in making too much of the Canadians. We were grateful to them for the manner in which they came to the aid of the Mother Country. We are indebted to them for many a gallant stand, and more than once they helped the Empire out of a very critical and perilous position. In our gratitude we were apt to make the utmost of the work of our Colonials. Over and over again they were extolled while our own lads, whose exploits were just as glorious and who individually did just as heroic deeds, were given little praise. That was a mistake because it gave to the Colonials an exaggerated idea of their part in the war, and it also left a grievance rankling in the minds of our own soldiers. . . . the Canadians and Australians were made much of when they came in our midst to recuperate and rest. The laudation and the friendliness shown had the effect of making some of the men unduly sensible of any slight and quick to resent a grievance, real or imaginary. Perhaps the chief cause of the culminating disturbance was the fact that in the Colonies life is more free of restraint. Many of these men have come from thinly populated areas where a man is very largely his own policeman and where law and order are of a primitive nature. Discipline in their armies is slack and they have found the restraint of camp in Epsom irksome. Coming as they have done into contact with our ordered conditions, under which they have not been able to run riot as they would do at home without interference, their exaggerated ideas of the meaning of the word freedom led to a revolt.[9]

In reality, the riots had very little to do with the free spirit of the frontier or the swelled heads of Canadian soldiers. They did not reflect anti-British or anti-imperial sentiment, but rather frustration with the slow pace of the repatriation process, poor conditions in the camps, the maintenance of heavy discipline, and delays in their pay. In a letter home to his mother, Harold Simpson, a schoolteacher from Prince Edward Island who had enlisted in 1915, described the situation much more clearly than either the military authorities or the local police ever did:

That little affair down at Rhyl [Kinmel Park] will liven things up a bit. In fact one can see a difference already and not before time. There was too much unfairness about it all, too much dilly-dallying too and it is a wonder that there wasn't trouble before. The boys showed marvellous patience and it was only when they saw that arguments were useless that they took matters into their own hands. The Canadian believes in a square deal and when he doesn't get it is going to know the reason why. Men should be demobilized according to service yet the RCRs and 42nd, fifty per cent of whom are conscripts, were sent home while '14 and '15 men, married and with families, were being held back, and held back under rotten conditions. Camp life in England in winter is by no means the most pleasant and camp rations are not the best. Yet men are paid once a month only and then only a pound even though they have a credit of twenty or thirty pounds and are making from three and a half to four pounds a month besides their assigned pay. The Canadian will never kick about hardships when they are necessary but when they could be avoided and when the authorities refuse to let him spend a part of his own money to make himself more comfortable he has too much go in him to take it sitting down and when he finds that camp limits are unheeded he strikes and strikes hard for his rights. He has sacrificed too much to be bullied now and he wants to get home when his turn comes without having a bunch of conscripts that have been away for less than a year butting in ahead of him.[10]

Whatever other effects they might have had, the riots jolted military authorities. The movement of men was accelerated as much as possible. In the two weeks after the Kinmel Park riot, some 15,000 were returned to Canada and by the late summer almost all of the CEF was home.

Tens of thousands of them did not come home alone, for Canadians were used to hearing the kind of news that William McLellan, a student at the University of Alberta when he enlisted, gave his girlfriend: "Fred Fansher is taking a bride home too. She was evidently his nurse in hospital—I wish him luck but she must have been the exception that

Wedding day for a Canadian artilleryman and his English bride

proves the rule for the majority of girls in this country. I think the ones around here are kept for a sort of Coast defense scheme."[11] Marriages between Canadian soldiers and British women had become common after August 1917, when the government cancelled the regulation barring a war bride from collecting her husband's separation allowance unless the couple had been engaged before the war. There were many theories on the attraction of war marriages, such as an army chaplain's observation that Canadian soldiers liked British women because they "are not so 'spoiled' by over-much attention as are many of the women overseas, where their comparatively fewer numbers make them very much in demand at social affairs. The English girls, too, have a splendid reputation for hard work among colonials."[12] Whatever the reason, after the Armistice, the rush to the altar became a stampede. The Bishop of London's marriage licence registry in London, which specialized in quick weddings, saw a sharp rise in business. Military authorities reported in December 1918 that Canadian soldiers were marrying at a rate of about 300 a week, and the special bureau that the government had set up in British Columbia House to process the paperwork for new dependants was swamped. Thousands of wives and children had returned to Canada before November 1918, but after the Armistice the need was of an entirely different magnitude.

Wherever possible, families were kept together for the move to Canada, so a special discharge depot was set aside at Buxton, a resort town in Derbyshire. Appropriately, it had once been the Empire Hotel, the most expensive in Buxton, where in 1911 a single room rented for six shillings sixpence. But the arrangements were far from simple. Married soldiers continued to be the responsibility of the Department of Militia and Defence, while their dependants came under the purview of the Department of Immigration and Colonization. The government provided free third-class passage (wealthier passengers could purchase an upgrade) and families travelled on specially designated ships that carried no other soldiers—although they were separated, with husbands and wives berthed in different sections. But with shipping space at a premium, arrangements often had to be made on the spur of the moment, leaving some British women a matter of days to take leave of their families and get themselves and their belongings to a port of embarkation. Thousands

The Canadian Discharge Depot at Buxton, in the old Empire Hotel

of war brides travelled unaccompanied and faced the prospect of being off-loaded in Halifax or Montreal, perhaps with infants in tow, to fend for themselves and make their own way to new homes. To ease the transition, the YMCA set up welcome stations at the Atlantic ports and in all major urban railway stations where volunteers met war brides and offered them a meal and accommodation (if they wished to break their journey), advice, and assistance.

When the Department of Immigration and Colonization balanced its books, it reported having helped to bring over 54,000 soldiers' dependants to Canada; some were women who had followed their husbands to Britain earlier in the war, but the majority of them were war brides. For many women, the move was a jarring experience. Manchester was not so very different from Toronto, or Southampton from Vancouver, but for Dorothy Abraham moving to her husband's shack on Vargas Island, BC, was about as far from her English village as she could imagine. There were few other people, no school, no pub, no roads, no fields, no grass— and no tennis. Elsie Houghton gave up the civilized seaside resort town of Dover to live with her husband, the son of a Micmac chief, on the Lennox Island Indian Reserve in Prince Edward Island. Peggy Holmes found that her delicate English trousseau, which would have been perfect for the genteel surroundings of Hull in northern England, where she was raised, was a little less suitable for the northern Alberta homestead, thirty miles beyond the end of the railway line, where her husband took her to live. But for all that, there were some comforting familiarities to prove that their new homeland was not entirely alien. Dorothy and Teddy Abraham went to a church service in Montreal on their way westwards, and Dorothy was thrilled when one of the hymns was the very same hymn she had sung in the last visit to her own parish church before leaving England.

Not all newcomers in the 1920s were war brides, for the federal and provincial immigration bureaus had been hard at work through the war years to make sure that Canada remained in the minds of prospective immigrants once the war ended. And it was not just homesteaders who were wanted. Brigadier-General J.G. Ross hoped that "many of the splendid women war workers of England" would emigrate to Canada—"we have plenty of room, and lots of nice boys who would be fond of them."[13] Joe Leggett would have come. His experiences with Canadian soldiers around Grigg's Green made such a deep impression on him that he did all the paperwork to emigrate to Canada. Ill-health kept him in Britain, but thousands of others made the journey. And although the overall numbers were smaller than they had been before the war— over 1.3 million immigrants from Britain in the first two decades of the twentieth century, only some 570,000 in the 1920s and 1930s—Britain remained the country of origin of about 40 percent of all immigrants coming to Canada.

The movement began in 1919, when the Colonial Office established an Overseas Settlement Committee to help Britons emigrate within the Empire. At first, it targeted ex-soldiers, the offer of free passage attracting nearly 27,000 British veterans and their families to Canada in the first three years after the war. The program expanded in 1922 with the passage of Britain's Empire Settlement Act, which brought over 107,000 British immigrants to Canada between 1922 and 1935. The Canadian government was leery of assisted immigration schemes, believing (with some justification) that they often brought the least desirable kind of person, the malcontent looking for a free ride. However, concern about non-British immigration and the attempt to bring to Canada people of

PLATE 14. This booklet encouraged Ontario schoolchildren to reflect on the greatness of the British Empire.

PLATE 15. The Canadian soldier bridging the Atlantic and bringing together Canada and Britain.

PLATE 16. As soon as Canadian soldiers got into action, battle scenes became more common in posters and graphic art.

PLATE 17. Cecil Merritt of the South Saskatchewan Regiment was awarded the Victoria Cross for gallantry at Dieppe—and was later featured in a poster by the Wartime Information Board.

PLATE 18. Patriotic stationery from 1942.

PLATE 19. Charles Comfort's "The Hitler Line"—the Canadian campaign in Italy was featured on this poster for Victory Bonds.

PLATE 20. The Canadian beaver and the British lion, the latter complete with bandaged tail and Churchillian cigar.

PLATE 21. Churchill's plea to the Allied nations, with the iconic symbols of Canada and Britain.

PLATE 22. The Rhythm Rodeo entertained tens of thousands of Canadian troops, and a good number of British civilians, in the months after the end of the war in Europe.

British stock was a more powerful motive, and Ottawa eventually gave lukewarm support to the plan.

The legislation spurred all sorts of religious, philanthropic, and welfare agencies to mount emigration schemes, with varying degrees of success. The 3,000 Families Scheme, intended to establish experienced British farmers on quarter-sections provided free by the Canadian government, appeared to work well, but in reality the settlers drew such generous subsidies from London that they would have been hard-pressed to fail. Over 23,000 young women came to Canada to work as domestic servants, and a Saskatchewan clergyman who had lost two sons to the war founded the quaintly named Fellowship of the Maple Leaf to bring British missionaries to the prairies. The Empire headquarters of the Boy Scouts had an emigration department that sent to Canada nearly a thousand Scouts—just the sort of "sound lads from the Old Country" that were wanted as emigrants. The import of 12,000 harvest workers in 1923 was a great success, 80 percent of them electing to stay in Canada, but a repeat of the scheme in 1928 could not have gone worse. Some 10,000 men were brought over, but many of them appeared to have little interest in either Canada or work. Only one-quarter of them opted to stay, and one-third proved to be so dissolute that the British government had to pay for their passage home. It was that kind of outcome that gave assisted immigration a bad name.

The migration was not only from the Old Country to the New, for Britain had made enough of an impression on some members of the CEF that they elected to make it their home. In fact, some of them didn't even bother to return to Canada before making the move. There was no particular opposition to an individual being discharged in Britain, so long as certain criteria were met: officers or nursing sisters could resign their commissions wherever they chose, but a soldier could only take his discharge in Britain if he had been born there, had no dependants in Canada, had dependants in Britain who required his support, and had an offer of employment or other independent means. During the war, roughly 7,100 Canadian soldiers opted to be discharged in Britain, a little more than twice that number after the Armistice. Most of them were recent immigrants to Canada whose roots were not deep, but some were Canadian-born who had never even been to Britain before war took them there. Beverley Baxter, Alfred Critchley, and Garfield Weston were three such men who made the transition from Canada to Britain after the war.

Beverley Baxter was the son of a Yorkshireman in Toronto, where he worked as a piano salesman and tried to make his name as a novelist. He enlisted in 1915 and was eventually commissioned as a lieutenant in the Canadian Engineers. While serving in France, he crossed paths with Garfield Weston, whose family owned a successful Toronto bakery and who also went to the front with the Canadian Engineers, although he never got beyond the rank of sapper. Alfred Critchley was born on a Calgary ranch to British parents (he had visited Britain, but only as a child), and in 1914 he was working in a Winnipeg bank and serving part-time with Lord Strathcona's Horse; he enlisted with the 1st Contingent and ultimately rose to become the youngest brigadier-general in the BEF. The three men shared a number of characteristics. All were of British stock (in Weston's case, his grandparents were immigrants), and all had left Canada to serve with the CEF. Military service seems to have been an incredible tonic for them. Weston, just a schoolboy when war began, clearly had natural ability but, as one writer said, his youthful energy was "whetted by contact with war, danger and victory."[14] The same holds true for Baxter and Critchley, who lived, it must be admitted, rather shiftless lives before 1914. In each case, the war seems to have sharpened an innate ambition of the kind that could not be fulfilled by the relatively limited opportunities available in Canada. Baxter aspired to be a writer—he was savvy enough to express the right opinions to the right people and instead of returning to Canada to be demobilized and toil in the barren fields of Canadian letters, he took his discharge in Britain and by 1922 was the editor of the *Sunday Express*. Alfred Critchley did go back to Canada to be demobilized, but by the mid-1920s he was back in Britain to make a fortune in cement and greyhound racing. Garfield Weston had also been demobilized in Canada, returning to Toronto in 1919 to take over the family bakery business. Having put his leave time to good use while in the army, he knew what British manufacturers had to offer, and he soon brought over William Doyle, a leading baker from Britain, to manage the technical end of the business. In advertising, Weston emphasized the Britishness of the bakery's products—"biscuits as they are made in

England," read a sign in the window of a Dickensian shopfront that the company built for the Canadian National Exhibition—and having been so successful in Canada, it made sense to try his hand in the home of English biscuits. He bought his first British bakery in 1933, added five more in 1935 (the same year that he relocated his family to Britain), and in 1938 opened a state-of-the-art modern bakery in Wales. Through this period of transition, Weston argued that the ambitious Canadian could do no better than to look for opportunities in Britain: "Come to the Mother Country," he said in 1938, "Britain needs your enthusiasm."[15] He believed firmly that the new British Empire, strengthened and modernized by the First World War, was on the verge of great things: "I am convinced that the Empire is just starting, that it is starting from here, and that the leadership must come from here."[16]

Baxter, Critchley, and Weston, as affluent members of the Anglo-Canadian community, may well have known each other socially, but they certainly knew each other politically—all three of them eventually sat in the British House of Commons, or the Imperial Parliament as it was

A taste of home for Canadians overseas: Weston's biscuits on their way to the CEF

still known. The tradition of Canadians being elected to Westminster as
MPs went back to the nineteenth century, and in 1922 the New
Brunswick–born Andrew Bonar Law became the only British prime
minister to have been born outside Britain. But the number of Canadians
at Westminster increased in the interwar era, after Canada had made the
transition from colony to nation. Is it ironic that after the First World War,
the crucible of Canadian nationhood, more Canadians than ever opted to
seek a political career in Britain? Hamilton Gault, after declining to run for
election in Montreal, was elected as the Conservative MP for Taunton in
1924—sixteen other Anglo-Canadians won seats in the same election, and
six more were defeated. In 1934 Critchley became the Conservative MP for
Twickenham, on his third try at campaigning in Britain, and the following
year Beverley Baxter was elected in Wood Green. Garfield Weston was
acclaimed to represent the constituency of Macclesfield in 1939.

That a Calgary farm boy, a Toronto piano salesman, and a Toronto
baker should all sit as members of the British Parliament is not as
strange as it may sound. Such people were Anglo-Canadians in every
sense of the word, as comfortable in Britain as they were in Canada.
Indeed, they would have seen no inherent contradiction between the two
identities—moving to Britain did not necessarily make them any less
Canadian. It was not so much leaving Canada as going to a different part
of the British world. For them, Canada was to Britain as a province was
to the dominion. For an ambitious entrepreneur who had conquered
Nova Scotia, for example, conquering Canada was the next logical step.
And once one had done well in the Dominion, where else to go but the
imperial capital (as London was frequently called) to test one's abilities?
After all, who would want to play for the farm team if one could play in
the majors?

This kind of trans-Atlantic existence was helped by the ease of
communications. We tend to think that with modern air travel the
continents are much closer together now than they were for earlier
generations. But in the interwar era, frequent steamship sailings made
the north Atlantic almost a commuter route for people like Baxter,
Critchley, and Weston. The fact that it was so easy to travel back and
forth in turn allowed their Canadian and British identities to co-exist
in a way that might seem contradictory, but was in fact entirely natural.

By the same token, that kind of co-existence can help make sense of the shifting policies that successive Canadian governments adopted towards Britain and the Empire in the interwar era.

In foreign policy, the nationalist imperative that Robert Borden had championed still carried the day, and would continue to do so under his successors, Arthur Meighen and Mackenzie King. In 1918, Borden declined to support Dominion contributions to an Imperial Grand Fleet, just as Wilfrid Laurier had done more than a decade earlier. At the 1921 Imperial Conference, Meighen deflected British demands for a new treaty with Japan, insisting that such an alliance was not in Canada's best interests in a North American context. In 1922, when a disturbance at a Turkish dustbowl called Chanak threatened to blow up into a war, King held firm against British calls for support, just as Sir John A. Macdonald had tried to do over the Sudan and Laurier over the Boer War. Canada might well send aid, but would not offer a blank cheque, and would do nothing without parliamentary approval. This manoeuvering, which was rooted in Dominion demands for change in the Empire at the meeting of the Imperial War Cabinet in 1917, culminated in the 1926 Imperial Conference, which fundamentally altered relations between Britain and the Dominions. The British Empire was now the British Commonwealth of Nations, its members equal in all respects. The mother lion and her cubs was a thing of the past; the new Commonwealth was an association of siblings.

But it was still a family, and there was little appetite for divorce or even separation. At the 1926 conference, Mackenzie King fought against the South African prime minister's desire for an expression of dominion independence from Britain, in the full knowledge that such a position could never be sold in Canada. The war had not taught Canadians that they should separate from the Empire, but that they could exert a positive influence in a new, reshaped Empire. In an essay entitled "Canada as a British Nation," journalist and editor John Castell Hopkins argued that the war gave no reason to fear a continued association within the Empire, for there were many examples of countries putting themselves under the control of others for the greater good, without surrendering any of their national rights. Had not Britain and the United States placed themselves under the French general Foch in the Supreme War

Council of the Allies? Had not the Canadian Corps fought as part of the British Expeditionary Force? "Surely there was no fundamental reason for the lover of autonomy to fear closer Imperial unity after the War or to deem a concentrated policy of co-ordinated self-defense in trade, finance and military or naval matters, either impossible or unnecessarily undesirable!"[17]

So for every Chanak, there was another occasion when the Canadian government was willing, even eager, to be supportive of British imperial initiatives. One such instance involved the new world of air travel. In May 1924 British prime minister Ramsay MacDonald announced his government's commitment to an imperial airship program: Britain would undertake a massive research and development program to build a brand new, five-million-cubic-foot airship (the R101) and mooring masts in England and India, while a private firm would receive a contract to build a second airship (the R100) to the same specifications. It was all part of a grand scheme of imperial transportation that emerged at the 1926 Imperial Conference. Sir Samuel Hoare, Britain's Secretary of State for Air, opened the deliberations with a stirring summary of imperial aviation efforts and future prospects. Land and sea transportation, he observed, was unlikely to improve enough to make any appreciable difference in travelling time around the Empire; it had taken sixty days for the Australian and New Zealand delegations to reach London, and "they are likely to continue to take sixty days for many Conferences to come"—unless the Empire embraced the air. In the not-too-distant future, the farthest reaches of the Empire would be days, not weeks, away from the Mother Country. Airplanes will be used on shorter routes, he believed, but "airships will carry out the long-distance non-stop air journeys of the future," cruising between the great cities of the Empire and uniting the dominions like never before.[18]

Mackenzie King, far from being alarmed at the spectre of new imperial entanglements, professed to being thrilled by Hoare's romantic vision. He promptly committed Canada to participation in the imperial scheme; the Canadian government would build a mooring mast to become part of the Empire's network, and would also host the first overseas visit by one of the new airships. Four years later, on a warm August day in 1930, the R100 drifted up the St Lawrence to begin its Canadian visit. For twelve days, it cruised over southern Quebec and Ontario as hundreds of thousands of Canadians craned their necks and gazed in awe at what they believed was the future. The airship program held the promise that the British Empire, hobbled by war, would return to its former status as the greatest empire the world had ever seen. Lord Thomson of Cardington, then the British air minister, wrote that the scheme's aim was "to give a unity to widely scattered peoples, unattainable hitherto; to create a new spirit, or, maybe, to revive an old spirit which was drooping and to inculcate a conception of the common destiny and mission of our race."[19] Dennistoun Burney, a British financier who was one of the program's biggest boosters, took every opportunity to introduce Canadians to a new Empire. "We must superimpose upon our existing structures," he told the Canadian Club of Toronto, "a method of transport which will allow great statesmen, great business men and leaders to travel from one end of the Empire to the other with little delay in a short time." Once that structure was in place, the Empire would be transformed. "It would affect the British Empire not only economically but socially and politically," he said. He envisioned a day when 1,400-foot-long airships would carry 100 passengers and ten tons of cargo across the Atlantic in perfect safety and comfort, in an all-British, twice-weekly service between Canada and England. It was an opportunity no one could afford to pass up: "the pioneer spirit of Canada should associate itself with this enterprise, and send us back to England with the word, 'If you do not see it, we do.'"[20]

Countless people were drawn to this vision of imperial unity. Mackenzie King announced that it was the "consummation of the combined efforts of the British and Canadian governments to provide, by air navigation, yet another avenue of trade and commerce between this country and the old land." R.B. Bennett, the Conservative leader who defeated King in the 1930 federal election, proclaimed that the airship's visit "will bring us closer to the motherland."[21] The mayor of Toronto regarded the voyage of the R100 as "not merely a trans-Atlantic flight but the first step in a far-sighted plan to bind together the distant parts of the Empire, to expedite a more rapid service which will not only serve in a commercial sense but will rouse all people to the realization that they are being brought into closer contact by regular air routes throughout the world." In newspapers, magazines, aviation journals, even advertisements for cheese and cigarettes, the same future was conjured: "Leviathan of the air . . . looming gigantic in the heavens . . . annihilating space . . . spanning oceans . . . droning out its message of empire unity . . . cruising majestically with goodwill as freight . . . thrilling millions in that Empire upon which the sun never sets."[22]

But the airship age was not the future. When the R100's sister ship, the R101, exploded in a ball of flame in northern France in October 1930, it killed not only Lord Thomson and most of Britain's leading airshipmen, but the dream of an imperial airship service as well. The crash proved that the future of air travel lay not with the dirigible, but with the airplane. And this time, it was competition, in the form of the aggressive and well-financed American carrier PanAm, that spurred the cause of imperial co-operation, again with Canada's active support. Since its creation in 1927, PanAm had been developing services on routes in Central and South America, China, and the Pacific, and by the mid-1930s it was also seeking a monopoly in trans-Atlantic passenger services. At a conference in Ottawa in November 1935, government delegates from Canada, Britain, Ireland, and Newfoundland tried to hammer out a common imperial air policy. Action was imperative: PanAm was attempting to extend its operations into Alaska, the Arctic, and Newfoundland, and Canada could not afford to be complacent. The delegates eventually struck a deal that they hoped would forestall PanAm's ambitions: Imperial Airways, Britain's national airline, would get a fifteen-year monopoly on landing rights in Newfoundland, a prerequisite if Imperial was to begin a trans-Atlantic service. To ensure Canada's co-operation, the privilege would be extended to Canada's soon-to-be created national airline. Rather than try to compete head-on with PanAm, Commonwealth delegates offered the American carrier a partnership of sorts. After preliminary experimental flights, the carriers would operate two regular flights a week for three months. If they were successful, a regularly scheduled service with mandatory stops in Canada and Ireland would begin. PanAm and the Empire consortium would have reciprocal privileges on each other's routes; the American and British services would begin simultaneously, to ensure that neither side got a head start.

The Canadian public was overtaken by enthusiasm as the trans-Atlantic air services came closer to fruition. That enthusiasm received a boost when Britain's new long-range flying boats took to the air in early 1937. The first two aircraft, the *Caledonia* and the *Cambria*, were to be used on Imperial Airways' north Atlantic run; PanAm would use the Boeing 314 *Clipper*. On 5 July 1937, as PanAm's *Clipper* was leaving its base in Port Washington, New York, the *Caledonia* departed from Foynes, Ireland, bound for Botwood, Newfoundland, and Montreal. It carried no passengers or freight; every non-essential, even the floorboards, had been stripped out to save weight. The *Caledonia* and the *Cambria* would make five round-trip Atlantic flights that summer, creating a sensation in Canada just as the R100 had done. When the *Caledonia* first landed in Montreal on 8 July 1937, "business practically ceased for about 15 minutes as thousands rushed to windows, roofs and streets." In September, the *Cambria* embarked on a tour of southern Ontario, including stops in Ottawa, Toronto, Windsor, and Hamilton. In Toronto, "the populace were warned of the arrival by blasts of factory whistles, also by flash broadcasts over local radio broadcast stations, given during the flight from Ottawa"; as many as 20,000 people crammed the CNE waterfront to watch the flying boat's arrival. It was the same wherever the *Cambria* and the *Caledonia* appeared; government officials estimated that 3.5 million people saw the aircraft on their demonstration flights.

Imperial Airways mounted further test flights in 1938, but problems with new equipment caused delays and PanAm was first out of the gate, beginning regularly scheduled trans-Atlantic service in June 1939. Carrying a full complement of luminaries, the *Yankee Clipper* left Port Washington at 1:21 in the afternoon on 24 June. On 28 June, after a three-day layover in Shediac and twenty-six hours in the air, the flying boat touched down on Southampton Water. The PanAm service was everything its promoters had promised: speedy, reliable, safe, and, above all, opulent. The passenger quarters were not spacious, but white-coated stewards served gourmet meals at tables set with crisp linen, fine china, and fresh flowers. Once Imperial Airways got its service up and running, it would be similar—fine food and wine as the flying boats ate up the miles between the great cities of the Empire. As Beverley Baxter, then writing for *Maclean's* magazine, put it, every journey would be like "a yachting party in the air."[23] But it was a yachting party with a decidedly British tone. There were strong reasons, both financial and practical, for

Canada to throw its lot in with PanAm, with its impressive track record of efficiency and profitability. But in the 1930s, those reasons couldn't outweigh the appeal of supporting an airline named Imperial.

If it was lobster and Chablis in the skies, it was gruel and water for the Canadian military. The peace, to be blunt, had been a nasty shock, for there were no grand imperial schemes to bolster morale and budgets. No one expected that the large wartime establishments would be maintained after the Armistice, but few could have predicted the depth of the cuts. By August 1922, the strength of the Permanent Force had been reduced to a little over 3,500 all ranks, and about 50,000 officers and men were supposed to have had some militia training. But as the federal government cut budgets to cope with the Depression, the three services faced a battle for survival. The Royal Canadian Navy came very close to being slashed out of existence, its vessels put on care and maintenance and its men paid off. The RCAF faced a budget that allowed it to add just two aircraft and thirty-eight airmen, not even enough to cover normal attrition. By May 1934, the air force had just nineteen aircraft, only one of which could be considered modern—and it was on a one-year loan from the British. Its nine fighter aircraft were Siskins, which the RAF had pulled from service as obsolete in 1932, and only one of them was armed. Perhaps it scarcely mattered, though, because the RCAF barely had enough money to fly at all.

The militia had its own problems. In 1925, its budget dropped below 1914 levels, and went down from there. In the early 1930s, its funding amounted to about $15 per militia soldier per year, and most units were kept going by the generosity of their officers. One battalion had a mechanical transport section but for thirteen long years was issued no mechanical transport of any kind; the officers used their own money to buy motorcycles for the unit, and for trucks they had to make do with two tired old vans that they begged from the post office, which had declared them unsafe for use. One artillery battery, for its training shoot, could muster just ten shells; had Canada been invaded in 1935, ordnance stores held sufficient ammunition for only ninety minutes of firing. The coastal defence guns in British Columbia were so decrepit that the crews were afraid to fire them, lest they came apart on the first shot. There was not a single anti-aircraft gun, not a single aerial bomb, in the country. Canada was, for all intents and purposes, defenceless.

Facing the government's budgetary knives, a small yet very vocal anti-military lobby, and a generally apathetic public, the military could at least take refuge in its British connections, in various forms. For an ambitious graduate of the Royal Military College of Canada, the only options for further professional training were in the Empire, at the Senior Officers School at Sheerness, the Staff Colleges at Camberley and Quetta, or the Imperial Defence College in London. Apprenticeships of a sort existed in the form of temporary postings to the War Office for training purposes, a program that had lapsed in 1914 but was reactivated in 1925. More and more Canadian units were granted permission to adopt the prefix "Royal" and militia regiments continued to invite members of the Royal Family to act as their Colonels-in-Chief. Maurice Pope, who had served in the Canadian Engineers during the First World War and stayed on to make the army his career, provided an evaluation of Canada's military between the wars that bears a striking resemblance to George Stanley's assessment of the pre-1914 military:

> The war establishment of our units and the composition of our formations were precisely those of the British Regular Army. All our manuals were British and so was our tactical training. Practically all our equipment had been obtained in the United Kingdom. . . . To qualify for higher rank our permanent force officers were required to sit for examinations set and marked by the War Office. . . . Our army was indeed British through and through with only minor differences imposed on us by purely local conditions.[24]

Critics accused Canada's soldiers of getting too close to Britain and becoming part of the imperial army in all but name. As one think tank observed in a 1934 report, "It was noted how members of the Canadian permanent forces are sent regularly to England for training, and how Canadian army regulations and equipment are co-ordinated with those of the British Army. At critical moments on the eve of war the advice of military authorities is apt to become only too influential, and in Canada

this advice would be imperialist in its sympathies." Soldiers would take
exception to the second suggestion, but the first was freely admitted,
for they really had very little alternative. Young men who yearned to
follow in the footsteps of the flying aces of the Great War could either
hope to win one of the few spots available in the peacetime RCAF, which
demanded a university degree, or travel to Britain to join the RAF, which
did not. Interested applicants with a private pilot's licence in hand could
present themselves at the Air Ministry in London and apply for a Short
Service Commission; if they were accepted, their travel expenses to
Britain would be reimbursed and they became an officer in the RAF for a
three-year term. It started slowly, with only three Canadians in the fifty-
two-man intake in 1934, but over time the restrictions were relaxed. A
pilot's licence was no longer required, and potential recruits could be
screened in interviews and medicals conducted by the RCAF in Canada;
by 1937, the RCAF was even providing preliminary flying training to
Short Service Commission volunteers. By this time, there were almost
certainly more Canadians in the RAF than in the RCAF—men like Ian
Bazalgette, whose father had served in the CEF and had moved his family
from Calgary to Britain in the mid-1920s; and Richard Denison, born
in London to a British mother and a Canadian soldier father, raised
in Vernon, BC, and a volunteer to the RAF in 1935. But in a very real
sense, it was government parsimony as much as sentiment that drove
men like Bazalgette and Denison, as well as the Canadian military more
generally, into the arms of the British. If the government declined to
pay for new training manuals or syllabi, what choice did they have but
to use Britain's? There was no money for staff training, so what could
be done but to send promising officers to Camberley or Sheerness? New
equipment was nowhere on the horizon, so it would have been foolish
to turn down British gifts or loans. One gets the kind of armed forces
one is willing to pay for and, since the federal government was not
willing to pay for a distinctly Canadian military, it got one that looked
very much like Britain's.

In any case, soldiers were far from the only Canadians who were
still imperialist in sympathy. From their earliest days in the classroom,
children received an education that was still strongly British and imperial
in tone. Their textbooks described the reshaping of the Empire that gave

the Dominions greater freedom from Britain, but insisted that those changes did not alter the general orientation of Canada:

> the British Empire will be stronger and more united when bound together by the silken threads of sentiment rather than by rigid links of law . . . the Crown of Great Britain is still the Crown of Canada; and even when negotiating separately with foreign countries, the Canadian government still speaks in the name of King George VI.[25]

Although the new Commonwealth was a family of equals, the parent/child relationship remained a popular metaphor. According to one textbook (that went through thirteen editions between 1928 and 1943), the war

> created a feeling of greater understanding and sympathy between the Mother Country and the Overseas Dominions . . . Great Britain is the Mother nation and the others are the daughter nations. Now, the daughter who leaves her mother's house to build a home of her own continues to love and respect her mother and to ask her advice on matters of importance. The wise mother leaves her daughter free to order her own home as she sees fit, but stands ready to help if the occasion arises. In a similar way the Mother Country has given her daughter nations all that each desires in the way of self-government. Canada and each of her sister nations can therefore say: "Daughter am I in my mother's house; / But mistress in my own."[26]

This blend of imperialism and nationalism was celebrated on special days throughout the school year. Many school districts adopted the idea of Flag Days, two days each month that marked significant historical events in British and Canadian history, such as the signing of the Magna Carta or the Battle of Trafalgar, and Empire Day remained one of the most important occasions on the school calendar. Although Member of Parliament Agnes MacPhail derided it as "the occasion for nothing but a strutty, silly, pompous, bombastic performance by military men and those who are backing them," it was clearly much more than that to those who celebrated it.[27] A pamphlet distributed by the Ontario government to mark Empire Day 1928 was typical of the sentiments. It contained, in fact, not a single mention of the military or war, but was a celebration of the Empire as something greater than the nation. It began with two poems by Colin J. Atkinson, "The Empire is Our Country" and "The Union Jack" ("Whenever British Children dwell / Or British folk may be, / On Empire Day our flag shall tell / That we are Britons free"), and included messages from prominent politicians. Provincial Minister of Education Howard Ferguson observed that "the Canadian is protected from narrow provincialism by the fact that his place in the Empire gives him a broad outlook. He is at home in Africa, in Asia, in Australasia, and in Europe because in all those continents the honour of being a British subject is held in high regard." Empire Day, in the minds of those who supported it, was not about subordinating nation to empire, but allowing the nation to grow and prosper within a greater entity. The new Empire was nothing like the old one; it was more like a United Nations: "The purpose of Empire Day is to develop the sense of national and imperial unity and to enlarge the ideas and ideals of citizenship . . . I cannot see Canadians giving up that primary principle on which their country is built, that is their determination to remain British. As British, Canada will continue to live."

Even in the memory of the First World War, which by common consent had brought Canada to a new sense of nationhood, the imperial context in which the nation flourished was always present. In memorial volumes, graphic art, war memorials, any context in which the war memory was expressed, national symbols—the maple leaf, the beaver, the caribou—shared space with British or imperial symbols—the lion, crowns, John Bull. One of the most popular paintings to come out of the war, with contemporaries if not with later critics, was Byam Shaw's *The Flag*, which shows a Canadian soldier, the Red Ensign draped around him, lying at the feet of a British lion—the consummate mingling of empire and nation. When British prime minister Stanley Baldwin arrived in Canada in July 1927 to dedicate the altar in the Peace Tower, becoming the first prime minister to visit an overseas dominion, Mackenzie King's welcome was anything but a declaration of independence from the Empire: "There never was a time in the history of Canada when its citizens were more conscious of their unity, or enjoyed a greater pride in their native land; and that at no time has Canada been happier in her relation with all parts of the British Empire or more loyal to the crown."

Veterans' organizations tend to be among the most nationalist groups in society, and the same was true in Canada. But when the Canadian Legion was founded in 1925, it was as a part of the British Empire Service League, which had been established in South Africa in 1921 (three times the League held its international conference in Canada, in 1925, 1931, and 1949). Similarly, the Canadian Legion stated proudly that it was "intensely national and British," with no contradiction implied.[28] "British" in this usage referred not to a nationality but to an historical legacy. It was entirely appropriate for the Legion to be a passionate defender of the Canadian nation and of the British tradition at the same time. Even the Vimy Pilgrimage of 1936, when over 6,000 Canadian veterans and their families travelled to France for the unveiling

Symbols of Canada and Britain intermingled at the unveiling of the war memorial in Essex, Ontario, on Victoria Day, 1929.

of the memorial on the battlefield that was proclaimed the birthplace of the Canadian nation, was a celebration of empire as well as nation. Much was made of the fact that King Edward VIII, the former Prince of Wales, unveiled the memorial as King of Canada. As the Pilgrimage's souvenir volume put it, "His Majesty co-operated whole-heartedly in demonstrating that the elements which unite Canada to the Motherland have a spiritual quality far more powerful and of infinitely greater value than words or documents or enactments."[29]

In his speeches during the Pilgrimage, the King often referred to his 1919 visit and the pleasure it had given him to be received so enthusiastically in the senior dominion. He never had the chance to come to Canada as its King, for shortly after the Pilgrimage he abdicated the throne to marry the woman he loved, the American divorcée Wallis Simpson. Edward VIII was the first monarch to act as King of Canada—his brother, as King George VI, would be the first monarch to visit as King of Canada. Mackenzie King and Vincent Massey had been working on the visit for some years, although each was prone to downplaying the other's role. Massey, the High Commissioner in London, was as anglophile as anyone, educated at the University of Toronto and Balliol College, Oxford, and an heir to the Massey-Harris empire, which had already set about conquering the world, one tractor at a time. King, for his part, was a man of sharp contrasts. He could be positively allergic to any kind of imperial centralization, seeing at every turn plots to ensnare his government in British wars, but at the same time he was vain and very fond of the kind of ritual that a monarchy could provide. For King, a royal visit would massage his vanity and pander to his love of pomp and circumstance, while at the same time providing a boost to his Liberal Party, of which he was obsessively partisan. B.K. Sandwell, the editor of *Saturday Night* magazine, thought in grander terms, seeing the visit as a boon to national unity: "So long as we have no King on the spot, and nothing but representatives, it is easy to remember the divisions and hard to remember the unity."[30]

On the 17th of May 1939, their majesties arrived in Quebec on the *Empress of Australia*, along with fifty tons of gold being sent to Canada for safekeeping in case things went bad in Europe. King George VI thus became the first reigning monarch to set foot on Canada—if one overlooks the elderly woman from Kirkland Lake, Ontario, who appeared on the dock at Quebec completely convinced that she was Queen Victoria. For the next four weeks, King George and Queen Elizabeth travelled across Canada in the deep blue and gold pinstriped Royal Train that came complete with a mauve-tiled bathroom, a twelve-person formal dining room, and a mobile post office that in one day could handle 250,000 pieces of specially postmarked mail. There was even a library on board for their majesties where they could learn about their surroundings by reading Stephen Leacock's *Sunshine Sketches of a Little Town*, Pauline Johnson's *Legends of Vancouver*, J.M. Gibbon's *Canadian Folk Songs*, or *The Golden Treasury of Canadian Verse*. If either of them had trouble sleeping, there was always W.P.M. Kennedy's *The Constitution of Canada*.[31]

Mackenzie King was never far from their royal elbows. The Governor General had no legal or ceremonial purpose when the reigning monarch was in the country; Lord Tweedsmuir, who had come to fame as the novelist John Buchan, saw the prime minister's determination to play host and took himself off on a fishing holiday. King spent much of his time watching carefully for any slight. His suspicions were raised when George McCullagh's horse won the King's Plate; McCullagh, founder of *The Globe and Mail*, was a staunch Conservative and King assumed that a Tory conspiracy had taken his horse to the winner's circle, the same conspiracy that was aimed at toppling his Liberals from power—today Woodbine raceway, tomorrow the House of Commons.

The paranoid prime minister aside, everyone else was content to bask in the regal glow. For a country struggling out from under the Depression and watching wearily as its leaders sniped at each other, it was a month of bliss. Enormous crowds greeted the royal couple wherever they went and people who lived off the train's route thought nothing about driving for hours just to be near as the train chugged past, to catch a few seconds' glimpse of the King and Queen waving from the rear observation platform. The King exceeded all expectations—painfully shy and apt to worry himself to exhaustion, he nevertheless appeared to be enjoying himself and carried off his speeches with a skill that deeply impressed his handlers. But it was the Queen who stole hearts. Stylishly dressed and always with a dazzling smile, she greeted everyone with genuine enthusiasm and charm, knowing apparently instinctively what should be said and to whom. Even the cynical and hard-boiled journalists who followed the tour were swept up by her spell. "Although we didn't see them in any way," wrote poet James Reaney in an ode to the stop in Stratford, Ontario, "I'll remember it to my dying day."[32]

More than anything else, the Royal Visit affirmed the value of the British connection. The King and Queen made it impossible to be anti-monarchist, or even anti-British. The *nationaliste* newspaper *La Presse* warned its readers to be wary of imperialist propaganda but admitted that there was nothing wrong in cheering George as King of Canada—so long as the cheers were in French. At the end of Queen Victoria's reign, a person could look at a map and glory at being part of the greatest empire the world had ever known. In the summer of 1939, Canadians could look at their monarchs and glory at being their subjects. Thirteen-year-old Ellen Higgins of Brantford, Ontario, was a winner in the Toronto *Star Weekly* poetry contest, her poem "Canada Welcomes Their Majesties" summing up what the visit meant to Canadians: "Our Canada is British as it was in days of yore . . . I know this is my country—from mountain unto sea; / I love it for 'tis British and I love its loyalty."[33]

On 21 May 1939, in the first week of the tour, the royal couple was in Ottawa to unveil the National War Memorial. Nearly twenty years in the making, it combined realism and allegory in one of the greatest achievements in modern commemorative art. And it seemed perfectly fitting that George VI, as King of Canada, should unveil the monument to a war that marked Canada's coming of age as a nation. When the formalities had concluded, the royal couple brushed aside the concerns of their security detail and took themselves into the crowd to mingle with war veterans—the first ever royal walkabout. It was a glorious day, and the deteriorating situation in Europe could be forgotten for a few hours. The week before, Nazi Germany had gobbled up much of the western half of Czechoslovakia, turning it into the Protectorate of Bohemia and Moravia in the Nazis' last "non-violent" conquest before turning on Poland to set in motion the Second World War. The glow of unveiling the memorial to Canada's first great war had barely faded when the nation's second great war began, and the children of the Canadian Expeditionary Force were called upon to take up their parents' quarrel with the foe.

FIVE

A NEW GENERATION IN THE OLD COUNTRY

In 1939, Stephen Leacock was resting comfortably on his laurels as one of the most beloved writers in the English-speaking world. Since before the First World War, the favourite son of Orillia, Ontario, had delighted readers in Canada, the United States, and Britain with his whimsical tales of small-town life, big-city preoccupations, and human foibles. Like all great satirists, Leacock was an exceptionally keen observer of the human condition—he saw through people, and understood them better than they might have understood themselves. Just before the British Empire went to its third war in his lifetime, he interpreted Canada's ties to Britain for readers of the American magazine *Atlantic Monthly*: "If you were to ask any Canadian, 'Do you people *have* to go to war if England does?' he'd answer at once, 'Oh, no.' And if you then said, 'Would you go to war if England did?' he'd answer, 'Oh, yes.' And if you asked 'Why?' he'd say, reflectively, 'Well, you see, we'd *have* to.'"[1]

That was the sentiment with which Canada went to war in 1939: the excitement of 1914 was missing, but there was the same underlying determination that a job had to be done. Few Canadians felt any sense of being compelled against their will to fight with Britain; it was simply the right thing to do. And so the men came forward to enlist in the first contingent, in even greater numbers than the men of their fathers' generation had done, and sailed for Britain to re-establish the Canadian empire there. The echoes of 1914 were powerful, but not entirely welcome. Charles Ritchie, a secretary at the Canadian High Commission in London, was saddened as another expeditionary force prepared to sail for Britain: "Surely one generation should be allowed to die off before another war is started," he observed.[2]

Prime Minister Mackenzie King was going about the business of governing in late August 1939, dividing his time between working at Kingsmere, his Quebec country estate, and attending to official duties in Ottawa. He had been monitoring the dispatches from Europe carefully, and on 30 August he warned his cabinet ministers that they should stay in Ottawa over the coming weekend—he well remembered the problems that might ensue should war come while members of the government were scattered across the country. On Friday morning, the 1st of September, King was awakened at 6:30 AM by the news that Germany had invaded Poland. He summoned his cabinet to meet at 9 AM, and read them a prepared statement. Canada was now in a state of apprehended war and, although Britain had not yet declared war on Germany, the Canadian government had already decided to stand at Britain's side. To give effect

On 4 September 1939, crowds gathered on Parliament Hill in Ottawa to hear a radio speech by King George VI.

to that decision, Parliament would convene the following Thursday so that King could seek from the House of Commons the authority for "effective co-operation by Canada at the side of Britain." This was King's fig leaf: Parliament will decide, even if the decision had, for all intents and purposes, already been made—King was just as shrewd an observer as Leacock, and he fully understood the public mood. The House met on 7 September, and on the 9th it approved the government's decision without a formal vote. Early on the morning of 10 September, King George VI accepted the government's advice and Canada was at war.

But this was not 1914 all over again; there were no marching bands or firecrackers in the streets, no crowds of giddy civilians singing with patriotic fervour. Public opinion was aroused when German torpedoes sank the Montreal-bound passenger liner *Athenia*, killing over a hundred passengers, including ten-year-old schoolgirl Margaret Hayworth of Hamilton, Ontario, who became Canada's first symbol of Nazi infamy. But beyond that, newspapers were restrained and Canadians stoic. It was the end of a dismal decade that had seen a third of Canadians lose their jobs, countless farms and businesses wiped out, and governments pushed to the very brink of bankruptcy. It was almost as if the country was too exhausted to get worked up over anything.

Yet when the call for recruits went out, it was picked up eagerly, despite the pervasive sense of ennui. Officially, the requirements stated that volunteers had to be between the ages of eighteen and forty-five, with a minimum height of 5'4"; they also had to be British subjects "of good character." To avoid wasting potential officers or experts in the infantry, various other classes were not permitted to enlist: university or college graduates in the engineering, scientific, or technical professions, graduates of medical programs or the Royal Military College, ex-cadets of the Canadian Officer Training Corps, bankers, and accountants. Even with these restrictions, the flood of volunteers overwhelmed many units. Occasionally wearing First World War uniforms and using twenty-year-old attestation forms, militia sergeants struggled to cope with the crush of volunteers. By the end of September, they had enrolled 58,337 volunteers, including over 4,000 veterans of the First World War.

Some of the volunteers were probably near desperation, for they might not have had a job in their entire adult lives, but we should not imagine that the idealism of the Great War had disappeared entirely. Many men spoke of patriotism, of a quest for adventure, of a desire to escape the boredom of everyday life, of the need to fight the Nazis before they overwhelmed the world. Claude Châtillon, who enlisted in the Royal 22nd Regiment (the Van Doos, and formerly the 22nd Battalion of the CEF), was moved by a vague feeling that something was deeply wrong in Europe: "something is happening over there that has profoundly touched me, my convictions and my principles. It's a reality I can no longer avoid . . . it's a war of ideas . . . of freedom, of rights, without discrimination as to origin, age, or colour . . . in Europe, it has gone out of control with cruel savagery." Soon, the songs, posters, and poems started to pick up the images and phrases of the last war. The metaphor for the family to describe the Empire was not as common, but there were plenty of other echoes of the past. Charles G.D. Roberts won a war poetry contest with an entry entitled "Canada Speaks of Britain"—honourable mentions went to "The British," "My England!" and "A Ballade of Canada and England," among others. Songs like Hugh Brodie's "My Flag and Yours," in which ". . . countless voices ring, / In grand acclaim, Britannia's name, / Hail Country, Flag and King," could easily have come straight out of 1914. Symbols of Britain continued to abound in visual art, whether it be the Union Jack (still Canada's official flag) or the British crown and lion. And in spite of the Statute of Westminster, "empire" remained a far more popular word than "commonwealth," at least amongst Canadian writers and politicians.

Unlike 1914, however, there would be no triumphant voyage of a contingent to Britain. There was no Sam Hughes, with his fondness for the dramatic gesture, just very organized and businesslike movements of troops. The top brass went first, and established Canadian Military Headquarters (CMHQ) on Cockspur Street in London—just a stone's throw from the Canadian High Commission and soon to be the nerve centre of Canada's new empire in Britain. On 17 December 1939 the first seven ocean liners, carrying 7,500 soldiers, docked in Scotland and Canadian units began heading south to take up residence in their training areas. Some of them ended up in the very same places as their predecessors a generation earlier. "The citizens greeted us with open arms," wrote Karl Butler, a young Sydney steelworker who enlisted in 1939, to his parents

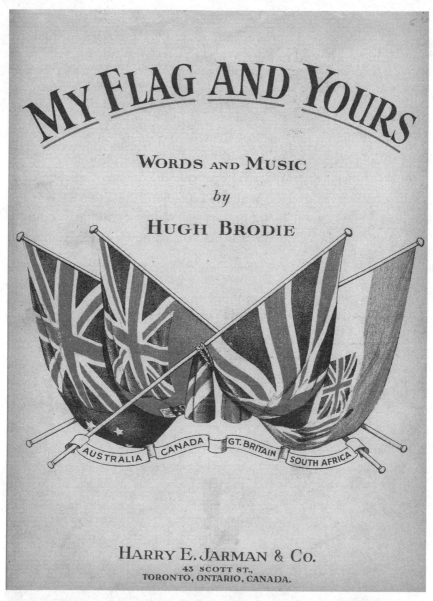

This song was published in 1940, but the illustration could easily have come from 1914 or even 1899.

in Cape Breton shortly after arriving in Britain. "We were treated like princes. . . . We were living off the reputation that our other boys made in the last war—I only hope that we keep up the reputation."[3] But the echoes of the past were sometimes too strong. The Royal Canadian Regiment took up residence at Pirbright, near Aldershot, to engage in intensive training in trench warfare. Every day the men learned the finer points of fire trenches, communication trenches, dugouts, and saps, just as their fathers had done. The Queen's Own Rifles paid homage to the past in a different way when Captain Warde Taylor and Rifleman William Sanders laid a wreath on the grave of Roy Gzowski. Taylor and Sanders had both been with the regiment on its 1910 trip to Aldershot, and had attended Gzowski's funeral after his death from typhoid. The two Canadian-born soldiers had served overseas with the Canadian Expeditionary Force in the First World War, and their pilgrimage to Aldershot Military Cemetery during the Second World War affirmed the continuity of the Canadian empire in Britain.

By the time the first Canadian units were settled, the Phoney War was in full swing. It was given that name only partly in jest, for there didn't seem to be a real war going on at all. Most people expected the Nazis, after overrunning Poland, to turn elsewhere immediately, but nothing happened. Weeks passed, then months, and still the German armies remained idle. Just as a sense of complacency began to take hold,

The 1st Division arrives in Britain, 1939.

in April 1940 the Nazis swept through Denmark and Norway. Then, after a brief pause, the *Blitzkrieg* crashed into the Low Countries and France. Within weeks, France and its powerful army of ninety-five divisions was humbled and the twelve divisions of the British Expeditionary Force, after fighting a string of bitter rearguard actions, had been lifted off the continent at Dunkirk. Britain would surely be the next target. The Empire stood alone.

The British Isles was transformed into an armed camp as its people prepared to meet the invasion that seemed inevitable. Farm fields were dotted with obstacles to prevent enemy gliders from landing, and road signs were taken down as a means of confounding the invader. Cement bunkers and blockhouses went up across the south coast, camouflaged to look like cottages, cafés, even haystacks. A strict blackout was enforced, while bridges, railway junctions, waterworks, hydroelectric plants, and a host of other critical sites were patrolled, often by the Home Guard— Dad's Army, mostly Great War veterans who were too old for front-line service but could still do their bit. And a few miles across the English Channel, German troops gathered. Adolf Hitler visited them and stood on the coast, gazing at the White Cliffs of Dover through field glasses.

Realizing that air superiority was essential for the invasion of England to succeed, German air force commander Hermann Göring directed his airmen to concentrate on destroying the Royal Air Force and its airfields. In July and August 1940, the *Luftwaffe* came very close to achieving that goal, as pilot losses and damage to Britain's communications network and airfields almost crippled the RAF. Guarding the skies were the men of Fighter Command, some 2,300 pilots on whom the survival of Britain depended. They represented a kind of united nations—more than half were British, but there were pilots from every part of the Empire, as well as Poles, Czechs, Frenchmen, Belgians, Irishmen, and Americans. Canada's colours were carried by two units. No. 242 Squadron RAF had been formed in October 1939, mainly from Canadians who had joined the peacetime RAF on Short Service Commission in the 1930s. During the Battle of France in May 1940, 242 was badly cut up; because most of the new pilots posted to the squadron, including the new commanding officer, were British, much of its Canadian character was lost. The unit fought gallantly during the Battle of Britain, only to be transferred to the Far East and annihilated in 1942 when the Japanese overran Java. The other Canadian squadron was No. 401 which (as 1 Squadron RCAF) had been stationed at Dartmouth, Nova Scotia, in the spring of 1940. Quickly shipped to Britain, it became operational on 17 August 1940, at the height of the Battle of Britain, although its first action a week later was one the pilots would sooner forget: the squadron shot down two British medium bombers that had been wrongly identified as German aircraft.

Ironically, on the same day the tide turned, although this only became clear in hindsight. On 24 August, two German bombers assigned to attack aircraft factories and oil storage tanks east of London lost their way. Unable to locate their targets and harried by anti-aircraft fire, they jettisoned their bombs over the city centre. It was the first air raid on London since May 1918, and British Prime Minister Winston Churchill was quick to order a retaliatory strike on Berlin. Neither raid caused significant damage, but the exchange shifted the focus of the German air offensive. Angered by the attack on Berlin and exasperated by the *Luftwaffe*'s failure to neutralize the RAF, Hitler ordered the air effort away from Fighter Command, which was then approaching the breaking point, and to London. On 7 September 1940, the Blitz began in earnest. The city would endure fifty-seven consecutive nights of bombing before Göring widened the attack to industrial centres, ports, and historic cities. On 14 November, ten hours of bombing left the centre of Coventry ablaze, its cathedral a ruin, its transportation and utilities infrastructure shattered. Large aircraft factories made Coventry a legitimate military target, but public outrage at the damage to the historic city was heightened by German boasts that the *Luftwaffe* could "Coventrize" any target at will. Attacks on English cities would continue until the spring of 1941, when the *Luftwaffe* withdrew its bomber force for the invasion of the Soviet Union. Some 40,000 civilians were killed and a million homes destroyed.

Those desperate months produced some of the most enduring images of the war: the dome of St Paul's Cathedral shrouded in smoke, the King and Queen stepping gingerly through the rubble of the imperial capital, aircraft condensation trails spidering across the southern English sky. It would be difficult to overestimate the impact of the Battle of Britain and the Blitz on Canadian opinion. They dominated the nation's newspapers with banner headlines, stories from the Canadian Press and other wire services, photographs, maps, and eyewitness accounts. Precise statements of damage and casualties were not permitted, but newspapers included as many human interest stories as they could. In early 1941, Hugh Templin of the Fergus *News-Record* was dispatched to Britain by the Canadian Weekly Newspaper Association to do a series of articles on the impact of the war in England. His eighteen-part series eventually appeared in more than 500 weekly newspapers across Canada. *Saturday Night* and *Maclean's* covered the Blitz extensively, with opinion pieces and first-hand accounts such as "This Was My First Air Raid" and "Democratic Bombs"; even specialist publications like *Canadian Banker* covered the bombing raids.

More important was CBC Radio, which provided on-the-spot reports from the heart of the Blitz, complete with recordings of bomb blasts and anti-aircraft guns. *We Have Been There* broadcast first-hand stories from Canadians in Britain, and was such a success that the CBC sold more than 25,000 printed copies of the text by the spring of 1942. Just as popular was *Old Country Mail*, excerpts from letters written by people across England; it was first broadcast on 13 September 1939, and by the end of 1940 excerpts from some 1,600 letters had been read on the air. There was even a radio soap opera entitled *Front Line Family*, which featured the residents of 88 Ashleigh Road, "an ordinary, common little semi-detached house, like thousands of other homes in England." It followed the family as they lived through the Blitz and became hugely popular, not only in Canada but in Britain and the United States as well. Britain's resistance fascinated the Canadian public. Accounts tended to be built on a cast of standard characters: the young fighter pilot dozing on a lawn chair in the sun, waiting for the order to scramble; the genial cockney matron brewing tea in the wreckage of her east London home; the stoic constable, unruffled by the destruction around him; and the children who played happily amidst the rubble of their neighbourhood. "The people are not only existing, they seem to be living normally, in fact happily," the *Montreal Standard*'s Davidson Dunton told CBC listeners in May 1941. "You hear them talking cheerily to one another. They chat about the latest bombing and prospects of more, as we would about the weather."[4] Account after account lauded their courage under fire and their determination to ensure that it was business as usual. Garfield Weston, in a talk from London, "the heart of the Empire, and tonight, the battlefront of civilization," that was broadcast in Canada on the CBC, paid tribute to British resolve:

> What an age in which to live! A second Elizabethan Era. Another Elizabeth graces the throne of England and a handful of her finest sons go forth to meet their Armada of the air. . . . Canadians, may your dearest dreams of childhood, in which you saw as a dazzling picture the greatness and glory of the Empire, your Empire, inspire you tonight. . . . there is hardly a person in this Old Mother Country who would not rather be here than any other place in the world. This is their shining hour; blessed with the power of supreme sacrifice, the hour in which a whole nation is knowing the glory of a resurrection and is ready to fulfil its destiny. And we Canadians here are proud indeed to stand in the front line with them and share their ordeal. The Battle of Britain is now at its height. With the prodigal abandon of a desperate gambler, Hitler is sending his bombers by the thousands. Day and night they come in, wave after wave, to rain destruction from the air in the hope of smashing Britain and her people into submission. But have no fear . . . the morale of the nation is higher than ever. Like fine steel tempered by the flame, this country stands firm and resolute.[5]

The experience of the Blitz was brought to Canadians in an even more personal and immediate way than over the airwaves. Since the First World War, when German bombs had devastated parts of urban England, fears had been growing of the civilian casualties that might be caused by air raids in a future war. Predicted death tolls were thrown around with abandon, and the popular media painted horrific pictures of the great cities of Britain reduced to rubble, their streets clogged with the bodies of the dead. The nightmare scenario was powerful enough to spur the British government to action. A House of Commons committee recommended evacuation of the most vulnerable people from urban areas in the event of war and divided the country into evacuable areas, reception areas (where evacuees would be billeted), and neutral areas (which could expect neither bombing nor evacuees). The evacuable areas were those deemed to be under direct threat of aerial attack: London and its environs; the cities of the industrial Midlands, including Birmingham, Manchester, and Liverpool; and major ports. It was estimated that roughly twelve million people in those areas were potential evacuees. The government also decided that it would determine the date of evacuation, rather than being forced to act by an enemy attack.

In the tense pre-war atmosphere, British parents faced a barrage of propaganda urging them to send their children away from vulnerable urban areas in the event of war. At the same time, many people in Canada came forward to offer them temporary homes. The National Council of Women began collecting the names of people who could take in evacuees; by September 1939, it had responses from 100,000 women. Ontario premier Mitch Hepburn endorsed the idea, while Lady Eaton offered her estate as a temporary home to child evacuees. The National Council of Education of Canada, which brought school groups from Britain on exchange programs, supported the notion wholeheartedly, and arranged for long-term billets in the event that war prevented groups of students from returning to Britain. Such measures were essential because the threat, according to the *Globe and Mail*, was all too real: "In recent months newspaper and newsreel pictures of little children, bewildered faces hidden behind ghoulish masks, being herded into dugouts have filled the gaps in the imagination. From the little Princesses in the palace to the babies of the slums, whole generations are as vulnerable as the troops in the front lines."[6] Although King George VI and Queen Elizabeth declined to send Princesses Elizabeth and Margaret out of London as a precaution, their decision was intended to provide inspiration rather than an example. For the sake of the Empire's future, British parents had a duty to evacuate their children, and Canadians had a duty to offer them shelter.

Britain's domestic evacuation scheme was set in motion on 1 September 1939, the day German troops invaded Poland and two days before Britain's declaration of war. Everything functioned just as it was supposed to, with remarkably few hitches. In the first four days of the program, some 1.4 million people were evacuated from British cities to rural areas; within another week, two million more had been moved. But they started to trickle back during the Phoney War, and by early 1940, more than half of the domestic evacuees had returned home. Then came the German *Blitzkrieg* in the west, which brought a second wave of evacuations. The list of cities declared evacuable grew longer, and the government announced a more generous billeting allowance to deal with the new exodus. Beginning in late May, some 1.25 million children again left their homes for safe zones. With the Nazis just a few miles across the English Channel, leaving the cities took on a new urgency. So too did leaving Britain altogether.

Only 253 children under the age of sixteen went to Canada in 1939, most of them from well-to-do families; after all, children being evacuated overseas paid a £15 transportation fee, which represented about a month's salary for three-quarters of the population, as well as £1 per child per week for expenses. No matter what the level of threat, this was simply beyond the means of the vast majority of Britons. But with the fall of France, a wave of desperation swept in and more parents began to look for ways to get their children to safety. At Canada House, the diplomatic staff was deluged with inquiries from people who wanted to ship their children to North America. The first to leave were mostly the wealthy and influential, who could push past the administrative obstacles that had been set up. But most Britons didn't have that much money or influence, so groups began making arrangements privately. Companies such as Ford and Kodak arranged evacuation for the children of their employees, and service clubs like Rotary and interest groups like the Eugenics Society also started group schemes. Canadian universities helped to bring over the children of their British faculty colleagues, and some private schools evacuated as groups. In June 1940 alone, some 10,000 civilians (including over 2,300 children) left Britain for the Dominions, most of them from affluent families. One concerned civil servant referred to the migration as "the rich swarming overseas."[7]

Prime Minister Winston Churchill objected to mass evacuation, telling the House of Commons that there was no military need for it, and no physical capacity to carry it out. Later, he stated that "a large movement of this kind encourages a defeatist spirit, which is entirely contrary to the true facts of the [war] position and should sternly be discouraged."[8] The headmaster of Winchester College argued in a letter to *The Times* that evacuation taught all the wrong lessons: "How can we with any consistency continue to speak of training in citizenship and in leadership while at the same time we arrange for them against their will to leave the post of danger? . . . I believe it is our duty to encourage those for whom we are responsible to stand fast and carry on."[9] But the most strident objections were raised against the inequality of current practice: the rich and powerful could easily get their loved ones out of harm's way, while the mass of the population could not.

Since the government couldn't ban private evacuation altogether, the only solution was to create a system that was accessible to everyone. The result was the Children's Overseas Reception Board (CORB), established under Sir Geoffrey Shakespeare to oversee a program of "carefully monitored child evacuation that would ensure that overseas evacuation represented a full cross-section of all classes." That wasn't the only benefit. Its promoters argued that the evacuated children would serve as ambassadors overseas because, as the executive director of Canadian welfare said, it was not just refugees "we plan to receive, it is not just evacuees, transferred from the range of the menace; it is part of Britain's immortality, part of the greatness of her past, part of all the hope of her future that we take into our keeping."[10] The Canadian government agreed to accept an unspecified number of children under the CORB, in very specific categories. They must be medically fit (stringent medical exams were required before a child could leave Britain), unaccompanied, and at least 75 percent of them had to be of British origin and not Roman Catholic. Sixteen years was the maximum age and most provinces preferred evacuees to be at least ten years old; there were few billets available for children under the age of five. Although all provinces agreed to accept children, the majority of evacuees went to Ontario.

The CORB's first day of business at its London office was 20 June 1940, and by ten o'clock that morning, the corridors were jammed and thousands of people were lined up outside the building. On the 23rd, Shakespeare gave a radio address to clarify the CORB's policy and perhaps stem the rush. He stated that the program's aim had never been to spur a mass exodus, but rather to spirit away a limited number of children to safe havens overseas. And he steadfastly refused to offer advice to parents: "You have to weigh the danger to which your child is exposed in this country, whether by invasion or air raids, against the risks to which every ship that leaves these shores is subject in wartime by enemy action, whether by air, submarine or mine. The risks of the voyage are obvious and the choice is one for which you alone are responsible."[11] But if Shakespeare hoped that his remarks would calm the public, he was wrong. Soon, the CORB had a large and growing backlog of cases. By the end of the month, the Board had expanded its staff to 620 employees and still could not keep up with the demand, which approached 20,000 applications a day. On 4 July 1940, Shakespeare decided to suspend registration, with over 210,000 children enrolled as potential evacuees. By the fall of 1940, some 3,500 CORB evacuees (christened CORB Limeys by some anonymous wit) had left Britain for the Dominions, and thousands more went under private arrangements. In total, some 5,500 children came to Canada under various programs in 1940.

But overseas evacuation was about to be dealt a death blow. In the summer of 1940 two passenger liners, the *Arandora Star* (carrying German and Italian internees to Canada) and the *Volendam* (carrying over 300 child evacuees), were torpedoed by German submarines. Although no children were killed, the willingness of U-boat commanders to attack passenger vessels (both were modern, fast vessels that sailed without naval escort—just the sort of ships that the CORB intended to use) set off alarm bells in the CORB. Then, on 17 September 1940, the *City of Benares*, four days out of Liverpool, was torpedoed by a German U-boat and sank in about thirty minutes. A British destroyer picked up survivors, but the loss was heavy: of the 406 passengers and crew, 248 died, including seventy-seven evacuees from the CORB. The program never recovered from the sinking of the *City of Benares*. Children who were en route to various ports were sent home and after October 1940, no more CORB evacuees left the British Isles. Through 1941 the flow of private evacuees dwindled to a trickle until it, too, stopped entirely. Altogether, 1,532 British children travelled to Canada under the auspices of the CORB; a thousand more went to other parts of the Empire. There is no reliable count of how many children were evacuated under private schemes, although the total may be as high as 15,000.

In their schools and host communities, evacuees became local celebrities. For most of them it was probably a disorienting experience, not least because of new classmates who stared at them with undisguised curiosity, as if they were visitors from another world. But in most situations they were quickly assimilated on the playground and in the classroom, although they never lost the exotic cachet of being refugees from the Blitz. They also quickly learned that they were objects of the generosity of relatives, neighbours, and local businesspeople who were keen to do what they could to assist them. Doctors would provide basic services at no charge, no small matter in the days before socialized medicine, and senior students at the University of Toronto's dental school were willing to work on evacuees at no charge. At least one summer camp was willing to accept evacuees at the deeply reduced fee of $10 per week, so that British children could experience this Canadian childhood ritual. Schoolmasters did what they could to reduce school fees, and the University of Toronto Schools even opened a special class for evacuees.

This depth of generosity towards Britons in need was expressed in all sorts of other ways as well. In Ontario, one of the biggest fundraising campaigns was the British War Victims Fund (BWVF). It was the brainchild of journalist C.H.J. Snider, who had been in Britain at the time of the Coventry bombing and, since then, had been looking for a way "to buck up the dauntless British spirit, and rush to the aid of the men, women, and children who have been under fire nightly for months that grow into years, in the front line of the war, while we wait safely at home."[12] Run by Snider's paper, the *Toronto Telegram*, it benefited from big events like the Fair for Britain, held in Toronto's Riverdale Park and featuring such attractions as Terrell Jacobs' Wild Animal Circus, the Phillips-Howard Swimcade, and the Conklin midway, which brought in $43,000 (over $560,000 in current values) in 1942 alone. However, the BWVF probably raised most of its money in smaller packets. Seven children in Tavistock dressed in costume and went door-to-door selling homemade candy and pot holders to raise money for the fund. Students at Port Hope High School held a tea dance and an operetta, which together netted $145 (nearly $2,000 today), and the City Hall Employees' Association in Toronto held a BWVF Blitz the Fritz Ball as a fundraiser. Trick-or-treaters on Halloween collected coins, while the Toronto and

York Mink Breeders' Association auctioned off eleven donated male mink and raised $610 ($8,000) for the fund. By the time it was wound down, the campaign had brought in $1.6 million (over $21 million).

The total is even more staggering when it is noted that at the same time dozens of other charitable causes were competing for Canadians' money, many of them aimed at helping beleaguered Britain. High school students in Fredericton, New Brunswick, chose the Queen's Canadian Fund for Air Raid Victims Throughout Great Britain as their pet charity, eventually forwarding a cheque for $1,100 ($14,000) to the *Daily Gleaner*, the fund's local organizer. Firefighters in Toronto sent £4,474 to the London Fire Service Benevolent Fund, while others could subscribe to the Milk for Britain Fund or the London War Orphans Fund. When these sums are added to the millions collected by the Canadian Red Cross Society and subscribed to the Victory Bond campaigns, it becomes clear that Canadians were remarkably selfless when it came to supporting the war effort financially.

Two causes were particularly appealing: food and fighters. With hundreds of thousands of Britons driven from their homes by air raids, the British government became increasingly concerned about feeding them—not only those whose homes had been destroyed by bombing, but those who spent nights in the Underground and other communal shelters. When the British cabinet minister responsible for feeding the nation made a public appeal for help, Garfield Weston put the resources of the family business behind the campaign. He pledged to purchase and staff twenty-five mobile kitchens capable of feeding 100,000 people a night, with plans to boost capacity to serve a quarter of a million people nightly if needed. But it was an ideal project for small community groups as well, for the cost was fairly modest, the impact obvious, and the publicity opportunities great. It took the Rotary Club of Windsor, Ontario, just fourteen minutes to raise enough money for a mobile kitchen. The Association of Rural Municipalities in Saskatchewan paid for a kitchen and had it presented to the city of Plymouth by Vincent Massey and the Astors. Massey also presented a mobile kitchen to the London borough of Southwark, on behalf of the Alpha Gamma Delta Fraternity at McGill University. Each unit (typically resembling a small house trailer, with cooking facilities similar to those found in a ship's galley) became a tangible sign of Canadian generosity and support, a load of coal and a hundred-gallon water tank making it possible to prepare soup, stews, chops, pies, sausages, bacon, and hot drinks for hundreds of emergency workers and bombed-out civilians.

Just as appealing was the opportunity to contribute very directly to the defence of Britain by purchasing an airplane. The ceremonial gift of

Ralph Betts of Toronto, in a mobile canteen donated by the Gyro Clubs of Canada

weapons is a practice that dates back to antiquity, but it was resurrected during the First World War when the Nizam of Hyderabad, one of the richest potentates in India, donated enough money to purchase an entire squadron of fighter aircraft for the Royal Flying Corps. In 1939, the Nizam promptly offered another £100,000 and the Wings for Britain Fund was born. The Air Ministry came up with a price list, from £5,000 for a fighter to £20,000 for a four-engine bomber (the pricing did not reflect the full cost of the airplane, but merely the basic airframe), and fundraising began across the British Empire, with a number of big donations grabbing headlines. In August 1940, after hearing that sixteen Spitfires had been lost in a single air battle over the south of England, Garfield Weston decided on the spur of the moment to hand over a cheque for £100,000 to pay for their replacement. "As a Dominion man, I've dug deep into my jeans to help with the war," he told reporters. "But I've got my money on a winning horse."[13] Weston's gesture captivated the newspapers, and soon other donors stepped forward. The Nizam

This Spitfire, christened Garfield Weston VI in honour of its donor, entered operations with 64 Squadron RAF in April 1941. It was destroyed by fire in November 1941.

came up with another £100,000, and J.W. McConnell, the publisher of the *Montreal Star*, donated $1 million to provide a squadron of aircraft built in Canada, to strike "a powerful blow at enemy squadrons which are seeking to enslave the Motherland from which his ancestors came," as the *Globe* put it.[14] Soon, the Canadian community in England joined the campaign with promises of donations, and Toronto mining executive J.P. Bickell offered to coordinate the fund with the Ministry of Aircraft Production. Another expatriate, former prime minister R.B. Bennett, often attended local ceremonies to accept cheques on behalf of the Ministry of Aircraft Production, charming the crowd with what one account referred to as "the easy, rich, and rolling drawl of a cultured son of Canada . . . a deep inspiring breath of Empire."[15]

Just as impressive was the sheer ingenuity that characterized local fundraising efforts. The Canadian Ladies' Golf Union raised $40,000 for the Wings for Britain Fund through tournaments, club donations, and the sale of posters showing the word "Spitfire" spelled out in golf tees.

Fundraising for Britain: the students of Lord Roberts Public School in London, Ontario, with the results of a paper drive

The children of Lord Roberts Public School in London sold pots and baskets, then sent a cheque for the proceeds to the Ministry of Aircraft Production, receiving in due course a receipt for £228. The manager of a bakery put his moustache on the line; he eventually sacrificed it for the cause, but it was commemorated by a Spitfire christened Sans Tache. When the city of Rochester, England, was bombed, Rochester, Alberta, joined other towns named Rochester around the world in banding together to raise funds for an airplane. Unwittingly imitating a British innovation from a year earlier, Dorothy Christie of Montreal (who, according to *Time* magazine, said most women's war work is "a lot of hooey") sold some of her evening wear and used the money to print cards that read "Is your name Dorothy? If so, rally around and help buy a Spitfire for Britain." She and her friends mailed them to every Dorothy they could find, eventually spawning a fundraising effort that held 20,000 tea parties (each hosted by someone named Dorothy), all-Dorothy musicales, car washes, rummage sales, and an auction of one of actress Dorothy Lamour's sarongs, which netted $151 ($2,000) for the Vancouver branch. In total, the Wings for Britain Fund raised enough money to pay for more than 2,200 aircraft, nearly 1,600 of which were Spitfires. Most of them proudly carried a name chosen by its sponsor, from Skysweeper (paid for by Hoover Limited, the manufacturer of vacuum cleaners) to Dog Fighter (presented by the Kennel Club of Great Britain). It is not entirely clear why a man named Herbert Morris paid for a Spitfire that he named Dirty Gerty Vancouver. Of those 1,600 Spitfires, a single aircraft is known to survive: Soebang, which was presented by Queen Wilhelmina of the Netherlands and is currently in the Canadian War Museum.

The speed and efficiency with which the Canadian community in Britain mobilized to support charitable causes like the Wings for Britain Fund demonstrates that Canada's empire in Britain from the First World War had never really disappeared. The banks, corporate offices, and government agencies remained, but more important was the large community of Canadian veterans in Britain. Some, like Garfield Weston and Beverley Baxter, had moved to Britain in the interwar era; others were among the thousands who opted to be discharged in Britain in 1919. The Weston family estate at Wittington, near Marlow in Buckinghamshire, became a magnet for expatriate Canadians, as did Canada House in London, but there were more modest outposts of empire as well. Frank Chillman had fought with the British Army in South Africa before emigrating to Canada before 1914. He enlisted in the CEF in Stratford, Ontario, fought at Vimy Ridge, and then moved back to Britain after the Armistice. In 1939, he was the owner of a pub called the Halfway House in Heath End near Aldershot, and became a father figure to Canadian soldiers stationed in the area during the Second World War. Soon after arriving in Britain, the Loyal Edmonton Regiment had a visit from twenty-two veterans of the 49th Battalion CEF who were living in Britain. One of them was a one-legged old soldier who hitchhiked eighty-six miles to get to the party; another was the brother of the mayor of Aldershot, and therefore a valuable ally to Canadians stationed around the city.

On such foundations the Canadian empire in Britain was quick to expand. It was much more spread out than it had been during the First World War, but a few areas saw a concentration of Canadians. The army laid claim to Aldershot and its environs, often the very same places that had been home to the CEF nearly thirty years earlier. RCAF squadrons were spread out across the British Isles, with the most intensive occupation being in the Vale of York. The Royal Canadian Navy's home in the UK was at Londonderry where, next to the British, Canadians comprised the largest national group. And of course, there was always a strong Canadian presence in the imperial capital. The bar at the Park Lane Hotel was all but taken over by Canadians, and they were almost always in the majority at the Dominion Officers Club. "Everywhere you go you see Canadians," wrote British-born soldier Fred Blancheon to his family in Saskatchewan. Time and time again, they remarked on the strangeness of being overseas, yet surrounded by Canadians. "I've seen so many boys I know that England is beginning to feel like home," wrote another prairie boy, Ted Schultz of 4 Field Company, Canadian Engineers.[16] And the familiar faces weren't always where they might be expected. Clarence Bourassa of the South Saskatchewan Regiment was finishing a tour of the famous Madame Tussaud's Wax Museum, and turned a corner to find himself facing the wax figures of Prime Minister Mackenzie King and General Andrew McNaughton.

The heart of the empire was "Little Canada," as Vincent Massey called it, the area around Cockspur Street in London.[17] The most recognizable landmark was Canada House, the Canadian High Commission, with its grand columns and classical decoration. Nearby, in the old Sun Life Assurance Company building, was CMHQ (the building also housed Sun Life's London office, the Royal Bank of Canada, and the headquarters of the Royal Canadian Air Force overseas); from the small advance party that set up shop there in October 1939, CMHQ grew to employ over 3,500 military personnel and 740 civilians by 1945. A little way down the street was the Canadian Officers' Club, organized by Alice Massey and, on account of its simple and hospitable lunches, affectionately known as Mother Massey's Hash House. A block or so away was the BC Services Club in British Columbia House, which provincial authorities opened within forty-eight hours of the first Canadian troops arriving in Britain in 1939. Further along Cockspur Street, past the offices of Canadian

Canadian Military Headquarters staff members enjoying an outing to Hampton Court Palace, 1945

shipping companies, the old London County Council building had been converted into the YMCA's Beaver Club. Masterminded by Vincent Massey, it opened in the spring of 1940 and offered a canteen with Canadian-style food, reading and writing rooms, games, an information bureau for those wanting to travel, banking facilities, showers, a barber shop, and at least one staffer who had worked in the Beaver Hut during the First World War. At first, Massey was annoyed at having "to keep the whole soul-saving tract-pushing tendencies of the YMCA personnel from getting out of hand," but within a few months he had everything sorted out. By July 1940, it sometimes hosted 9,000 servicemen in a single week, about half of them Canadian. It was often the first stop on any leave, for it was the best place to read a local newspaper or track down a pal from home.

The YMCA was one of four aid organizations chartered by the government to be responsible for soldiers' comforts. It took care of

British Columbia House, an outpost of Canada's empire in Britain during the Second World War

sports and recreation, the Canadian Legion was in charge of concerts and entertainment, the Salvation Army operated canteens and cinemas, and the Knights of Columbus took care of hospitality and social functions. Unlike the last war, Canada's empire in Britain would be far more carefully controlled. There would be no more private hospitals or convalescent homes established by eager philanthropists or soldiers' wives who came over from Canada, for in the summer of 1940 the government prohibited women from travelling to the war zone except on official business. All such facilities—including Cliveden, the estate at Taplow that the Astor family once again turned over to Canada for a hospital, at a rent of a shilling a year (the Masseys also loaned their country house to the Canadian military, as did a number of other prominent people)—were put under the control of the Royal Canadian Army Medical Corps. But the empire was no less extensive by being more organized. Again, the main effort was directed towards giving Canadians places to go where they could surround themselves with comforting familiarities and be protected from the unhealthy influences that beckoned in any big city. In 1940, the Salvation Army rented an empty London hotel and turned it into the Canadian Red Shield Hostel, which offered bed, bath, and breakfast for half a crown. Originally staffed by locals, the Salvation Army soon brought workers over from Canada to staff the kitchens— and before long, the food was completely Canadianized. Later additions to the hostel boosted its capacity to 600 men a night, but the Salvation Army didn't stop there. By 1944 there were eleven hostels in London and eleven more in other cities that offered a piece of home to Canadian servicemen and women.

What most Canadians wanted, however, was to spend some time with a family—not in a service hostel, although they certainly had nice facilities—but in a normal family home, where they could remember what it was like before the war. The hospitality service that had been so popular during the First World War was taken over by the Knights of Columbus Canadian War Services, which by war's end had opened twenty hospitality bureaus in various cities. British families willing to open their homes simply registered with a bureau, indicating the facilities they had available and how many people they could accept. A soldier on leave had only to contact the bureau to be matched with a host family.

"Home Away from Home"—a souvenir postcard of the Canadian Salvation Army Hotel in London

There was a similar program run by Lady Frances Ryder, who before the war had arranged private hospitality for dominion students studying in Britain. In 1939 it was expanded to dominion officers, and two years later the Knights of Columbus took it over for all ranks. As RCAF navigator William Watson wrote to his family in Grand Valley, Ontario, "after school, we all make a dash for Lady Ryder's where we get tea and peanut butter & jam sandwiches free. She really does a wonderful job of keeping us happy and on the go. Sunday she arranged it for Tommy and I to go to a doctor's for supper. It really turned out lovely."[18]

Private arrangements were even more common. The Westons, with plenty of space at Wittington, seemed always to have military visitors, many of the invitations coming through Miriam Weston, who worked at CMHQ and was a supporter of the RCAF officers' club in London. At Christmas 1940, the family was joined by some twenty-five guests, "all of whom are Canadian soldiers, airmen or naval boys from Toronto, with a sprinkling of Canadian nurses to give them some excitement." In the summer of 1941, it was "three Canadian boys from one of the Bombing Squadrons spending their whole week's leave with us. . . . To have the intimate knowledge of what they are doing is not only amazing but very encouraging," wrote Garfield Weston. For Christmas 1943 they had

> nine extra boys from the Army, Navy and Air Force for almost three days and frankly, while we had a wonderfully merry time, it was a bit exhausting on everybody, so that for a couple of days this week I am trying to get Mrs. Weston to stay in town for a complete change before tackling the New Year's festivities, for which we expect to have another nine or ten . . . we felt particularly pleased at being able to add to the general gaiety of those boys from every part of Canada.[19]

The Wittington guest book is filled with the names of Canadians who visited the estate, beginning with a contingent from the Toronto Scottish Regiment in December 1939. In a small, neat hand, someone has made note of the many who never survived the war.

Christmas 1939, and Garfield Weston's estate Wittington was already hosting its first Canadians in uniform.

But a modest home was just as welcome. While on leave one day, Nova Scotian Karl Butler happened to ask a young woman in uniform for directions to the nearest tea room, a chance encounter that led to friendship. The woman's parents invited him to stay at their home in Northampton whenever he could, and he was deeply impressed by the hospitality of such people "who thought it was their sole duty to entertain us while we are here—or it seemed to me for they spared no end to see that we enjoyed ourselves."[20] It would be difficult to over-estimate how much such hospitality was appreciated. As one anonymous Canadian wrote to his family at home,

> there isn't anything better you can do to make these lads feel good than to have them in for meals and an evening in a soft chair with pleasant company. I can tell you it is just like a breath from Heaven to go into someone's home and have that sensation of being in a place where people "live." . . . I think it is one of the greatest aids there is to the war effort, because it has such a stimulating effect on the morale of the men.[21]

By the end of the war, Canadians had become quite used to invitations from complete strangers who were delighted to provide a little hospitality to young men and women so long separated from their own homes and families.

Such a refuge was even more important to this generation of colonists, who faced circumstances that were entirely different than for the previous generation during the First World War. Hundreds of thousands of Canadians had passed through Britain between 1914 and 1918, but most stayed for just a few months before moving to the continent. During the Second World War, the colonists really put down roots, with over a quarter of a million Canadians living in Britain for three, four, or five years. Even more important was their origin. Almost half of the CEF had been British-born, so the war represented a kind of homecoming for them. In contrast, during the Second World War, fully 85 percent of Canadian military personnel were born in Canada. For them, Britain was essentially a foreign country, and they were strangers in a strange place.

There was the same tendency to comparison, often on the same grounds as their predecessors. Men from rural areas still marvelled at British farming techniques, wondering how they produced so much food with methods that seemed, at least to them, to be fifty years behind the times. Accustomed to the grid pattern of North American streets, they complained about roads that wandered across the countryside for no apparent reason. "I don't know who laid out the roads over here who ever it was made quite a mess of the job," wrote Vancouver artilleryman Ted Loney to a friend. "For my part I think it must have been a drunk the way they wander around."[22] The small British trains still drew chuckles, but the lack of central heating was no laughing matter. "What I miss most of all is the Canadian system of heating," Toronto airman Frank Scandiffio told a friend. "There are no furnaces here. You come in out of the cold and you stick your feet into a fireplace. The draft seems to go down your neck, out of your shoelaces and into the fireplace. The best way to keep warm is to put on another coat and go for a walk."[23] Everything seemed so small, and even claustrophobic. "Everything was in miniature," wrote infantry officer Arthur Stone, "tiny fields, houses, roads, even the trees looked smaller. The horizon was closer and trees were set in picturesque little groves of neat, broad and bushy boughs."[24] Canadians were mystified by a British class system that seemed to hold people in place, generation after generation. They didn't understand the British sense of humour, they couldn't get used to the damp, and British coinage was a mystery. "I found it hard to get on to their [English] ways and I was born here," wrote Fred Blancheon.[25] "It would be hard to figure two more different types than the Canadian and the English," artilleryman Elmer Bell wrote to his parents in Drew, Ontario.[26]

And that was the heart of the problem: despite their shared history and common heritage, Canadians and Britons didn't seem to understand each other very well. Charles Ritchie thought that, to the average Briton, "the soldiers from the Dominions are invading armies of irresponsible younger brothers . . . an army of friendly barbarians who for some incomprehensible reason have come to protect him from his enemies."[27] The mythology of the First World War, which had portrayed Canadian soldiers as hardy backwoodsmen from colonial wastelands, had been

Men of the Royal Canadian Artillery seeing the sites, Stonehenge, 1943

exaggerated by interwar popular culture, by silent films about Mounties and outlaws, and cheap novels like the one Hugh Templin saw a British factory worker reading: "*Love in the North* . . . On the cover was a huge Canadian youth dressed in fur parka, hugging a beautiful girl, while the aurora borealis made a brilliant background." Not all Britons were so ill-informed, but airman William Watson ran into plenty of locals who "pictured Canada as a very wooded country with log cabins and cowboys riding miles into town—a place where you had to go out and shoot your meal and cook it over a campfire."[28]

When it reached Britain in December 1939, the 1st Division was almost completely untrained and quickly lived up to the stereotype of undisciplined colonials. It was the coldest winter since 1894, and barracks that were austere at the best of times became downright unpleasant. The accommodations were not all sub-standard, but there were enough problems to cause bad feelings. The Calgary Highlanders found themselves in Talavera Barracks in Aldershot, which they were told had been condemned after the First World War but never actually demolished. Morval Barracks, the temporary home of the Loyal Edmonton Regiment, was unfinished when they arrived, and often had no running water—because the pipes ran outside the building, and frequently froze and burst. This was still a problem five years later, when the Lorne Scots from Toronto arrived to take up residence in the barracks. Soldiers complained about the mattresses at Aldershot, each made up of three pads known as biscuits—of course the Canadians referred to them as sons of biscuits—and about the poor heating in barracks, even though they already received a larger coal ration than British units. Park benches started to disappear as enterprising Canadians stole them to burn them, which didn't help their reputation any. To escape the dismal barracks or, even worse, the tent cities, they descended en masse on the nearest town where, unused to the more liberal liquor laws, they drank more than they should have.

The regular censorship of Canadian-bound mail revealed the deteriorating situation. Over that first winter, there were frequent complaints about food, weather, boredom, and inactivity. The pervasive tone of pessimism merely made things worse. "We were so sure of ourselves," wrote the war diarist of the Loyal Eddies, "and yet Britain was unsure of anything. It seemed, if one listened to the newspapers, that there was nothing but recriminations, accounts of blunders and [it was] virtually impossible to do anything right. Everyone said we would muddle through somehow but there were doubts in their tones perhaps as never before."[29] The military assumed that morale would improve with the coming of spring, and it did, but only temporarily. After Christmas 1940, British officials were appalled by the extent of Canadian dissatisfaction that was revealed in the mail:

> The damp to which they were unaccustomed made them miserable; inactivity and a feeling of being unwanted lowered the morale of many and made them disconsolate and homesick. They did not understand the English, and the English did not always understand them . . . there is more than a suggestion of an active and growing dislike of the Englishman, though seldom

of the Scot. . . . The Canadian does not appear to be adapting himself at all willingly to wartime conditions and restrictions; he grumbles repeatedly about the food; and he does not readily submit to discipline. Yet on the other hand his suggestion that the Englishman cold-shoulders him may not be without foundation.[30]

A year later, censorship reports were just as gloomy: "much is due to lack of understanding and outspoken comments on both sides, leading to recrimination and ill-feeling. Of course there are also the brawls caused by the unmannerly acts of men on both sides, especially in public bars, and under the influence of drink, when views become somewhat distorted and there is a certain amount of acrimony."[31] It merely made matters worse that, for the second winter in succession, the British Isles were hit with record-breaking cold spells.

Discontent and dissatisfaction boiled over in petty acts of disobedience. In October 1940, General McNaughton wrote to Canadian commanders to draw their attention to "the many complaints that are reaching me regarding drunkenness and disorderly behaviour, damage to private property, slovenliness in dress, misuse of mechanical transport, dangerous driving and loss of equipment, and the indications amounting almost to a certainty that there is a considerable traffic in petrol and, to a lesser extent, in blankets and other public property."[32] Chicken stealing was almost epidemic, although many Canadian soldiers scarcely considered it a crime—it was a kind of hunting, rather than theft. It became so common that many units, on arriving in a new area, immediately put local poultry yards out of bounds. Drunken brawls were a constant problem, as were road accidents caused by alcohol or excessive speed. In fact, Canadian recklessness was so legendary that Brookwood Cemetery became known at the Despatch Riders Holding Unit. Even Lord Haw-Haw, the German radio propagandist, was familiar enough with the Canadians' reputation to mention it in one of his broadcasts: "The Canadians arriving in your midst will not be of much help in your war effort. Lock up your daughters and stay off the roads. Give these men a motorcycle and a bottle of whisky and they will kill themselves."[33]

The crime rate involving Canadian soldiers was probably no higher than it was for other forces, or for the civilian population for that matter, but it certainly got more publicity. Against the advice of some British justices, Canadian military authorities allowed that serious crimes involving Canadian personnel would be handled by British civilian courts; the US, on the other hand, insisted that the British justice system would have no jurisdiction over Americans. This meant that violent crimes involving US personnel were reported only in brief, while the press enjoyed full access to all the lurid details of serious crimes involving Canadians.

There were a number of cases of armed robbery that led to convictions, and at least one in which a Canadian was acquitted in the murder of an elderly women who was killed in a botched robbery. Another Canadian was committed to an asylum for the criminally insane after stealing a weapon and hundreds of rounds of ammunition and shooting two policemen to death. But the most serious cases involved affairs gone wrong. A Métis from Saskatchewan was hanged after confessing to the murder of a teenaged girl with whom he had been having a relationship. A dispatch rider was convicted of manslaughter in the shooting death of his pregnant girlfriend, who had taken up with another Canadian soldier. A Jamaican in the Canadian Ordinance Corps was executed for the stabbing death of another pregnant teenager. A regimental policeman stole a Bren gun and shot up his married mistress's house in Brighton, killing her and wounding her new lover. Such crimes were rare, but they made for just the kind of publicity that Canadian military authorities were desperate to avoid.

The winter of 1941–42 marked the low point for the Canadian empire in Britain, as the boredom and discontent that plagued Canadian bases was worsened by bad news from the fighting fronts. Canada's seamen had been thrown into action in the North Atlantic to protect the vital convoy lifeline between Britain and North America, but had neither the training nor the equipment to do the job effectively. In September 1941, convoy SC42 lost sixteen merchant ships, with RCN escorts claiming a single U-boat in exchange. In November, a Canadian-escorted convoy was ordered back to port (for the first and only time during the war) because of fears that it would be ravaged by German submarines. Britain, losing faith in the ability of Canada's navy, insisted that RCN escort groups be reinforced with British (and eventually American) ships to guard against catastrophe. In the air, RAF Fighter Command had beaten back the German air armada, but the attempt to carry the bombing war to the Reich had yielded disappointing results. Operational research in the fall of 1941 showed that only 30 percent of any attacking force got within five miles of the aiming point; one crew, ordered to attack Düsseldorf, in Germany's Ruhr Valley, mistakenly bombed Dunkirk on the French coast, over two hundred miles away, as a result of navigational errors. The loss rate climbed alarmingly, with the average bomber completing just eleven operations, and the British press began to question openly the resolve of Bomber Command. By early November 1941, big raids had become so costly and ineffective that Churchill ordered Bomber Command to conserve its aircraft for the present—a polite way of telling it not to try anything too ambitious.

In the Canadian army, morale was falling not because of military defeats but because the force wasn't involved in any military action at all. The mood of the soldiers was not helped by news that two infantry battalions had been sent to defend Hong Kong—not from the divisions in Britain but from the home establishment in Canada. As their third Christmas in Britain approached, the fact that they had gone two years without facing the enemy rankled Canadian soldiers—"a galling situation for men of high mettle and indomitable spirit, but a situation, nevertheless, dictated by the exigencies of the war," said one British newspaper.[34] "The Canadians are known as the 'Home Guards' by the civilian population," wrote one soldier to his parents, "because they are taking about as active a part in the war as the home guard are."[35] The more realistic among them had to admit that, for the moment, they were hardly prepared for battle—after all, the British Columbia Dragoons, supposedly an armoured unit, had just three tanks, none of them fit for action. Over Christmas week 1941, there were numerous reports of battles between British and Canadian troops in the south of England, as boredom and drink mixed with Christmas homesickness to boil over into violence. Some incidents saw the supposed allies battling each other in the streets with bayonets and broken bottles. A letter in the Sussex Daily News denounced Canadian "hooliganism" and suggested that, "unless the officers in charge of these brutes can control them it would be a good thing for the authorities to apply for their removal."[36]

Things were no better for the Allied war effort as a whole. On all fronts, the enemy was in the ascendant. Yugoslavia, Greece, and Crete had fallen and Malta, the last British possession in the Mediterranean, was barely hanging on. The Soviet Union had joined the Allied side, but in the six months after the Germans launched Operation Barbarossa, the Nazi armies had pushed hundreds of miles into Russia, reaching the outskirts of Moscow. Japan had struck in the Pacific but the good news of the US entry into the war was overshadowed by a string of defeats as Allied outposts—including Guam, Wake, Hong Kong, Malaya, the Philippines, and Singapore—fell in quick succession, taking the Japanese to within a few hundred miles of Australia, deep into Burma, and within striking distance of India. In North Africa, German armies were about to begin an offensive that would see them push deep into Egypt, to within a few miles of Alexandria. With bad news coming from all fronts, Canadian morale in Britain was wrapped up in a much bigger question: could the Allies even survive?

SIX

THEY CAME, THEY SAW, THEY CONQUERED

The 26th of January 1942 was a day to remember in the port of Belfast, in Northern Ireland. Two American vessels were about to disembark the 34th US Infantry Division, the Red Bulls, and assembled on the dock were as many dignitaries as could be mustered. As newsreel cameras clattered and bands played, Milburn Henke, a young soldier from Hutchinson, Minnesota, walked down the gangplank and into history as the first US soldier to land in Britain during the Second World War. It was strictly a public relations exercise—the headquarters elements of the Red Bulls had landed two weeks earlier, and there were already plenty of US soldiers on the dock to shake the hand of the first US soldier in Britain—but it signalled the dawning of a new era in wartime Britain.

The Red Bulls were the first wave of a new friendly invasion of over two million Americans who would descend on Britain during the war years. This influx of newcomers—over-paid, over-sexed, and over here, as the locals irreverently observed—would push Canadians and Britons closer together by highlighting their similarities, after two years during which their differences seemed more apparent with every passing month. And as the Allies went on the offensive for the first time, Canadians swapped roles, becoming participants instead of bystanders. No longer would Canadians see themselves, and be seen by others, as spectators, on the outside of action looking in. Although it hardly seemed so in the early months of 1942, the tide was turning. Soon, the situation would stop deteriorating—the Allied war effort would bottom out and prospects would slowly start to brighten. In November 1942, Winston Churchill would utter one of those phrases for which he has become justly famous. "Now, this is not the end," he said in a speech at London's Mansion

House. "It is not even the beginning of the end. But it is, perhaps, the end of the beginning." The same could be said of Canada's empire in Britain. It was about to emerge from the bleak winter of 1941–42.

The arrival of the Americans fundamentally changed the social equation in Britain. For two years, the Canadians had been the exotics. With their strange accents, odd social habits, and frontier mentality, they seemed to have more money than they knew what to do with, and were apparently incapable of enjoying themselves unless noise was involved. The Englishman had expected "a dominion cousin who would think like an Englishman and respect English ways," according to one journalist.

> Instead he found an incomprehensible North American character who for an Englishman's taste drank too much, bragged too much, had too much money. And even with a good Scottish or Welsh or Yorkshire name he was quite capable of materializing as an Eskimo from Hudson Bay, a Ukrainian from the wheat prairies, a French Canadian from the logging camps, or a Nova Scotia fisherman.[1]

Now, the Americans brought stranger accents, more unusual social habits, and an even more pronounced frontier mentality; they had even *more* money, and seemed even *more* addicted to creating a racket. In the face of these new invaders from across the Atlantic, the Canadians were suddenly much more familiar. "The British," wrote journalist Charles Murphy in *Fortune* magazine, "discovered that while the Americans had all the peculiarities of the Canadians, only in twice the intensity, they were an entirely different brand of North Americans."[2] And the locals found that they weren't entirely comfortable with the newcomers. "London no longer belongs to England," wrote Donald Duncan, a Winnipegger who held a commission in a British regiment, "but has been taken over lock, stock and barrel by the Americans . . . who have the money, the gals and the best hotels . . . with their fists-full of money, and tendency towards noisiness, many of them have gotten thoroughly into the hair of the English."[3] When Karl Butler's name came up for leave in September 1942, he was glad to retreat north, to his friends in Northampton. "All the popular spots in England are just crowded with Americans," he wrote to his parents. "J.C. was up to London last week-end and he had to sleep on a bench in Hyde Park. All the clubs were filled up."[4] In this new reality, Canadian accents didn't seem quite so broad, or their parties quite so noisy. The fact that they packed the pubs, causing a serious shortage of beer glasses and forcing the locals to fight for the attention of the barmaids, started to seem a little less annoying. Many Britons were coming to terms with the fact that they had more in common with the Canadians than with any of their other allies.

The Canadians themselves were quite aware of the changing relationship. They had always been more comfortable in the old world than the Americans who, according to Charles Ritchie, "seem completely incurious. They look as though they are among strange animals. The Canadian soldiers up against the British try at once to establish human contact—they make jokes, pick quarrels, make passes, get drunk, and finally find friends."[5] As more and more Americans poured into the British Isles, Canadians gravitated not to the newcomers with whom they shared a continent, and increasingly a culture, but to the British. "The Canadians in Britain did not identify themselves with the Americans," wrote Charles Murphy. "Their particular experience in England, as the years there passed, brought them closer to the British people and gave a new reality to the Commonwealth connection."[6]

That growing sense of connectedness and the rediscovery of the fact that, accents and social habits aside, Canadians and Britons shared a common heritage put the Canadian empire in Britain on a different course. The ill-will that had simmered for the first couple of years didn't disappear entirely, but relations started to improve dramatically, in almost every respect. Crime rates dropped and there were fewer bitter complaints in letters home. Most important, Canadians began to feel less out of place; for the newcomers, Britain was no longer a strange and forbidding place with awful weather, deplorable living conditions, and cold people. There were now enough reminders of home to take away some of the sting of separation, and they were seeing a side of Britain that contrasted strongly with the cool English reserve that had been so annoying in the past.

And so Canadians became more and more involved in the lives of the villages around their bases. Early in the war, the contact had been more reactive than proactive, and rarely went beyond smoothing ruffled feathers—it was said that the last vehicle in any military convoy was the regimental paymaster, so he could pay for damages caused by the vehicles that preceded him. CMHQ now realized that disciplinary problems were more serious in areas where Canadians lived in tented camps and used local pubs, cinemas, and restaurants as playgrounds. It was a different story where they were billeted in private homes and could become part of a community. Then, they were no longer seen as transients with little attachment to their hosts, but members of the family. The kind of community events that garrison towns had grown used to during the First World War again became a feature of life. Regimental bands played for local dances—in his letters home, Clarence Bourassa of the South Saskatchewan Regiment gave the impression that he spent more time practising the trumpet and performing at local functions than training as a rifleman. Canadian sports teams competed against local sides to raise money for charity. Camps held open days when townspeople could tour the base and see what was happening in their backyard. Canadian soldiers were on call to help local firefighters, and soldiers and locals pulled together in the event of tragedy. When the parish church at South Mertsham was demolished by German bombs, Canadian troops stationed nearby built a replacement. At the consecration, the Bishop of Southwark praised "our Canadian kinsmen [for going] out of their way to build a place in which our people might worship."[7]

But nothing symbolized the close relations more than the children's Christmas party. With wartime shortages and rationing, children missed out on all the treats that brightened the holiday season—from oranges to toys to sugar plums. It was just the sort of situation to which the visitors could bring some welcome cheer. Weeks before Christmas, soldiers asked their families in Canada to send treats for local children, to be distributed by volunteers from the regiment. When the big day came, trucks circulated through nearby villages, picking up groups of children here and there. Back at the camp, there might be games, a concert by the unit's band, or even the latest Hollywood cartoons, the cinema equipment coming from the YMCA. Regimental cooks would put on a big buffet, with the kind of food that civilians hadn't seen since before the war. But the highlight was always the arrival of Santa Claus,

Meeting the locals: men of the Royal Canadian Ordnance Corps talking to children near their base, 1943

usually in a decorated jeep. Most units could produce someone who met the physical requirements (in the Queen's Own Rifles, it was Ben Dunkelman, a Jewish officer whose height and booming voice made up for any shortcomings in girth), and he made sure that the children went home with their pockets full of sweets and other trinkets, and perhaps some cigarettes for their parents—the kind of treats that were hard to find in wartime Britain. The War Diary of the Argyll and Sutherland Highlanders of Hamilton, Ontario, based at Uckfield in Sussex, gives a hint of what such a party must have meant to the local children:

> The children's party, for which the men had been saving candies and other edibles from their parcels, used the Sally Ann theatre as a general rendezvous, where two Popeye pictures were shown. After the show the children were divided into groups and taken in TCV's to the various company parties. However, those selected for the Support Company had the added thrill

of marching there behind the bagpipes. Each party featured a Christmas tree and of course a Santa Claus, all of whom were unmasked by the most precocious youngsters. One Santa Claus whose garb failed to completely hide the battle dress pulled a neat strategic withdrawal by explaining that he had been "caught in the draft." The chocolate bars, gum, etc, so carefully husbanded were distributed to the children, cocoa and cookies served and everyone, soldiers certainly included, had a fine time.[8]

Another apocryphal story has it that, when meeting local children, a Canadian's first question was always, "Do you have an older sister?" With so many young men concentrated in certain parts of Britain—in the Aldershot area, the ratio of men to women was about fifteen to one—romantic entanglements were inevitable. Local lore in Aldershot told of a complaint sent to military authorities: "A Canadian soldier on leave has visited my home. As a result, both my daughter and I are pregnant. Not that we hold it against your soldier, but the last time he was here he took my daughter's bicycle which she needs to go to work. Can you get him to return it?"[9] Twenty-two cases of bigamous Canadian soldiers came before the courts (it being almost impossible to verify from an ocean away a Canadian marriage or the death of wife), and British civil courts informed military authorities of over 400 maintenance orders involving Canadian soldiers. And we have heard about the relationships that ended in violence.

Even though such cases were the exception, military authorities were leery of romantic entanglements. Quite apart from the principle involved in wartime unions (as one CMHQ officer wrote, "It might be considered that each marriage overseas is robbing some Canadian girl of a husband"), they were administratively inconvenient and required a good deal of paperwork. So, obstacles were set up to dissuade soldiers from marrying in haste only to repent at leisure (the first marriage took place at Farnborough on 29 January 1940, between a British woman and a sergeant of the Saskatoon Light Infantry—a unit that had landed at Glasgow on 17 December 1939, just six weeks earlier). The prospective groom was required to secure the permission of his commanding officer—this applied to all junior and warrant officers under the age of twenty, and all non-commissioned officers and men; any soldier who was under nineteen and any fiancée under twenty-one had to show the written permission of their parents. After December 1941 (by which time 4,200 marriages involving Canadian soldiers had been recorded), the regulations were tightened even more: a man had to certify his marital status and agree to a $10 monthly pay deduction, to be banked until $200 was collected, to pay for family's passage back to Canada; the fiancée had to show a certificate of good character, and a two-month waiting period was imposed.

But once a marriage was solemnized, the military did all it could to make the bride feel welcome. The first club for Canadian war brides was established in Kent in September 1941, and by 1945 there were thirty-five such organizations around the UK, many of them established by the Salvation Army and all working under the auspices of the Canadian Wives Bureau at CMHQ. The clubs gave women a chance to socialize with other war brides and be initiated by guest speakers into the mysteries of the Canadian domestic arts. "It is a topic of interesting conjecture," Gillis Purcell told CBC radio listeners, "whether the south of England will be more changed by the friendly invasion of the Canadians than post-war Canada will be by the home-coming of thousands of Anglicized war veterans with their English, Scottish and Welsh wives."[10]

But it wasn't just the newlyweds who were anglicized. After the arrival of the Americans, more and more Canadians began to remark on the closer ties that were developing with the natives. Vincent Massey's comment that "we are the more British for being honestly Canadian, just as we are the more Canadian for keeping alive and treasuring the precious legacy of the traditions which are British"[11] might be dismissed as the wishful thinking of a committed anglophile, were it not for the fact that he was far from the only Canadian to express such sentiments. "Curious how I instinctively consider myself Canadian isn't it and yet with ever so close a tie to England and ever willing also to be known as a son of England?" Edmonton airman Dennis Quinlan wrote to his mother, "I am strangely thankful for being a 'Canadianized' Englishman."[12] Indeed, Canadians were often surprised at the unusual ways their anglicization was manifest. Charles Murphy quoted a Canadian soldier in Italy, who observed that "our years in England have I suppose made us more

English than we realized." He and his pals frequented a typical Italian wine shop, but instead of christening it the Maple Leaf Club or the Beaver Tavern, they called it the Sussex Inn and taught the Italian waiter to say "Time, gentlemen, please" in the fashion of the English publican. "You run into things like that quite often which illustrate our 'anglicised' outlook," he mused.[13] Harry Crerar, commander of First Canadian Army and Canada's highest ranking general of the Second World War, told the troops in Sussex that such feelings would be deep and long-lasting:

> Those of us who return to Canada will take with us the intention that the ties which have previously existed between this country and our own should be strengthened; that more effective means to co-operate in preventing a recurrence of war should be mutually developed; and that, in the evolution of a better world order, the British Empire—tested and purified by the experience through which we are passing—will have a vital part to play.[14]

But Crerar was looking to the future. There was a vital part to be played in a much more immediate sense. The Russians, who had borne the brunt of the land war for a year, were pressing the western Allies to open a second front in France, a goal that the US supported. For their part, the British were keen to put new tactics and equipment for amphibious warfare to the test as a prelude to the eventual invasion of German-occupied Europe—the last major amphibious operation had been at Gallipoli in 1915. After much deliberation, British commanders decided to mount a reconnaissance in force against the French coastal resort town of Dieppe, a favourite with tourists for decades. General Andrew McNaughton, Crerar's predecessor, had referred to the Canadian army as a dagger pointed at the heart of Berlin but because boredom and inactivity were blunting the weapon, Canadian commanders clamoured for the assignment.

Looking back, it is easy to see how the raid went wrong. Security was certainly lax, especially after the operation was cancelled for the first time, only to be resurrected, renamed, and launched. Even if there is no direct evidence that the Germans were expecting the raid, it was far from secret in the south of England in the summer of 1942. Tactically, there were also serious problems. There was no aerial or naval bombardment to provide cover for the landing forces, and it would have been difficult to find a spot on the French Channel coast that was less favourable for an amphibious landing with tank support. However, planners didn't necessarily know that, for intelligence preparations were appallingly shoddy.

As always in such situations, the soldiers paid heavily for the failures of their commanders. In the plans, units of the 2nd Division were to capture the town of Dieppe, establish a defensive perimeter, and hold it while key facilities were destroyed. Then, they would simply re-embark and return to Britain—with some prisoners and enough stories to keep them in beer for weeks. But mistakes and delays were compounded by bad luck and missed opportunities, and very few of the attacking units reached their objectives. Most of the men were pinned down on the stony beaches, where incessant machine-gun fire kicked up lethal shards of rock. It wasn't even 9 AM before the first Canadian units were forced to surrender, and for the rest of the day the few small groups that had actually pushed inland slowly retreated to the seaside. But there was nothing for them there. Many of the landing craft that came to collect them were sunk—the Royal Navy lost over a quarter of the vessels it committed to the raid—and by late afternoon, surrender was the only option. Most of the Canadian infantry units sent around 600 men to Dieppe. Toronto's Royal Regiment of Canada brought only sixty-five men back to Britain; the Essex Scottish Regiment from southwestern Ontario, just fifty-two. More than 900 Canadian soldiers had been killed and nearly 2,000 captured; over 100 Allied aircraft were downed (the largest single-day loss since the war began). Less than half of the attacking force returned to Britain, and nearly 600 of them were wounded.

After the Dieppe raid, Aldershot was a very different place. It wasn't just the seemingly endless line of ambulances along the road to the Cambridge Military Hospital, or that the numbers had dwindled so noticeably—before, it had seemed as if there were thousands of Canadians in and around the town, but now locals had the streets to themselves. Most striking was the new sense of purpose that had settled over the Canadian empire in Britain. No longer were they undisciplined colonials whose first priority was enjoying themselves. With thousands of their comrades dead, wounded, or in captivity, the Canadian Army smartened up. One day they would get the chance to avenge the men of the 2nd Division and show the Nazis what they could do in battle. Until then, it was time to get down to business. Everyone noticed the change. One local lad who delivered papers to the Canadian camps around Aldershot was used to having his run of the place, waving cheerily to the sentries and exploring the base as he did his rounds. After Dieppe, he was brought into the guardroom and told that in future, all papers would be left there for soldiers to deliver. The carefree days were past.

At least there were signs elsewhere that the Allies' fortunes were looking up. The Royal Canadian Navy worked through its early growing pains once Canadian escort groups were transferred to the eastern Atlantic to gain much needed training under the watchful eyes of the Royal Navy. By the spring of 1943, the RCN had improved enough that it was given charge of all escort work (Canadian, British, and American) in the northwestern Atlantic. Merchant shipping losses remained high—108 vessels were sunk in March 1943 alone—but escort groups began having greater success, sinking increasing numbers of U-boats that the Nazis could ill afford to lose. With Londonderry serving as the base for five RCN escort groups in the British Isles, the city hosted as many as 3,000 Canadian sailors at any one time. However, they were essentially transients for whom the city was a source of entertainment and amusement rather than a home. Their brushes with the law caused constant headaches for their superiors; "there are too many sailors milling round in Londonderry with nothing to do but get drunk and break up the place," observed the commander of a Canadian escort group. One solution was to ask the YMCA to open a rest and recreation camp in a disused army base, but that didn't eliminate the problem. It was not unknown for Canadian ships to sail ahead of schedule, simply to get the crew out of port. But as an Irish historian notes, once American sailors began to use Londonderry in significant numbers, the Canadians started to seem "comparatively civilised" to the locals.[15]

The Royal Air Force, after two years that (save for the triumph in the Battle of Britain) could only be described as disappointing, had a new commander and a new sense of resolve. In May 1942, the RAF scraped together 1,043 bombers and sent them to Köln for Operation

Millennium—the first thousand-plane raid of the Second World War. In July 1942 the US 8th Army Air Force joined the offensive, and would soon take round-the-clock bombing to every corner of Germany. This expansion brought with it a rapid increase in the strength of the RCAF and, by extension, greater political pressure for a policy known as Canadianization. In personnel matters, the air forces followed a very different practice than the army or the navy. No matter where newly minted airmen enlisted or trained (and by war's end, more than 250,000 of them came from Canada), the British Air Ministry retained control of their operational posting, and rarely paid attention to nationality. In practical terms, this meant that if an RCAF squadron needed a replacement pilot and there was a Canadian pilot waiting to be posted to an operational unit, he *might* be sent to the Canadian squadron—or he might find himself on the way to an RAF squadron while the RCAF squadron received an Australian or a Welshman.

Canadian officials had been grumbling about this practice since early in the war, for a number of reasons. They were anxious that Canada's contribution to the war was properly acknowledged, something that was much easier with distinct Canadian squadrons than with Canadians dispersed through the Commonwealth air forces. The government also wanted to exercise some control over where Canadians fought and died. No infantry battalion had been committed to the Dieppe raid without the express consent of Ottawa, but half a dozen RCAF squadrons were involved in air operations over the Dieppe beaches without the permission or even the advance knowledge of the Canadian government. Finally, Canada's air minister, Montreal Member of Parliament C.G. Power, didn't like the appearance of things. Canadian squadrons were representatives of a sovereign nation that had gone to war as a full ally; having Canadian airmen scattered through the RAF seemed to reduce their status to "hirelings or mercenaries in the service of another State."[16]

British officials insisted that funnelling reinforcements to specific squadrons made the system impossibly complicated, an excuse that Canada said revealed more about administrative inefficiency than anything. The other argument had more merit. A multi-national squadron was a better squadron, for it symbolized the unity of the Allied cause and took advantage of the different strengths of the various nationalities.

More than one Air Ministry official argued that Canadians benefited from the tighter discipline that typically characterized British squadrons, while Canadians brought a higher level of operational creativity and élan—the frontier mentality, in other words. No one wanted to see crews or squadrons split up in the name of Canadianization, but there could be no disagreement with the attempt to make RCAF squadrons Canadian in more than name only by ensuring that they received Canadian replacements. This was relatively easy in fighter squadrons, which had more than 90 percent Canadian personnel for most of the war, but much more difficult in squadrons that flew multi-engine aircraft, especially in Bomber Command. A bomber crew included a number of different tradesmen—pilot, wireless operator, gunners, navigator, bomb aimer—and the training schools didn't produce them all in equal numbers. Flight engineers, for example, were mostly British, largely because so many of them were trained there; not until 1944 did the first class of flight engineers graduate in Canada. However, inequality in trades training alone couldn't explain the fact that in January 1943 only 17 percent of the aircrew in 431 Squadron RCAF, for example, were actually Canadian.

Ottawa kept pushing the British government, although progress was slow. The first success was in Fighter Command, with the establishment of an all-Canadian fighter wing at Digby in Lincolnshire in April 1941 (the second was formed at Kenley some eighteen months later). It took longer to reach an agreement that a Canadian bomber group would be formed to bring together a number of RCAF squadrons under Canadian command. On 1 January 1943, 6 Group RCAF became operational. Its squadrons flew from a number of airfields in the Vale of York, an area that was used to Canadian colonists, thanks to the demobilization depot that had been established there at the end of the First World War. The men of 6 Group flew from airfields scattered around the lowlands between York and Darlington. To the east lay the North Yorkshire Moors, whose rocky crags and low peaks would claim many a careless or damaged aircraft. Beyond the moors was the North Sea, and the routes to targets in Germany and occupied Europe.

In the Vale of York, airmen created the kind of Canadian colony that had been growing around Aldershot since 1939. However, the RCAF enclaves had a different character than army bases, if only because the people were more transient. An army unit might be billeted in one area for two years or more, giving the soldiers plenty of time to become part of the local community. A fighter or bomber squadron, on the other hand, had a much more rapid turnover, at least as far as aircrew were concerned. Casualty rates were higher (many airmen were with a squadron for a matter of days before being shot down on their first or second operation) and, unlike soldiers, airmen had a fixed term of duty. After completing thirty operations (and then a second tour of twenty), a bomber crew would be screened, or transferred away from the squadron for instructional or administrative duties. Even before completing a tour of operations, any airman might be posted from his squadron to an elite unit if he was especially skilled or to the manning pool if his nerves had broken. It was quite normal for a soldier to spend the better part of two or three years in the same area; an airman in a similar situation would have been rare indeed.

Furthermore, a big bomber airfield was a self-contained community that could provide most of the comforts of home. Linton-on-Ouse had separate messing facilities for various ranks—the Sergeants' Mess, brand new in the summer of 1943, boasted leather couches and a sixteen-foot bar; the old mess was converted to a YMCA recreation hut, with Canadian newspapers and magazines, a Canadian hostess, and a much appreciated taste of home, Pepsi. A cinema at the base showed a different film every week, and live shows were available two or three times a month at the Navy, Army, and Air Force Institutes hut. There was a station orchestra, the Lintonaires, that played for dances almost every week, but perhaps the most distinctive feature of airfield life was the presence of women from the RCAF Women's Division and the Women's Auxiliary Air Force, who provided so many of the communications and administrative services that were essential to operations. There were, in short, all sorts of reasons for the men and women of the RCAF to spend their leisure time on their airfields rather than venturing into the local community.

They weren't completely cloistered, however. They supported local charities—426 Squadron adopted the Hull Sailors' Orphans' Home, for which it held fundraising concerts and organized an annual Christmas party. Nearby pubs and hotels offered a very welcome change of scenery and a chance to rub shoulders with people who weren't in uniform. The

College Arms pub at Linton (affectionately known as the College of Knowledge) was a favourite, but they seemed happier mingling with their own. Perhaps the favourite haunt for the men and women of 6 Group was Betty's Bar in York, where they could relax, fill up on spam fritters or corned beef hash, and perhaps sign the long mirror just inside the front entrance. But it wasn't really a local pub, so much as a service club that just happened to be in the centre of York. In March 1945, airman James Baker described the scene to his parents:

> Jack—my mid-upper gunner and I went in to York, had a wonderful time; it was such a grand relief! We did nothing spectacular—just had a meal, went to a show and then to our favourite pub called "Betty's Bar" (or more familiarly amongst us) the "Briefing Room" because all the crews from all the operational stations in our Base foregather there to "swap yarns and renew old acquaintances." Even if you don't drink, you go there to be with the boys. I don't believe there was a "civvy" in the place last night, just Ops. boys and their girlfriends. I only stayed about ½ an hour—time to consume about one pint, yet I met about five fellows that I know. We had a great time swapping yarns and experiences![17]

Clearly, members of the RCAF lived in a very different world than soldiers. An infantry regiment lived amongst civilians for months or years but when it went into action, it left the comforts of civilian society and lived in the field. Airmen and airwomen, on the other hand, lived a life of jarring contrasts. A pilot could be dodging flak over the Ruhr in the early morning, and lunching at a village pub in Yorkshire a few hours later. An airwoman knew full well that any of the aircrew at a dance one night might well be dead the next. In such situations, spending leisure time with peers was more relaxing than making the difficult mental adjustment from military to civilian worlds and back again every day or two. Another contrast lay in the fact that bomber crews seemed to be fighting a war of attrition in which the outcome was rarely more than inconclusive. An infantry company might take heavy losses but at the end of the day a result, for good or ill, was relatively clear. But from thousands of feet in the air, it was impossible to know what impact the bombs were having, and reconnaissance flights the next day might not clarify the situation. Even if a raid was deemed a complete success, there was always another target on another night. The Ruhr Valley, Germany's industrial heartland, afforded an apparently inexhaustible supply of targets to be attacked and no matter how many times a squadron was sent to bomb Berlin, another trip to the capital was always a possibility. Not until after the war would it become clear how much devastation Allied bombing raids had caused. At the time, the crews must have felt like Sisyphus, forever pushing the same boulder up the mountain.

The ground war at least offered a little more clarity. In July 1942, the British and Indian Armies stopped the German advance in the Western Desert, at El Alamein; they would hold firm for the rest of the summer, and in November started to push the enemy back, out of Egypt and west across North Africa. At the same time, British and American forces landed in Morocco and Algeria in Operation Torch and began driving eastward. By the spring of 1943, they had linked up with the 8th Army moving west from Egypt and had the German *Afrika Korps* pinned in a small corner of Tunisia. In the Pacific, Japan's advance was halted in May 1942 at Midway Island, where almost the entire Japanese aircraft carrier fleet was sunk. Later in the summer, successful landings by US and Australian forces at Guadalcanal and New Guinea seemed to offer proof that the tide in the Pacific was turning. On the Russian front, the war of annihilation that would eventually claim twenty million civilian lives ground on, but the Soviets were starting to gain the upper hand. A string of successes in the east was capped in February 1943 by the surrender of an entire Nazi army at Stalingrad, a crushing blow to German morale.

But as far as most Canadians were concerned, these campaigns were more or less sideshows. The main event was continental Europe, and the beginning of the end wouldn't come until Allied soldiers were on the mainland. With the net closing around the German armies in Tunisia, Allied leaders met at Casablanca in January 1943 to decide on the next move. The Americans pushed hard for a cross-Channel invasion of France, but the British insisted that there would not be enough landing craft available until 1944. In any case, with the Soviets having turned things around on the east, it was no longer so critical to draw German divisions away from the Russian front. And then there were the hundreds of thousands of British and American troops in Tunisia, who would be idle as soon as the *Afrika Korps* was defeated—how could they be put to the best use? More and more, it looked like another major offensive in the Mediterranean made practical sense. If the region could be secured, it might draw Turkey into the war on the Allied side, opening the Black Sea route to the Caucasus and Russian oilfields. If Italy could be knocked out of the war, Germany would be forced to defend the peninsula. And Sicily was less than a hundred miles from the port of Tunis, the ultimate target of 380,000 British, American, and French soldiers. Sicily it would be.

The original plan for what was eventually code-named Operation Husky envisioned an amphibious assault by ten British and American divisions. There would be no Canadian participation. This was a heavy blow, made worse by confirmation that a cross-Channel invasion that year was out of the question. The morale of the Canadian Army in Britain had been resting on an imminent landing in France; now they faced the prospect of another year, or more, of idleness. The situation was as frustrating as it was embarrassing. Every other Commonwealth army had been in action—the Australians and New Zealanders in Greece, Crete, and the Far East, the South Africans in the Western Desert, the Indian Army almost everywhere. The Canadians' battle experience was confined to a single bad day at Dieppe and two bad weeks at Hong Kong. Ottawa began to lobby, and eventually the persistence paid off: in April, the Canadian government learned that a British division would be withdrawn from Operation Husky and Canada's 1st Division would take its place.

Soldiers are constantly being moved, sometimes on very short notice, and they quickly develop a kind of sixth sense for knowing when a move is out of the ordinary. In late April 1943 it was clear that something different was going on in the 1st Division. The men of the Seaforth Highlanders knew that something was up when all leave was cancelled and they were ordered to go through their gear and pack away for storage anything non-essential. When battalion headquarters staff began burning piles of documents and announced tough new security measures, it "sent the rumour-mongers off into new ecstasies of embellishment," as the unit's War Diary put it so colourfully.[18] When the Royal Canadian Regiment was ordered to Scotland for intensive training, the hope of seeing battle rippled through the men—in the words of the War Diary, "Not a hole-in-the-ground battle but one which will put the name of our Regiment on the lips of every Canadian at home and on people throughout the world! 'No more Home Guard' is our feeling! At last our training and our courage is going to be put to the test."[19]

The training involved amphibious landings, which dissolved any last doubts of what lay ahead. As the units of the 1st Division made their way to Scottish ports in late June, the only uncertainty concerned their exact destination. On Dominion Day 1943, the last vessels in the invasion convoy slipped anchor in the Clyde and drew out into the North Atlantic; the same day, the troops learned that on 10 July, they would put ashore on Sicilian beaches to begin the invasion of Italy. Spirits were high on the way south—except for the loss of three transports carrying Canadian soldiers and their equipment, the trip was uneventful—and by lunchtime on 9 July the invasion convoy of some 2,600 vessels, some from the UK, some from North Africa, had come together in the waters south of Malta. Jockeying for position in a carefully choreographed dance, they slowly got ready for the last run to the Sicilian coast.

The target for the 1st Division was the extreme southern tip of the island, near the town of Pachino. After capturing the airfield, the only one in that part of Sicily, they would push to the north, between the British divisions driving up the east coast of the island and the American divisions to the west. At 1:34 AM on 10 July 1943 the first Canadian assault troops left their transports; a little over five hours later came confirmation that all of the first objectives had been secured. Enemy fire had been, at the worst, sporadic; most of the defenders were all too happy to surrender. The station master at Pachino welcomed the invaders, the Royal Canadian Regiment diarist recording that he telephoned stations up the line to say, "be good to the Englishmen in funny hats; they are kind to our children and treat prisoners well."[20] The next four days were similar, the Canadians encountering only Italian units that gave up at the first opportunity. But on the 15th, they ran into German troops; moving into the hills north of Pachino, their advance was slowed by the difficult topography of Sicily. Spines of stony hill chains, frequently cut by steep ravines and dry stream beds, crossed the countryside while roads that were often little more than foot tracks straggled between villages. Every small ridge could become a defensive position, for the soft rock was easily dynamited into roadblocks. It was dry and dusty, and the hot sun beat down on Canadian infantrymen who had spent the last three years in the British climate. Few of them had heeded advice to purchase sunglasses.

The Sicilian campaign was a difficult test in harsh, unfamiliar conditions, but the Canadian division was up to the challenge. Twelve days of fighting brought them to the town of Leonforte, where they wheeled due east; with the Americans clearing the north coast of Sicily, they pushed towards Mount Etna. On the 25th of July came news that Italian dictator Benito Mussolini had been overthrown, but that did little to weaken the resolve of the island's German defenders. It was another three weeks before Allied armies took the port of Messina and even then, skilled rearguard actions allowed the Germans to evacuate most of their troops and heavy equipment to the Italian mainland. Thirty-eight days of fighting had cost the three Allied armies over 19,000 casualties. The 1st Division alone had sustained 2,310, including 562 dead. One of them was Karl Butler of the West Nova Scotia Regiment, killed in action just days before the end of the fighting in Sicily.

As the campaign was winding down, Allied leaders met to plot the next step. From the available options, they chose a two-prong strategy: an Anglo-Canadian assault across the Strait of Messina and an American landing farther up the Italian peninsula, at Salerno. In the early hours of 3 September, British and Canadian units began crossing to Calabria. There were no beach obstacles or barbed wire, no land mines or pillboxes—there weren't even any defenders in evidence, one unit diarist reporting that "the stiffest resistance of the day came from a puma that had escaped from the Reggio zoo and which seemingly had taken a fancy to the Brigade Commander."[21] By nightfall, Canadian units were as far as five miles inland and had suffered just seven casualties, all of them wounded and none from the attacking infantry battalions. On 8 September, the West Novas prevailed in a short, sharp clash with Italian troops, the last time they would face the Italians in battle. That night came news that Italy had capitulated—defence of the peninsula now fell to the Germans. With that, the complexion of the campaign changed dramatically. No longer could the Allied armies expect the enemy to retreat headlong at the first shots. The Germans would perfect the tactic of mounting a stiff defensive action and then, when the tide was turning against them, abruptly melt away, only to take up equally strong defensive positions a few miles back. The farther north the Allies advanced, the higher their casualties would climb. The landing at Salerno, after some tense early hours, had established a beachhead and, as Canadian and British units pushed north along the Adriatic coastal highway, the Americans were fighting inland. On the 16th of September, elements of Princess Louise's Dragoon Guards from the Ottawa area met up with a patrol from an American airborne division moving east from Salerno. Five days later, after the Canadians captured the town of Potenza, the Allies had established a line from Salerno to Bari, on the Adriatic coast.

The town of Campobasso, captured in early October, was converted into a forward leave centre known as Maple Leaf Town (although many of the troops preferred to call it Canada Town), with the Aldershot Club and the Royal York Hotel for officers, and the Beaver Club for other ranks, the latter in the former headquarters of the local fascist youth club. It was an indication of the anglicization of the 1st Division that they christened the main thoroughfares Piccadilly Circus and Pall Mall rather than Yonge Street or Dorchester Boulevard. The Salvation Army brought in a mobile movie cinema that showed films in the warm evening air. Living off the land was discouraged, to avoid poisoning relations with the populace, but sometimes temptation was too much to resist. When one Canadian officer found his men plucking chickens (not on the ration rolls and clearly stolen), he took them to task for looting—only to have the men tell him, with completely straight faces, that they had acted in self-defence after being attacked by what were obviously fascist poultry. Over the next month, as the division pushed north, Canadian soldiers enjoyed forty-eight-hour passes to Campobasso. They would need them, for the Italian campaign was about to become much tougher. Adolf Hitler had decided that Rome would be held, and ordered the construction of a defensive position, the Bernhard Line. The Allies' prospects for late 1943 were daunting. Shipping shortages meant that they would be outnumbered and out-supplied by the Germans for the foreseeable future. Yet despite that numerical inferiority, they would have to assault newly prepared positions in terrain that already favoured the defender. For their part in the coming operation, the Canadian division drew the eastern end of the

Bernhard Line, on the Adriatic coast. The anchor of the line was a town that few of the Canadians had ever heard of, but fewer still would ever forget: Ortona.

At any other time, Ortona would have delighted the visitor—a medieval castle overlooked the tiny harbour, a legacy of the town's origins as a trading community; old cobbled streets, shadowed by the tall buildings that lined them; a picturesque ravine that bordered the town to the south. For the attacker, Ortona was a nightmare. A relatively small force, if well stocked with supplies, could in theory defend the castle for weeks. The picturesque ravine meant that the only useful access to the old town was by road, but most of the streets were too narrow for tanks to pass through. Although Canadian armour and artillery gave valuable support, the bulk of the work fell to small groups of Canadian infantrymen fighting house-to-house along the streets of Ortona. The Loyal Edmonton Regiment began to move into Ortona at dawn on 21 December; not until the night of the 27th–28th did the Nazi defenders cut their losses and abandon the town. It cost 650 Canadian casualties, with the Loyal Eddies and the Seaforths taking the heaviest losses. "I used to like hunting," Private Norman Latender told the diarist of the Loyal Eddies after the battle, "but when I get home I never want to see another rifle."[22]

It was fortunate that the Italian front entered the off-season after Ortona, for the Allied armies badly needed a rest and refit. For the Canadians, the three months' lull permitted some much needed reorganization, as it had been decided to send the 5th Armoured Division and headquarters' elements from Britain to Italy and establish the 1st Canadian Corps. The units had begun to arrive in Naples in November 1943, and by mid-January the new formation launched its first attacks; it was May before the Corps as a whole went into action. By that time, an American landing at Anzio had given the Allies a foothold within sixty miles of Rome and the fight for the Italian capital was about to begin. In a series of bitter, costly battles, the Canadian Corps and other Allied divisions punched through the much vaunted Hitler Line. Roy Durnford, the chaplain to the Seaforth Highlanders, recorded his first impressions of the newly disabled fortifications: "Deep entrenchments. Tunnels of cement and steel, and steel and concrete pillboxes. Wire very deep. Vastly fortified. We go back to cemetery and bury 42 in the dark. Bodies keep coming in, mute testimony to awful victory. The cemetery is filling up fast."[23]

With the Allied armies poised to take Rome, the Canadian Corps was pulled from the fighting and placed in reserve. Casualties had been heavy—over 3,200 in under three weeks—and the experienced 1st Division badly needed a rest. The rest of the Corps had shown some inexperience and British commanders believed the Corps would benefit from a chance to catch its breath and ponder some of the lessons learned in its first battles. As the Canadians were getting settled in the reserve area, Rome fell. For many of the Corps' soldiers, the capture of Rome was less memorable than days spent wandering in the countryside or swimming in the warm waters of Salerno Bay or the Gulf of Gaeta. A special beach was set aside for the Canadian Corps at Mandragone, north of Naples (the city itself was eventually placed off limits because of a near-epidemic of venereal disease), and a few lucky soldiers were taken to the Vatican for an audience with the Pope. The Canadian Army Show set up shop to entertain the troops, and the band of the Royal Canadian Army Service Corps played as often as it could. Such diversions provided a stark contrast to the job they were doing, as Padre Durnford observed: "Adriatic is beautiful. Sands lovely. Whole district evacuated by German orders. Every man gets his own villa to live in. Luxury for a day. Yesterday kill and being killed, dodging from hole to hole, crawling in darkness and danger—today lolling on sands, swimming and lounging."[24]

The next order of business was the Gothic Line, the last prepared defensive network in Italy. Beyond it lay the city of Bologna, with its critically important rail junctions, the Po River, and the north Italian plain where, Allied commanders assumed, their tanks could finally escape the narrow tracks and steep ravines of central Italy and really stretch their legs. Because of the mountainous terrain in the American sector, the planners' gaze fell on the eastern end of the Gothic Line, where the Adriatic coastal plain gave the attacker more options. When the advance went forward in late August, the Canadians and the Poles found it easier than they had expected to breach the Gothic Line itself, but the rapid progress was misleading. First, the weather turned. Soldiers were glad to see the rain—anything was better than merciless heat and choking dust—but changed their minds after a few days' downpour turned the dust into mud. As the soldiers and their vehicles splashed and slid along the now greasy tracks, a few of them probably recalled wistfully the days of dust and sure-footedness. The weather, in turn, caused delays, just what the Germans needed to shore up their defences and bring in reinforcements. They fought tenaciously and well, making Allied units pay dearly for every ridge line and ravine they passed on the way north. Nor did the going get any easier beyond Rimini, where the stony hills at last gave way to low-lying fields formed by a network of dykes. The rains had given the Germans the opportunity to breach dykes and flood the fields as they retreated, so the Allied advance was no quicker or less costly than it had been in the mountains.

When the campaign closed down for the season in January 1945, with the Allies holding a line stretching from Ravenna on the Adriatic to north of Pisa, the 1st Canadian Corps learned it was about to leave the Italian theatre. The government in Ottawa had made no secret of its desire to keep Canadian units together, under Canadian commanders; any expansion of the commitment in Italy was always undertaken on the assumption that Canadian units would be reunited in northwest Europe before the end of the war. By late 1944, with the Italian campaign winding down and the British making noises about sending divisions to Greece, Canada pressed the case and eventually prevailed: the 1st Canadian Corps would be taken out of the line and transferred to the Netherlands—just in time to get in on the closing act of the campaign in northwest Europe.

Since the summer of 1942, Allied planners had been studying the problem of invading France. The landings at Dieppe, North Africa, and Italy had given them a good deal to think about, including the critical importance of air cover and a naval bombardment and the need for specialized vessels to carry assault forces to the beaches. The limits of Allied air cover dictated that the landing would have to take place on the northern coast of France, where the topography permitted just two options: the Pas de Calais and Normandy. The former was tempting— one could stand on the White Cliffs of Dover and see the French coast quite clearly—but that was precisely why the Germans had defended it so heavily. Normandy, although farther from British ports, was more lightly defended, and so was the preferred option. The timing hinged on the availability of landing craft to carry the men and tanks to the beaches. Everything possible was being done to speed up the manufacturing process, but 1 May 1944 remained the earliest invasion date; commanders would eventually settle on 5 June 1944 as D-Day. Canada's contribution, after late changes in the plan boosted the assault force from three divisions to five (as well as three airborne), consisted of the 3rd Division and the 2nd Armoured Brigade. They would land at Juno Beach, the easternmost of the invasion beaches, the first wave comprising the Regina Rifles, the Royal Winnipeg Rifles, the North Shore Regiment from New Brunswick, and Toronto's Queen's Own Rifles, Roy Gzowski's regiment.

No one outside the Allied high command knew these specific details, but for anyone living in the south of England that spring, it was impossible to miss the signs that something was up. "Everybody seems to be on tiptoe these days in anticipation that our attack on Europe may start at any moment," wrote Garfield Weston to a friend in Toronto.

> You have no idea what a tension has been created throughout the whole country! Every morning when we awaken we wonder whether it has started. . . . Great squadrons of bombers are passing over us every hour of the day and night, bombing vital targets and coastal and military areas in the hope of creating chaos behind the German lines—and they must be doing so! Meanwhile, the roads are very heavy with military traffic and moving guns—but no doubt you have read it all in the newspapers, only until the second front has been firmly established in the west, I don't think anybody here in England will relax quite the same.[25]

With the volume of military traffic, caused by regiments streaming back to the south from intensive training in all corners of the British Isles, the main streets of Aldershot came to resemble a parking lot, with jeeps, trucks, and Bren carriers sitting two and three deep along the tree-lined avenues. To avoid a repeat of the lapses that had preceded the Dieppe raid, new security precautions came into effect in late April

1944, and in late May the assault units were sequestered altogether. No one was allowed in or out of the camps—there were even armed guards posted to keep them honest. Once the camps were sealed, the last-minute preparations began. Regimental officers were fully briefed, and the men were issued with water purification tablets, escape kits (in case they were cut off behind enemy lines during the advance), and vomit bags for the journey across the Channel. With hundreds of thousands of soldiers crowded into the south coast, it left a void elsewhere, as Charles Ritchie noted: "The soldiers who have been left behind in London look forlorn and subdued. The town seems empty. The gaiety and sense of pressure and excitement have gone. There is a morning-after feeling abroad. The taxis have become plentiful again and the drivers are beginning to be quite polite now that the American debauch is over."[26]

Had Ritchie been living in one of the southern counties rather than London, he would have remarked instead on the carefully controlled chaos, especially the near-constant rumble of truck engines as vehicle convoys wound towards the embarkation ports, movement control parties at every crossroads to guard against wrong turns. This was true even in Kent, where troop movements (real and notional) went on as part of an elaborate deception plan to convince the Germans that the Pas de Calais was the real target. The Canadian units were bound for Portsmouth and Southampton, where they boarded the transports that would take them to within a few miles of the French coast to transfer to landing craft. The transports waited in the Solent to join the invasion fleet, an immense armada of 7,000 ships—more than three times as many as in the Sicily invasion fleet. Above them aircraft from over 170 squadrons would shuttle back and forth from their airfields in Britain to soften up the coastal defences and hit road and rail targets inland.

Bad weather forced a twenty-four-hour postponement but the seas were hardly any calmer in the early hours of the 6th of June as the men transferred from the transports to the landing craft. Heavy swells churned the stomachs of the already nervous assault troops, but there was little sound beyond the crashing of the seas and the distant roar of explosions as heavy bombers pounded the areas behind the invasion beaches. Then, not long before the first units were due to hit the beaches, the naval bombardment opened up. Any soldier who had a notion to sneak a look at the French coastline had good reason to keep his head down, although the combination of a heavy overcast, spray from the seas, and smoke from the bombardment meant there wasn't much to see anyways. Visibility was so poor that many of the supporting fighter-bombers were grounded and the air operations to soften up the beaches were nowhere near as intensive as they were supposed to be. At least the terrible weather meant that the Germans weren't expecting anything when, at 7:49 AM, the first landing craft to approach Juno Beach dropped their ramps and the infantry clambered out.

This was much harder than it sounded. The beaches were festooned with iron and concrete obstacles that, thanks to the rising tide, were quickly disappearing from sight. Many landing craft were forced to drop anchor hundreds of yards from the water's edge and disgorge their cargo into water that was six feet deep or more. The men were so happy to be off the churning seas—"we were so sea-sick that we preferred to be shot on the beaches rather than go back on those Landing Craft," recalled one infantryman of the Royal Winnipeg Rifles[27]—that they ignored the depth of the water. Most quickly bobbed to the surface but a few, weighed down by extra equipment, simply vanished beneath the waves. Enemy fire was intense in places, the spotty bombardment having left many of the beach defences intact, and some platoons took heavy casualties within minutes of hitting the beach. But by 9 AM, the first waves of all four Canadian battalions were ashore and getting ready to move inland.

Once the beach obstacles had been cleared, the assault units had to get past the seawall, which in some places rose ten feet above the level of the sand. But by mid-morning, that obstacle too had been overcome and the forward infantry companies and their supporting armour were moving into the towns of Bernières, Courseulles, and St Aubin. Pockets of fierce enemy resistance slowed the advance in some sectors; elsewhere, congestion on the beach held up reinforcements and kept the leading elements from moving inland as quickly as they might. But success was virtually complete. A Canadian battalion (precisely which unit is still a matter of heated debate) was the first in the 2nd Army to reach its objective and by nightfall, the 3rd Division had achieved almost all of its objectives, at a cost of over 900 killed, wounded, and captured. The

British divisions on either side of Juno beach had also done well, but to the west the Americans had taken heavy casualties at Utah and especially Omaha beaches.

The first forty-eight to seventy-two hours after D-Day were the most critical; if the invasion was to fail, it would probably fail in the first few days. And the defenders did their best to push the Allied armies back into the sea. In the eastern end of the sector, the heaviest blows fell on the Canadian front. For six days, elements of an elite SS panzer division tried to dislodge the Canadians from villages and crossroads north of Caen. As well trained as they were, the battalions of the 3rd Division were hard pressed by the experienced and fanatical Nazi soldiers and the thin-skinned Allied tanks were at the mercy of far superior German armour and anti-tank guns. Canadian casualties were horrific—nearly 3,000 killed and wounded over a week. The 3rd Division had suffered some serious tactical reverses, but hadn't been pushed back to the beaches. They went into two weeks of rest and refit with the bridgehead stabilized and the invasion secured.

The division returned to the front lines just in time to be thrown against Caen, the home of William the Conqueror that was supposed to have been captured on D-Day. Then, the 2nd and 3rd Divisions (the former having arrived in France in the last week of July) fought a series of bitter, costly, and in some cases mismanaged battles south of Caen that took a heavy toll in Canadian units; amongst the dead was Clarence Bourassa of the South Saskatchewan Regiment, killed by a sniper on 20 July 1944. The object of those battles was to tie down the best German units at the eastern end of the bridgehead, to allow the US divisions at the western end to break out from Omaha and Utah beaches and move into open country in western France. In that, it succeeded. It also drew the Germans into the battle. Adolf Hitler insisted on attacking the Americans, which meant that his forces would have to drive westwards across the Anglo-Canadian front. If the US divisions could dodge the punch and push east to the south of the German advance, it might be possible to link up with the Anglo-Canadian divisions moving south from Caen and encircle an entire enemy army. As the Allied armies rumbled towards a rendezvous, the German corridor of escape, near Falaise, narrowed. With Allied fighter-bombers blasting German vehicles from tree-top height and the roads becoming clogged with shattered tanks and trucks, Canadian and Polish soldiers fought desperately to close the gap. When they finally did, on 21 August, the troops got a glimpse of what they had wrought. "We marched to high ground north of Falaise Gap," wrote Harry Ruch of the Argyll and Sutherland Highlanders in his diary a few days later. "Could see signs where Jerry was definitely on the run. The road was clogged with wrecked tanks, trucks, dead horses, and dead Jerries. . . . As we progressed through the valley we could see the beating Jerry had taken. It must have been pure Hell for him. Wrecked tanks, trucks, and wagons everywhere. Jerry dead all over the place. Horses both dead and living by the thousands."[28] The closure of the Falaise Gap brought German losses for this stage of the Normandy campaign to 300,000 men and over 2,000 tanks. Nazi Panther and Tiger tanks were superb fighting vehicles, but they simply couldn't be replaced in sufficient numbers. The Allied Shermans might have been under-gunned and under-armoured, but there were dozens more of them rolling off transport ships every day. The weight of numbers was beginning to tell.

But for how long? The invasion forces had been supplied through huge artificial harbours anchored off the beaches, but the harbours had been badly damaged in a savage Channel storm, and the Allies were starting to have trouble supplying their advancing armies. Unless some large ports were captured, and soon, the liberation of France might grind to a halt for want of fuel and replacement vehicles. It was essential to clear the ports along the French coast as a stopgap, until the Allies could capture the real target, Antwerp. Because the Canadians were on the coast, the job fell to them. Over the course of a month, the 2nd and 3rd Divisions cleared Dieppe, Le Tréport, Boulogne, and Calais, opening their harbours to Allied shipping. And although the British captured Antwerp, the port itself was of little use. Between Antwerp and the North Sea was the fifty-mile-long Scheldt estuary, both sides of which were strongly held by battered but not yet broken German divisions. To complicate the situation, the lands on either side of the estuary, as well as the heavily defended South Beveland isthmus and Walcheren Island, were low-lying and subject to flooding. By blowing the dykes that held back the sea, the Germans could turn the region into a network of small lakes. Of all the Canadians' battlefields of the Second World War, the

Scheldt most resembled the very worst of Flanders from a generation earlier. The defenders were firmly dug in and determined to hold their positions; the attackers were under-strength and exhausted, yet gamely accepted the near impossible tactical jobs given to them. And everywhere there was water, sometimes chest deep—the historian of the Queen's Own Rifles recalled "the utter misery of the conditions and the great courage required to do the simplest things."[29] It took the Canadians five weeks and over 6,300 casualties to clear South Beveland, Walcheren, and the south shore, and the tragedy was that it didn't need to happen. The British army that took Antwerp had every opportunity to clear the estuary before the Germans dug in, but timidity won out—and the Canadians paid dearly.

In 1917, the Battle of Passchendaele had coincided with a conscription crisis as the government conceded that the voluntary system could no longer provide enough men to sustain the Canadian Corps. In 1944, it was the Battle of the Scheldt that marked the turning point. Infantry casualties had been intense since D-Day, and there simply weren't enough volunteers coming forward to fill the gaps. No one could predict if the high loss rate would persist, and the army had no choice but to plan for the worst. The obvious source of manpower, as far as the generals were concerned, was the Zombies, men who had been conscripted for home service only under the 1940 National Resources Mobilization Act. The solution seemed as easy as converting them to General Service and sending them to northwest Europe. But to Mackenzie King, conscription was a catastrophe and to avoid it he wriggled and squirmed like a child dodging a dose of castor oil. Looking back, his political manoeuvring makes sense, for it proved to the Canadian public that he had indeed tried every possible alternative before converting the Zombies as a last resort. But to members of the Canadian forces overseas, King was a weakling whose waffling cost Canadian lives at the front. The most polite of military audiences greeted him with a stony silence. Most booed him lustily. For his part, the prime minister deeply wished he could connect better with military men, and he lamented the fact that he just didn't understand the soldier or the world in which he lived.[30]

Now with sufficient reinforcements coming through the system, First Canadian Army had two main tasks in the early months of 1945. Clearing the west bank of the Rhine River near the Dutch border was the first order of business. The Americans were moving towards the industrial cities of Duisburg and Essen, but to the northwest was a wedge of land through which the invading armies had to pass on the way to the Netherlands. Low lying and dotted with thick forests, it offered many advantages to the defender and few to the attacker. From 8 February to 10 March 1945, Crerar's divisions fought through the Reichswald Forest, Moyland Wood, and the Hochwald Forest before battling through the town of Xanten to the Rhine. Now that they were defending the fatherland, German units fought even more doggedly, inflicting over 5,300 Canadian casualties in the campaign. Crerar insisted that the dead be taken to cemeteries in the Netherlands; he would not allow Canadian troops to be buried on enemy soil.

The sands were running out for Hitler's Germany by the time 1st Canadian Corps arrived from Italy in April. The newcomers, used to equipment and ammunition being carefully husbanded in Italy, were amazed at how freely everything was used—a thundering artillery barrage would be called down on the most unpromising of targets, for the supply of shells was apparently limitless. One gunner noted that over 4,100 guns were in action against the enemy in Operation Plunder, the crossing of the Rhine River in late March 1945; to breach the Hitler Line in 1943, Allied units in Italy had fewer than 800. With enormous firepower at its disposal, Crerar's army wheeled north, fanning out across the Netherlands and delivering the Dutch from their occupiers. The jubilation of the civilians was intense, their gratitude profound, and it seemed a fitting conclusion to the campaign in northwest Europe. There were still pockets of stiff resistance to be flushed out, but the ultimate outcome could no longer be in doubt. The 1st Division was taken out of battle, having lost heavily in the Netherlands—the 48th Highlanders lost their commanding officer to shellfire just a few weeks before the end of the war, while the Royal Canadian Regiment's last officer casualty had been the first officer to land on the beach in Sicily, nearly two years earlier. On 4 May, two days after the remaining German armies in Italy gave up, Crerar suspended offensive operations; surrender negotiations were underway and, with memories of visiting Mons in November 1918 as a young artillery officer, he had no desire to lose any men unnecessarily.

At 8 AM on 7 May, the Thousand-Year Reich ceased to exist. The war in Europe was over.

It would be another three months before the war in the Pacific ended. Not until August 1945, after Hiroshima and Nagasaki had been flattened, did the agony end for the Allied troops who had been island-hopping across the Pacific, or for the prisoners of war who had suffered unimaginable abuse at the hands of their Japanese captors. But for the Canadian empire in Britain, the party began on 8 May 1945. It was just like the 11th of November 1918 all over again, but in glorious spring weather and without the threat of a deadly pandemic hanging over everyone. It was also eagerly awaited. The German surrender documents were signed at 2:41 AM on the 7th of May, and British newspapers were able to announce in their morning editions that the following day would be observed as VE day—by the time midnight tolled, Londoners were well in the party mood. In Piccadilly Circus, crowds sang "There'll Always be an England" while in Trafalgar Square, steps from Canada House, some teenagers climbed Nelson's Column and decked it out with flags as civilians joined hands and danced around its base. Prime Minister Winston Churchill seemed to be everywhere. At 3 PM, he spoke from Downing Street, his remarks carried by loudspeakers to the multitudes in the streets. Later, he was at Buckingham Palace with the King and Queen, and then he spoke from the balcony of the Ministry of Health in Whitehall, overlooking the Cenotaph that had been erected in 1919 to honour the dead of the last war. All around the city, the crowds continued to celebrate through the night. The blackout was technically still in force, but Buckingham Palace and the government buildings were bathed in floodlights, and there were more than a few bonfires in the streets. At Linton-on-Ouse, the RCAF broke out the refreshments that had been carefully put aside for the occasion, and there was more than enough drink to keep the party going through that day and into the next. The revellers were boisterous but generally well behaved, and there was almost no damage to property—the station commander reported only two broken windows, both apparently caused by tipsy airmen who mistook them for doors. In Aldershot, local schoolchildren donned fancy-dress costumes for the occasion, and one lad whose tenth birthday fell on VE day was given the honour of lighting the victory bonfire. For many of the children, it had been a good war—the Canadians, after all, had brought sweets and chewing gum, cartoons and Christmas parties, baseball games and motorcycle rides.

Not all Canadians celebrated with equal vigour—one soldier from the Perth Regiment, at the end of a long hospital stay in Aldershot after being wounded in Italy, noticed that the most enthusiastic partygoers were men who, thanks to the surrender, would never see combat. And for most of them, the desire to celebrate was quickly replaced by the desire to get home. This time there could be no grumbling about demobilization plans being left to the last minute, as many in the Canadian Corps

Members of the Canadian Women's Army Corps buying flags in celebration of VE day, London, 8 May 1945

believed in 1919. The Mackenzie King government had begun planning for the process as early as December 1939, long before it had any idea of the magnitude of the task, and various committees put in countless hours hammering out a system to get Canadians home and back into civilian clothes. It was an enormously complex process that had to account for the needs and desires of those in uniform, principles of fairness, the demands of postwar industry, military obligations, and logistics. First in, first out (or first over, first back) seemed fair, but should a soldier who spent five years in Britain with the pay corps get home before one who enlisted in 1943 but spent months with the infantry, slogging through the battlefields of northwest Europe? NRMA men serving in Canada could be discharged quite easily, but was it fair to give them the pick of postwar jobs, while men and women with overseas service sifted through the leftovers months later? "Surely the Government will not be so foolish this time as to consider giving the first and best jobs to the men who remained in Canada," wondered a concerned soldier in 1943.[31] As the planning proceeded, the questions only became more complicated.

The federal government had already committed publicly to a modified first-in, first-out system, based on a point scale that took into account length of service and family needs. To see what soldiers wanted, the army prepared to poll them as the war in Europe drew to a close: did they want to be discharged immediately, or would they be willing to stay in uniform for occupation duties, or even to join the 40,000-strong force that was being readied to help finish the war in the Pacific? But the desires of the soldiers themselves could never be the primary consideration. It was made clear that the manpower requirements of the army would be paramount; General Crerar was very much in favour of discharge by unit, for all the same reasons that Sir Arthur Currie had advanced in 1918. And again, there was the problem of shipping space. The shortage of troopships simply didn't allow six years of immigration, not only by Canadians but by Americans, Australians, New Zealanders, and others, to be reversed in a matter of months. Until all the arrangements could be sorted out, Crerar wrote, "the essential thing is to keep all ranks mentally and/or physically active, and interested, for most of their waking hours."[32]

Some parts of the demobilization puzzle were easier to solve in the air force. Squadrons had no territorial basis, so there could be no argument for demobilizing them as units. A squadron had far more officers than an infantry battalion (the RCAF insisted that anyone who flew operationally hold commissioned rank), but aircrew officers had no command function over the ground crew, who were mostly NCOs and enlisted men, so the presence of a large officer cadre was not essential for the maintenance of discipline. And each operational squadron was small—a typical bomber squadron had fewer than half as many members as an infantry battalion—so individual units were relatively easy to demobilize. Still, the air force was in the same queue for shipping space as everyone else, and unforeseen delays were all too frequent.

As soldiers from the continent moved back to Britain, it was becoming clear that the problems of 1919 hadn't been avoided altogether. Crerar felt that Canada was getting shortchanged on shipping space because CMHQ and Ottawa were too timid in pushing Canadian demands. The points system had its own problems. It may have been fair, for it was designed to reward long-service soldiers with speedy repatriation. But it ignored the fact that those same veterans, whether or not they were commissioned officers, were the natural leaders in their units; without them, discipline started to slip. The situation boiled over in Aldershot on 4 July 1945. A group of Canadian soldiers, bored and likely hung over from the night before, gathered in a park and convinced themselves that the local police were holding three of their pals in the cells. In a repeat of the 1919 Epsom riots, they marched on the station, collecting support as they went. One of their officers showed them that the cells were empty but the crowd was already out of control. Frustrated by their inability to liberate anyone, they descended on the shopping district, smashing windows as they went. In two days of rioting, they attacked over 200 businesses and caused £15,000 in damages. But unlike Epsom, there were no serious injuries and almost no looting. British officers suggested that their own soldiers might be needed to restore order, but Canadian military policemen responded swiftly and decisively. One hundred Canadian soldiers were arrested and five went to jail.

The Aldershot riot was certainly the most serious outbreak, but it wasn't the only one. In February 1946, RCAF ground crew at Odiham in Hampshire began a strike to protest the lack of information being given to them about repatriation; days later, men at another airfield struck, until nearly 2,000 Canadians were engaged in the protest. There was no violence involved—the men made it clear that they had no complaints against their commanders in Britain, and being on strike didn't prevent them from attending local dances. Their actions technically constituted

Soldiers behaving badly: the Aldershot riot, July 1945

mutiny, but the strike drew enough sympathy from Canadian newspapers that the RCAF wisely decided not to pursue charges.

Fortunately, such disturbances were out of the ordinary and scarcely hurt the good relations that had developed between the colonists and their hosts. As the final departure of Canadian troops from Aldershot drew near, the borough council decided to confer the freedom of the town on the visitors. On 26 September 1945, in front of a huge crowd at the sports ground, the mayor and town clerk paid tribute to the relationship that had grown:

> This ceremony may be said to be not merely a gesture on the part of Aldershot, but rather as coming from the whole of the British Isles. . . . Friendly men they were, three or four thousand miles from home, yet keenly conscious of home ties, and warmly appreciative of every effort we made to offer them a share in our home life. . . . Many are the lasting friendships formed, many the attachments which have led to the altar, and not a few Aldershot families have been saddened and grieved by the loss of friends who have made the supreme sacrifice. . . . Our Canadian visitors . . . have expressed their gratitude in many ways by whole-heartedly co-operating in our communal life, and not least by their most generous treatment of our children.

As General P.J. Montague, the chief of staff at CMHQ, said in response, the warm feelings were mutual:

> Aldershot has been more than a place of bricks and mortar, training grounds and huts. It has been the centre of our life in England. Here we have always been a good, happy family. A lot of our men have taken charming women as their wives and they have formed many friendships. . . . Thank you for the great kindness and forbearance which has been shown to the men and women of the Canadian Army during the past five and a half years. . . . We give you this assurance, that as long as the winds blow and the rivers run in Canada we will remain loyal to this Mother Country, and we shall never forget Aldershot.[33]

The ceremony in Aldershot was just one of many that combined a send-off with an expression of thanks. In the Vale of York, 426 Squadron RCAF held Linton-at-Home Day on 20 May 1945, with the Lord Mayor of York and 3,000 locals in attendance. Security demands had prevented civilians from getting close to the big bombers while they were operational; now that the squadron was about to return home, the townspeople were given a chance to get a close look at the aircraft they knew only as muffled roars overhead. At Godalming in Surrey the Rhythm Rodeo, a spectacular variety show that had been entertaining Canadian soldiers from a nearby repatriation depot, was opened to the locals in December 1945, with a special children's performance on Christmas Day. The Canadians also mounted a farewell Christmas parade in Godalming, complete with the chuck-wagon racers and chariots from the Rhythm Rodeo and a Farewell to Britain float featuring Johnny Canuck shaking hands with John Bull across the Atlantic Ocean.

Even as these celebrations were going on, the Canadian empire was rapidly shrinking. This time, discharge in Britain was allowed only in cases of serious hardship; fewer than 6,000 Canadians were demobilized in Britain, less than half the number from the First World War and few enough that it made no impact on the repatriation process. Despite the minor disturbances, the process was moving with commendable efficiency. On VE day, there were over 281,000 members of the Canadian Army in Britain; six months later, fewer than 100,000 of them remained. The RCN, never a large presence in Britain, had mostly cleared out as well, and the RCAF was making good progress in sending air and ground crew home. The other significant contingent in the westbound migration was war brides. This Canadian occupation produced nearly as many war brides as the First World War. By the end of 1946, there had been nearly 45,000 marriages, some between Canadians in uniform but most with British civilians, and over 21,000 children born in Britain of wartime unions. Canadian officials did all they could to pre-empt some of the problems that had appeared in 1919. A Civilian Repatriation Section in London (and later the Immigration Branch of the Department of Mines and Resources) handled the arrangements, with the Canadian Red Cross Society providing escorts to accompany war brides on the journey. Usually, women and children were added to troopships as space became available, but in February 1946 a sailing of the RMS *Mauretania* was reserved for war brides and their children—Operation Daddy, the press called it.

These newcomers faced the same jarring adjustments as their predecessors, made worse by the fact that not all Canadians were scrupulously honest. The woman who was told that her new home was "not far from Regina" could be forgiven for being comforted by the prospect of moving to a provincial capital, especially one named after Queen Victoria. She didn't reckon on the different Canadian perception of time and space—"not far" was actually Climax, Saskatchewan, more than 300 kilometres from Regina. But the train only ran three days a week, and then just in the summer. At least in that case there was no outright deceit. Less fortunate was the young bride whose soldier husband showed her a photo of an imposing stone building that he claimed was the family mansion. Only when she got to the Prairies did

Women of the Canadian Red Cross serving supper to the children of war brides en route to Canada, April 1946

she discover that she had been shown a photo of the Moose Jaw public library. Even so, this generation of war brides proved to be every bit as resilient as the previous one. Not all of the marriages survived—perhaps 10 percent of them ended in divorce—but the vast majority of British women who came as war brides decided to remain in Canada, even if they couldn't remain with their husbands.

Even after most of the people had gone, the traces of Canada's empire in Britain remained. The dead became permanent Britons. All over the British Isles, the Imperial (later Commonwealth) War Graves Commission buried the men and women who had succumbed to wounds or disease, in training accidents or traffic mishaps, or whose bodies had been lifted from aircraft that limped back to base, carrying the dead and the dying to be buried in friendly soil. In June 1917, a CEF band played while more than 1,500 local schoolchildren brought flowers to decorate the graves of Canadians who were buried at Shorncliffe Military Cemetery. The plot would become a small piece of Canada in Folkestone, said a local dignitary. "Canadian parents would be bound closer to the Mother Country by the action of the little children" who brought flowers.[34] In St Mary's Churchyard in Bramshott, a Canadian memorial was erected in 1921, and every year on Dominion Day, the women of Liphook gathered to place flowers on Canadian graves. The same ritual occurred at All Saints Churchyard in Orpington, where a plot had been set aside and christened Ontario Cemetery, or more commonly the Canadian Corner.

But Canada's empire in Britain had a living legacy as well. After 1918 and 1945, the infrastructure that had been built for war was put to peaceful purposes. The Ontario Hospital in Orpington was turned over to the Ministry of Pensions to house wounded veterans, and by 1939 it had become the area's municipal hospital. At Bushy Park, the King's Canadian Red Cross Hospital was given to the London County Council to treat "delicate" children, while Upper Lodge became a holiday school for boys from London's East End. The Canadian Red Cross gave to the city of Birmingham parts of the Duchess of Connaught's hospital at Taplow, specifically Queen Alexandra Wards 1 and 2, the Saskatchewan and Manitoba Wards, and the nurses' sleeping quarters (the rest of the buildings were later razed). The same thing happened in 1946, when

Viscount Bennett, as chair of the overseas advisory committee of the Canadian Red Cross Society, presented the new Second World War hospital at Taplow to the British people, as a war memorial. It would address a grave shortage of hospital beds in the district, and eventually become a special hospital for research into cardiac rheumatism in children until its closure in 1985. The CEF's prefabricated huts at Bramshott also found a second life in the 1920s; some became private homes, one a school sports pavilion, and another a classroom. The Second World War headquarters building of the Canadian Army (Overseas) in Aldershot is still used by the British Army; it has been renamed Wavell House, but Crerar and McNaughton Closes in nearby Farnborough still bear witness to earlier inhabitants.

Other outposts of the Canadian empire have disappeared altogether, or show no trace of their former use. The Empire Hotel at Buxton, which became the Canadian Discharge Depot at the end of the First World War, was used by the British Army in the Second World War, and then fell into disuse. After two decades at the mercy of squatters and vandals, it was pulled down in 1964. Wittington, the Weston estate that was such a welcome destination for so many Canadian men and women on leave, now houses the offices of a software company. All around Aldershot, cement pads that had been laid to take the weight of Canadian armoured vehicles have been used for sports, community events, or new construction. Canada House in London is still the centre of the nation's peacetime empire in Britain, but the other buildings that once housed the Overseas Military Forces of Canada, Canadian Military Headquarters, the Canadian Red Cross Society, and a host of other organizations have returned to more conventional uses. In most cases, there is not even a plaque to note that occupying that spot had once been an outpost of the Maple Leaf Empire.

EPILOGUE

It is easy to say that the Canadian empire in Britain quickly became a mere shadow of its former self, but its decline has never been as precipitate nor as absolute as it might seem. In 1957 Beverley Baxter wrote a tongue-in-cheek column in *Maclean's* (part of his long-running "London Letter" series) that revealed the degree to which expatriate Canadians (like himself) had found their way into positions of influence in the UK. Britain had been the victim of many invasions, he wrote, and "in modern times there has developed a steady infiltration from Canada, which flows like a river and never recedes." After listing over a dozen Canadians who had achieved a degree of celebrity in the UK (the majority of them connected to one of the wartime empires), he imagined the House of Commons at Westminster debating a quota on Canadian immigration to Britain, or measures to deport Canadians who were long-time residents and showed no inclination to return home. "Will the growing Canadian influence in Britain end?" Baxter mused. "Might as well ask if the Thames will stop."[1]

The Thames still ebbs and flows, as does the influence of the British connection. Contemporaries were fond of referring to a silken thread binding the two countries together—a thread that was not so tight that it chafed but strong enough to endure the strains of war. In the decades since the end of the Second World War, the thread has been stretched, thinned, and reshaped, but never severed. Ambitious Canadians are still drawn to stand for election to Westminster (although it's no longer known as the Imperial Parliament) or try their hand in British business, but perhaps not for the same reasons that Beverley Baxter, Alfred Critchley, and Garfield Weston did after the First World War. And yet there is surely still some truth in the analogy that, having succeeded in the minor leagues of Canada, it was only natural to crave the challenge of the big leagues in Britain. Robert Borden was the last prime minister to accept a knighthood (the Nickle Resolution of 1919 barred Canadians from accepting royal titles, forcing Conrad Black to renounce his Canadian citizenship so he could become Lord Black of Crossharbour in 2001), but Mackenzie King maintained his own brand of anglophilia— he certainly treasured his appointment to the Privy Council, not least for the snappy uniform that accompanied the honour. John Diefenbaker was the last avowedly pro-British prime minister, his fondness fostered by a short time spent with the CEF in Britain before being injured in a training accident and invalided home. His successor Lester Pearson also spent many years in Britain—with the CEF, at Oxford University, and at Canada House. It didn't rub off on him to quite the same degree, but Pearson certainly understood the sentiment well enough to be prepared for the wrath he incurred when he replaced the Union Jack with the Maple Leaf flag in 1965.

And if Canadians no longer glow with pride in the knowledge that they were part of an empire that covered a quarter of the globe, a weakness for things British is manifest in other ways. Generations of sports car enthusiasts fell in love with Triumphs and MGBs, revelling in their Britishness even though they were completely unsuited to Canadian winters. Porsches and Alfa Romeos sold here too, but never captured hearts like a TR3 in British Racing Green and spoked wheels. Britcoms and *Coronation Street* have legions of fans in Canada—we seem to understand them better than the Americans—and Canadian militia units still celebrate their links to sister regiments in Britain, and honour the royals who serve as their Colonels-in-Chief. Members of the Queen's Own Rifles still visit Roy Gzowski's grave in Aldershot to leave flowers and pay their respects. Royal visits and weddings continue to take our fancy, even among people who consider the Monarchist League of Canada to be vaguely old-fashioned.

No one talks about the Mother Country anymore—as Charles Ritchie observed, the phrase was rarely heard in Britain anyways[2]—and the notion of subservience to an imperial capital an ocean away has vanished from our thinking. But we shouldn't lose sight of what made the British connection so attractive and important to earlier generations. When Canadians went to Britain during the two world wars, they found themselves in a familiar land, even those who had never been there before. Donald Duncan of Winnipeg, who had only scant contact with Britain before he arrived as an infantry officer in May 1944, remarked on the feeling of familiarity, and concluded that it stemmed from a childhood spent reading English literature, "a memory from Dickens or Hardy."[3] The newcomers already knew of Shakespeare's Stratford-upon-Avon and Blake's green and pleasant land, of William Wallace and Queen Boadicea. Leslie Frost was certainly not the only Canadian soldier to experience a strange thrill "to stand within a few feet of the dust of such people as Gladstone, Peel, Charles II, Mary Queen of Scots, Queen Elizabeth,"[4] while Saskatchewan farm boy Frank Selinger wrote that the years spent learning British history in school came alive when he visited the Tower of London in 1945.[5] Whether or not they had any personal connection to Britain before enlisting, these visitors appreciated the country as a source of the legacies that they valued—the parliamentary tradition, liberalism, religious tolerance—even if neither country always lived up to the ideal. Indeed, many of them came to believe that Canada had preserved in a finer form the heritage that had lost some lustre in the Mother Country. For them, the colonization of Britain during the twentieth century was a way to reinvigorate those values. In doing so, they built a Canadian empire that left its mark on Britain, sometimes for ill but mostly for good. And Britain left its mark on them.

APPENDIX

Given the adjustment problems that Canadians in Britain experienced in the early years of the Second World War, it became clear that military authorities were not doing enough to prepare men and women headed overseas for the social and cultural differences they would encounter in Britain. One product of that concern was *A Guide for Guys Like You*, distributed in 1943 by the Royal Canadian Artillery to enlighten gunners on some typical British characteristics, habits, and preoccupations. In it, the sadly anonymous author captured the essence of the Mother Country that 85 percent of Canadians in uniform had never before visited and knew only second-hand.

A GUIDE FOR GUYS LIKE YOU
A Gunner's Guide To Great Britain

To help you see it through
We guys who've seen
Are sincere and keen
To help you, it's up to you!

Introduction

During the course of this War, you may find yourself in England, or as you have heard your folks call it sometimes, the "Old Country". During your stay there, you will be a guest of Great Britain, and the purpose of this guide, is to try and acquaint you with the British people, their country, and their ways. Although we are a part of the British Empire, speaking the same language, believing in representative government, in freedom of worship, and in freedom of speech, some things are a little different over there from what we have been accustomed to here in Canada.

For instance: The people of the British Isles are often more reserved in conduct than we. So if they sit in trains or busses without striking up conversation with you, it doesn't mean that they are being haughty or unfriendly. Probably they are paying more attention to you than you think. But they don't speak to you because they don't want to appear intrusive or rude.

Another difference. They have phrases of their own that may sound funny to you. You can make just as many boners in their eyes. It isn't a good idea for instance, to say "bloody" in mixed company in Britain—it is one of their worst swear words. To say: "I look like a bum" is offensive to their ears, for to the British this means that you look like your own backside. It isn't important—just a tip if you are trying to shine in polite society. Near the end of this guide you will find more of these differences of speech.

British money is in pounds, shillings and pence. The British are used to this system and they like it, and all your arguments that our decimal system is better won't convince them. They won't be pleased to hear you call it "funny money", either. They sweat hard to get it (wages are much lower in Britain than in Canada) and they won't think you smart or funny for mocking at it.

DON'T BE A SHOW OFF. The British dislike bragging or showing off. Canadian wages and Canadian soldier's pay are among the highest in the world. When pay day comes, it would be sound practice to learn to spend your money according to British standards. They consider you highly paid. They won't think any better of you for throwing money around; they are more likely to feel that you haven't learned the common-sense virtues of thrift. The British "Tommy" is apt to be specially touchy about the difference between his wages and yours. Keep this in mind. Use common sense and don't rub him the wrong way.

You will find many things in Great Britain physically different from similar things in Canada. But there are also important similarities—our common speech, our common law, and our ideals of religious freedom

all come from Britain. Remember that in Canada you like people to conduct themselves as we do, and to respect the same things. Try to do the same for the British and respect the things they treasure.

THE BRITISH ARE TOUGH. Don't be misled by their tendency to be soft-spoken and polite. If they need to be, they can be plenty tough. The English language didn't spread across the oceans and over the mountains and jungles and swamps of the world because these people were panty-waists.

Sixty thousand British civilians—men, women and children—have died under bombs, and yet the morale of Great Britain is unbreakable and high. A nation doesn't come through that, if it doesn't have plain, common guts. You won't be able to tell Great Britain much about "taking it". They are not particularly interested in taking it any more. They are far more interested in getting together in solid friendship with us, so that we can all start dishing it out to Hitler.

The Country

AGE INSTEAD OF SIZE. On furlough you will probably go to the cities, where you will meet the Briton's pride in age and tradition. You will find that the people of Great Britain care little about size, not having the "biggest" of many things as we do. For instance, London has no skyscrapers. Not because English architects couldn't design one, but because London is built on swampy ground, not on a rock like Ottawa and skyscrapers need something solid to rest their foundations on. In London they will point out to you buildings like Westminster Abbey, where England's kings and greatest men are buried, and St. Paul's Cathedral with its famous dome, and the Tower of London, which was built almost a thousand years ago. All of these buildings have played an important part in England's history.

The largest English cities are all located in the lowlands near the various seacoasts. In the southeast, on the Thames (pronounced "Tems") is London which is at the heart of our far-flung British Empire. The population of greater London is twelve million people, this is equal to the total population of Canada. The great "midland" manufacturing cities of Birmingham, Sheffield, and Coventry are located in the central part of

England. Nearby on the west coast are the textile and shipping centres of Manchester and Liverpool. Further north, in Scotland, is the world's leading ship-building centre of Glasgow. On the east side of Scotland is the historic Scottish capital, Edinburgh, scene of the tales of Scott and Robert Louis Stevenson which many of you read in school. In southwest England at the broad mouth of the Severn is the great port of Bristol.

REMEMBER THERE'S A WAR ON. Britain may look a little shop-worn and grimy to you. The British people are anxious to have you know that you are not seeing their country at its best. There's been a war on since 1939. The houses haven't been painted because factories are not making paint—they're making planes. The famous English gardens and parks are either unkept because there are no men to take care of them, or they are being used to grow needed vegetables. British taxicabs look antique because Britain makes tanks for herself and Russia, and hasn't time to make new cars. British trains are cold because power is needed for industry, not for heating. There are no luxury dining cars on trains because total war effort has no place for such frills. The trains are unwashed and grimy because men and women are needed for more important work than car-washing. The British people are anxious for you to know that in normal times Britain looks much prettier, cleaner, neater.

The People—Their Customs and Manners

The best way to get on in Great Britain is very much the same as the best way to get on in Canada. The same sort of courtesy and decency and friendliness that go over big in Canada will go over big in Britain. The British have seen a good many Canadians and they like Canadians. They will like your frankness as long as it is friendly. They will expect you to be generous. They are not given to back-slapping and they are shy about showing their affections. But once they get to like you they make the best friends in the world.

In "getting along" the first important thing to remember is that the British are like us in many ways—but not in all ways. You will quickly discover differences that seem confusing and even wrong. Like driving on the left side of the road, and having money based on an "impossible" accounting system, and drinking warm beer. But once you get used

to things like that, you will realise that they belong to England just as baseball and jazz and coca-cola belong to us.

THE BRITISH LIKE SPORTS. The British of all classes are enthusiastic about sports, both as amateurs and as spectators of professional sports. They love to shoot, they love to play games, they ride horses and bet on horse races, they fish. But be careful where you hunt or fish. Fishing and hunting rights are often private property.

The great "spectator" sports are football in the autumn and winter and cricket in the spring and summer. See a "match" in either of these sports whenever you get a chance. You will get a kick out of it.

Cricket will strike you as slow compared with baseball, but it isn't easy to play well. You will probably get more fun out of "village cricket" which corresponds to sandlot baseball. The big professional matches are often nothing but a private contest between the bowler (who corresponds to our pitcher) and the batsman (batter) and you have to know the fine points of the game to understand what is going on.

Football in Britain takes two forms. They play soccer, which is known here, and they also play "rugger", which is a rougher game, but is played without the padded suits and headguards we use. Rugger requires fifteen on a side, uses a ball slightly bigger than our football, and allows lateral but not forward passing. The English do not handle the ball as cleanly as we do, but they are far more expert with their feet. As in all English games, no substitutes are allowed. If a man is injured, his side continues with fourteen players and so on.

You will find that English crowds at football or cricket matches are more orderly and more polite to the players than we are. If a fielder misses a catch at cricket, the crowd will probably take a sympathetic attitude. They will shout "good try" even if it looks to you like a bad fumble. Here the crowd would probably shout "take him out". This contrast should be remembered. It means that you must be careful in the excitement of an English game not to shout out remarks which everyone here would understand, but which the British might think insulting.

In general more people play games in Britain than in this country, even if they are not good at it. You can always find people who play no better than you and are glad to play with you. They are good sportsmen and are quick to recognize good sportsmanship wherever they meet it.

INDOOR AMUSEMENTS. The British have theaters and movies (which they call "cinemas") as we do. But the great place of recreation is the "pub". A pub or public house, is what we call a bar or tavern. The usual drink is beer, which is not an imitation of German beer, but ale. (But they usually call it beer or "bitter".) Not much whiskey is now being drunk. Wartime taxes have shot the price of a bottle up to about $5.00. The British are beer-drinkers—and can hold it. The beer is now below peacetime strength, but can still make a man's tongue wag at both ends.

You will be welcome in the British pubs as long as you remember one thing. The pub is "the poor man's club", the neighborhood or village gathering place, where the men have come to see their friends, not strangers. If you want to join a darts game, let them ask you first (as they probably will). And if you are beaten it is the custom to stand aside and let someone else play.

The British make much of Sunday. All the shops are closed, most of the restaurants are closed, and in the small towns there is not much to do. You had better follow the example of the British and try to spend Sunday afternoon in the country.

British churches, particularly the little village churches, are often very beautiful inside and out. Most of them are always open and if you feel like it, do not hesitate to walk in. But do not walk around if a service is going on.

You will naturally be interested in getting to know your opposite number, the British soldier, the "Tommy" you have heard and read about. You can understand that two actions on your part will slow up the friendship—swiping his girl, and not appreciating what his army has been up against. Yes, and rubbing it in that you are better paid than he is.

KEEP OUT OF ARGUMENTS. You can rub a Britisher the wrong way by telling him "we have come over to win the war". Neither do the British need to be told that they lost the first couple of rounds in the present war. Use your head before you sound off, and remember how long the British alone held Hitler off without any help from anyone.

In the pubs you will hear a lot of Britons openly criticizing their government and the conduct of the war. That isn't an occasion for you to put in your two-cents worth. It's their business, not yours. You sometimes criticise members of your own family—but just let an outsider start doing the same, and you know how you feel!

The Briton is just as outspoken and independent as we are. But don't get him wrong. He is also the most law-abiding citizen in the world, because the British system of justice is just about the best there is.

Once again, look, listen, and learn before you start telling the British how much better we do things. British railways have dinky freight cars (which they call "goods wagons") not because they don't know any better. Small cars allow quicker handling of freight at the thousands and thousands of small stations.

British automobiles are little and low-powered. That's because all the gasoline has to be imported over thousands of miles of ocean.

British taxicabs have comic-looking front wheel structures. Watch them turn around in a 12-foot street and you'll understand why.

The British don't know how to make a good cup of coffee. You don't know how to make a good cup of tea. It's an even swap.

The British are leisurely—but not really slow. Their crack trains held world speed records. A British ship held the trans-Atlantic record. A British car and a British driver set world's speed records in America.

On the whole, the British people—whether English, Scottish or Welsh—are open and honest. If you are on furlough and puzzled about directions, money or customs, most people will be anxious to help you as long as you speak first and without bluster. The best authority on all problems is the nearest "bobby" (policeman) in his steel helmet. British police are proud of being able to answer almost any question under the sun. They're not in a hurry and they'll take plenty of time to talk to you.

The British will welcome you as good friends. But remember that crossing the ocean doesn't automatically make you a hero. There are housewives in aprons and youngsters in knee pants in Britain who have lived through more high explosives in air raids than many soldiers saw in first class barrages in the last war.

Britain at War

At home in Canada you were in a country at war. Since your ship left port, however, you have been in a war zone. You will find that all Britain is a war zone and has been since September, 1939. All this has meant great changes in the British way of life.

Every light in England is blacked out every night and all night. Many a highway signpost has come down and barrage balloons have gone up. Grazing land is now ploughed for wheat and flower beds turned into vegetable gardens. Britain's peacetime army of a couple of hundred thousand has been expanded to over two million men. Everything from the biggest factory to the smallest village workshop is turning out something for the war. Hundreds of thousands of women have gone to work in factories or joined the many military auxiliary forces. Old-time social distinctions are being forgotten as the sons of factory workers rise to be officers in the forces and the daughters of noblemen get jobs in munition factories.

But more important than this is the effect of the war itself. The British have been bombed, night after night and month after month. Thousands of them have lost their houses, their possessions, their families. Gasoline, clothes, and railroad travel are hard to come by and incomes are cut by taxes to an extent we Canadians have not even approached. One of the things the English always had enough of in the past was soap. Now it is so scarce that girls working in the factories often cannot get the grease off their hands or out of their hair. And food is more strictly rationed than anything else.

THE BRITISH CAME THROUGH. For many months the people of Britain have been doing without things which Canadians take for granted. But you will find that shortages, discomforts, blackouts, and bombings have not made the British depressed. They have a new cheerfulness and a new determination born out of hard times and tough luck. After going through what they have been through it's only human nature that they should be more than ever determined to win.

You are going to Britain from a country where your home is still safe, food is still plentiful, and lights are still burning. So it is doubly important for you to remember that the British soldiers and civilians have been living under a tremendous strain. It is always impolite to criticise your hosts. It is militarily stupid to insult your allies. So stop and think before you sound off about luke-warm beer, or cold boiled potatoes, or the way English cigarettes taste.

If British civilians look dowdy and badly dressed it is not because they do not like good clothes or know how to wear them. All clothing is rationed and the British know that they help war production by wearing an old suit or dress until it cannot be patched any longer. Old clothes are "good form".

One thing to be careful about—if you are invited into a British home and the host exhorts you to "eat up—there's plenty on the table", go easy. It may be the family's rations for a whole week spread out to show their hospitality.

WASTE MEANS LIVES. Most British food is imported even in peacetimes, and for the last two years the British have been taught not to waste the things that their ships bring in from abroad. British seamen die getting those convoys through. The British have been taught this so thoroughly that they now know that gasoline and food represent the lives of merchant sailors. And when you burn gasoline needlessly, it will seem to them as if you are wasting the blood of those seamen—when you destroy or waste food you have wasted the life of another sailor.

BRITISH WOMEN AT WAR. A British woman officer or non-commissioned officer can—and often does—give orders to a man private. The men obey smartly and know it is no shame. For British women have proven themselves in this war. They have stuck to their posts near burning ammunition dumps, delivered messages afoot after their motor-cycles have been blasted from under them. They have pulled aviators from burning planes. They have died at the gun posts and as they fell another girl has stepped directly into the position and "carried on". There is not a single record in this war of any British woman in uniformed service quitting her post or failing in her duty under fire.

Now you understand why British soldiers respect the women in uniform. They have won the right to the utmost respect. When you see a girl in khaki or air-force blue with a bit of ribbon on her tunic—remember she didn't get it for knitting more socks than anyone else in the community.

SOME HINTS ON BRITISH WORDS. British slang is something you will have to pick up for yourself. But even apart from slang, there are many words which have different meanings from the way we use them and many common objects have different names. For instance, instead of railroads, automobiles, and radios, the British will talk about railways, motorcars, and wireless sets. A railroad tie is a sleeper. A freight car is a goods wagon. A man who works on the road-bed is a navvy. A streetcar is a tram. Automobile lingo is just as different. A light truck is a lorry. The top of a car is a hood. What we call the hood (of the engine) is a bonnet. The fenders are wings. A wrench is a spanner. Gas is petrol—if there is any.

Your first furlough may find you in some small difficulties because of language difference. You will have to ask for sock suspenders to get garters and for braces instead of suspenders—if you need any. If you are standing in line to buy (book) a railroad ticket or a seat at the movies (cinema) you will be queuing (pronounced "cueing") up before the booking office. If you want a beer quickly, you had better ask for the nearest pub. You will get your drugs at a chemist's and your tobacco at a tobacconist, hardware at an ironmonger's. If you are asked to visit somebody's apartment, he or she will call it a flat.

Ubique Quo Fas Et
Gloria Ducunt

Be proud of your
regiment.

Be proud of Canada.

Canada is proud
of you.

NOTES

CHAPTER ONE The Senior Dominion

1. *Canadian Illustrated News*, 2 December 1871, 354.
2. *Quebec Mercury*, 11 November 1871; *L'Événement de Québec*, 25 October 1871.
3. Quoted in Elinor Kyte Senior, *British Regulars in Montreal: An Imperial Garrison, 1832–1854* (Montreal: McGill-Queen's University Press, 1981), 20.
4. Charles Boulton, *Reminiscences of the North-West Rebellions, with a Record of the Raising of Her Majesty's 100th Regiment in Canada, and a Chapter on Canadian Social & Political Life* (Toronto: Grip Publishing, 1886), 15.
5. Isaac Weld, *Travels through the States of North America, and the Provinces of Upper and Lower Canada, During the Years 1795, 1796, and 1797* (London, 1800), 351–52.
6. Quoted in George Stanley, *Canada's Soldiers: The Military History of an Unmilitary People* (Toronto: Macmillan, 1974), 240.
7. Quoted in Senior, *British Regulars in Montreal*, 182.
8. Mrs [Anna] Jameson, *Sketches in Canada, and Rambles among the Red Men* (London: Longman, Brown, Green, and Longmans, 1852), 42.
9. Edward Robert Cameron, *Memoirs of Ralph Vansittart, a Member of the Parliament of Canada, 1861–1867* (Toronto: Musson, 1902), 54.
10. Letter to Sir Charles Tupper, 12 March 1885, in Sir Joseph Pope, ed., *Correspondence of Sir John Macdonald: Selections from the Correspondence of the Right Honorable Sir John Alexander Macdonald, First Prime Minister of the Dominion of Canada* (Garden City, NJ: Doubleday Page, 1921), 337–38.
11. Diary for 5 October 1884, in C.P. Stacey, ed., *Records of the Nile Voyageurs, 1884–1885: The Canadian Voyageur Contingent in the Gordon Relief Expedition* (Toronto: Champlain Society, 1959), 97.
12. Henry Brackenbury, *The River Column: A Narrative of the Advance of the River Column of the Nile Expeditionary Force, and its Return Down the Rapids* (London: William Blackwood, 1885), 278.
13. Quoted in T.G. Marquis, *Canada's Sons on Kopje and Veldt: A Historical Account of the Canadian Contingents* (Toronto: Canada's Sons Publishing, 1900), 1–2.
14. Stanley McKeown Brown, *With the Royal Canadians* (Toronto: The Publishers' Syndicate, 1900), 18.
15. Walter Moodie's correspondence can be found at the Canadian Letters and Images Project, http://www.canadianletters.ca.
16. Gaston P. Labat, *Le Livre d'Or (The Golden Book) of the Canadian Contingents in South Africa, with an Appendix on Canadian Loyalty* (Montreal, 1901), 177.
17. Marquis, *Canada's Sons on Kopje and Veldt*, 69, 107.
18. Quoted in Carman Miller, *Painting the Map Red: Canada and the South African War, 1899–1902* (Montreal: McGill-Queen's University Press, 1998), 111.
19. William Green diary, 16 October 1900 (author's collection).
20. Green diary, 26 December 1900.

21. Stanley, *Canada's Soldiers*, 305.

22. Marquis, *Canada's Sons on Kopje and Veldt*, 62.

23. Marquis, *Canada's Sons on Kopje and Veldt*, 191.

24. Quoted in Mark Maclay, *Aldershot's Canadians in Love and War, 1939–1945* (Farnborough: Appin Publications, 1997), 33.

25. J. Castell Hopkins, *Canada at War: A Record of Heroism and Achievement* (New York: George H. Doran, 1919), 21.

CHAPTER TWO The First Colonies

1. Robert Rhodes James, ed., *Memoirs of a Conservative: J.C.C. Davidson's Memoirs and Papers, 1910–37* (London: Weidenfeld and Nicolson, 1969), 19–21.

2. W.L. Mackenzie King diary, 4 August 1914.

3. Quoted in A. Fortescue Duguid, *Official History of the Canadian Forces in the Great War, 1914–1919* (Ottawa: King's Printer, 1938), vol. 1, pt. 2, 7.

4. "Rally, Boys, to the Standard," words by Mrs M.J. Payton, music by Edward W. Miller (Toronto: Mrs M.J. Payton, 1916).

5. Duguid, *Official History of the Canadian Forces*, 111.

6. Quoted in Duguid, *Official History of the Canadian Forces*, 10.

7. G.W.L. Nicholson, *Canadian Expeditionary Force, 1914–1919: Official History of the Canadian Army in the First World War* (Ottawa: Queen's Printer, 1964), 18.

8. Katherine Hale, "The Departure" in *The White Comrade and other Poems* (Toronto: McClelland, Goodchild & Stewart, 1916), 23.

9. *St Croix Courier*, 3 September 1914, 6.

10. Letter of 29 August 1914, at http://www.canadianletters.ca.

11. "A Valcartier Letter," *Temiskaming Speaker*, 4 September 1914, 5.

12. Letter of 25 September 1914, at http://www.canadianletters.ca.

13. Letter of 13 October 1914, at http://www.canadianletters.ca.

14. Diary/memoir for 1914, at http://www.canadianletters.ca.

15. Letter of 18 October 1914, at http://www.canadianletters.ca. Crerar will reappear later in the story as the commander of 1st Canadian Army.

16. Quoted in J. Castell Hopkins, *Canadian Annual Review of Public Affairs for 1915* (Toronto: Annual Review Publishing, 1916), 370.

17. Duguid, *Official History of the Canadian Forces*, 123.

18. Letter of 3 November 1914, at http://www.canadianletters.ca.

19. Letter of 3 December 1914, at http://www.canadianletters.ca.

20. *Manchester Guardian*, 20 July 1915, 6.

21. Letters of 20 October 1914, 11 January 1915, at http://www.canadianletters.ca.

22. *St Croix Courier*, 7 January 1915, 1.

23. Letter of 10 January 1915, at http://www.canadianletters.ca.

24. Letter of 24 January 1915, collection of Audrey Sollis, Victoria, BC.

25. William Smith Duthie, *Letters from the Front: Being a Record of the Part Played by Officers of the Bank in the Great War, 1914–1919* (Toronto: Canadian Bank of Commerce, 1920), vol. 1, 78.

26. Douglas Leader Durkin, "Colonials" in *The Fighting Men of Canada* (Toronto: McClelland, Goodchild & Stewart, 1918), 68.

27. Letter of 29 December 1914, at http://www.canadianletters.ca.

28. Letter of 10 January 1915, at http://www.canadianletters.ca.

29. Letter of 4 December 1914, at http://www.canadianletters.ca.

30. *Times* [London], 10 November 1914, 5.

31. Letter of 25 April 1915, at http://www.canadianletters.ca.

32. Letter of 22 April 1915, at http://www.canadianletters.ca.

33. *Canada in Khaki*, vol. 1 (1916), 18.

34. *Canada in Khaki*, vol. 1 (1916), 61.

35. *Times* [London], 22 May 1915, 18.

36. *Canada* 42/538 (29 April 1916).

37. Minutes of the Senior Literary Society, Harbord Collegiate Institute, Toronto, 25 October 1915, Weston Corporate Archives.

CHAPTER THREE Growing Up At War

1. Marjorie Barron Norris, ed., *Medicine and Duty: The World War I Memoirs of Captain Harold W. McGill, Medical Officer, 31st Battalion C.E.F.* (Calgary: University of Calgary Press, 2007), 62.

2. Castell Hopkins, *Canadian Annual Review for 1915*, 376.

3. *Canada in Khaki*, vol. 2 (1917), 40.

4. W.W. Murray, *The History of the 2nd Canadian Battalion (East Ontario Regiment), Canadian Expeditionary Force, in the Great War, 1914–1919* (Ottawa: Mortimer, 1947), 91.

5. R.C. Fetherstonhaugh, *The Royal Montreal Regiment, 14th Battalion, C.E.F., 1914–1925* (Montreal: Gazette Printing, 1927), 84.

6. Murray, *The History of the 2nd Canadian Battalion*, 94.

7. Edith Lelean Groves, *Britannia: A Play* (Toronto: McClelland, Goodchild & Stewart, 1917); *Canada Calls*; *We'll Fight for the Grand Old Flag*; and *Primary Pieces* (Toronto: McClelland, Goodchild & Stewart, 1918).

8. Public Archives of Nova Scotia [PANS]: Violet Black Collection, MG100 vol. 194 #34, notebook.

9. PANS: 85th Battalion miscellaneous material, MG23 vol. 57 f. 6, supplement to *Journal of Education*, 14 February 1916.

10. Quoted in J. Clinton Morrison Jr., *Hell upon Earth: A Personal Account of Prince Edward Island Soldiers in the Great War, 1914–1918* (privately published, 1995), 34.

11. Donald Stuart Macpherson, *A Soldier's Diary: The WWI Diaries of Donald Macpherson* (St Catharines: Vanwell, 2001), 31.

12. Letter of 14 January 1917, author's collection.

13. Dale McClare, ed., *The Letters of a Young Canadian Soldier during World War I: P. Winthrop McClare of Mount Uniacke, N.S.* (Dartmouth: Brook House Press, 2000), 18.

14. Letter of 13 July 1918, *Waterdown Review*, 15 August 1918, 1.

15. McClare, ed., *The Letters of a Young Canadian Soldier*, 15.

16. John M. Hughes, ed., *The Unwanted: Great War Letters from the Field* (Edmonton: University of Alberta Press, 2005), 14; J.P. Pollock, ed., *Letters from Angus, 1915–1916* (Victoria: Trafford Publishing, 2005), 45.

17. Norma Hillyer Shephard, *Dear Harry: The Firsthand Account of a World War I Infantryman* (Burlington: Brigham Press, 2003), 74.

18. McClare, *The Letters of a Young Canadian Soldier*, 55, 64.

19. Letters of 26 September and 2 November 1916, at http://www.canadianletters.ca.

20. Letter of 25 September 1916, at http://www.canadianletters.ca.

21. Quoted in Harley Lashbrook, *West Elgin at War: Letters, Stories and Pictures of Local Men and Women in Our Armed Forces in the 1st World War* (West Lorne, ON: privately published, 2007), 98.

22. Letter of 9 May 1917, Weston Corporate Archives.

23. Undated letter (1915), at http://www.trentu.ca/admin/library/archives/ftransclettpg.htm.

24. Alan Mann, *"No Return Ticket": Wallaceburg's War Casualties and Selected War Memories* (Wallaceburg, ON: Mann Historical Files, 2002), 15.

25. Hughes, *The Unwanted*, 13.

26. Dwight Whalen, ed., *War Christmas: Letters to Niagara* (Eugenia, ON: Battered Silicon Despatch Box, 2010), 27–28.

27. Milly Walsh and John Callan, eds., *We're Not Dead Yet: The First World War Diary of Private Bert Cooke* (St Catharines: Vanwell, 2004), 53.

28. Letter from Seaford Camp, Sussex, of 24 October 1917, Weston Corporate Archives.

29. Castell Hopkins, *Canadian Annual Review for 1916*, 453; *Canadian Annual Review for 1917*, 518.

30. *Canada* 42/543 (3 June 1916).

31. J. Castell Hopkins, *The Province of Ontario in the War: A Record of Government and People* (Toronto: Warwick Bros. & Rutter, 1919), 102–3.

32. *British Journal of Nursing*, 14 July 1917, 20.

33. William Perkins Bull, *From Brock to Currie: The Military Development and Exploits of Canadians in General and of the Men of Peel in Particular, 1791 to 1930* (Toronto: Perkins Bull Foundation, 1935), 462–63.

34. *Canadian Red Cross Society Bulletin* #31 (November 1917), 5.

35. *Canadian Red Cross Society Bulletin* #31 (November 1917), 5.

36. Deborah Cowley, ed., *Georges Vanier, Soldier: The Wartime Letters and Diaries, 1915–1919* (Toronto: Dundurn Press, 2000), 43–44.

37. Helen Fowlds diary, at http://www.trentu.ca/admin/library/archives/fdiaries.htm.

38. *Halifax Morning Chronicle*, 15 July 1915.

39. J.C. Carlile, *Folkestone during the War: A Record of the Town's Life and Work* (Folkestone: F.J. Parsons, 1919), 167–68.

40. Letter of 8 October 1916, at http://www.canadianletters.ca.

41. R.B. Fleming, ed., *The Wartime Letters of Leslie and Cecil Frost, 1915–1919* (Waterloo: Wilfrid Laurier University Press, 2007), 93.

42. Letter from Crowborough Camp, of 9 May 1917, Weston Corporate Archives.

43. *Canada* 42/534 (1 April 1916).

44. Nicholson, *Canadian Expeditionary Force*, 408, 424.

45. Castell Hopkins, *Canada at War*, 348.

46. *Canada* 42/534 (1 April 1916); *Canada* 42/536 (15 April 1916).

47. Quoted in Castell Hopkins, *The Canadian Annual Review for 1915*, 376.

48. Fleming, *The Wartime Letters of Leslie and Cecil Frost*, 93.

CHAPTER FOUR Canada: A British Nation

1. D.J. Dickie and Helen Palk, *Pages from Canada's Story* (Toronto: J.M. Dent, 1928), 434–36.

2. Canada, Overseas Military Forces, *Report of the Ministry, Overseas Military Forces of Canada* (London: OMFC, 1918), 517.

3. *Times*, 8 March 1917, 7.

4. Quoted in Howard G. Coombs, *Dimensions of Military Leadership: The Kinmel Park Mutiny of 4–5 March 1919* (Kingston, ON: Canadian Forces Leadership Institute, 2004).

5. *Times*, 8 March 1919.

6. *Canada* 53/687 (8 March 1919), 293.

7. 'The Pity of It!' in *Canada* 53/688 (15 March 1919), 326.

8. *Epsom Herald*, 20 June 1919.

9. *Epsom Advertiser*, 27 June 1919.

10. Letter of 9 March 1919, at http://www.canadianletters.ca.

11. Letter of 11 November 1918, at http://www.canadianletters.ca.

12. *Toronto Star*, 14 December 1917, 25.

13. *Canada* 53/679 (11 January 1919).

14. *Financial Post*, 20 January 1934.

15. *Toronto Star Weekly*, 11 June 1938.

16. *Weston Cavalcade* (London, 1938).

17. Castell Hopkins, *Canada at War*, 335–36.

18. Statement by Sir Samuel Hoare, 28 October 1926, in *Imperial Conference, 1926: Appendices to the Summary of Proceedings* (Ottawa: King's Printer, 1927), 155–56.

19. Quoted in Peter Masefield, *To Ride the Storm: The Story of the Airship R101* (London: Kimber, 1982), 7.

20. Dennistoun Burney, "Aviation and the Empire," in *Addresses Delivered Before the Canadian Club of Toronto, Season of 1930–31* (Toronto: Warwick Bros. & Rutter, 1931), 11; Ian Shaw, "Future Atlantic Airship Services as visualized by Sir Dennistoun Burney," in *Canadian Aviation* 3/9 (September 1930), 20.

21. *Toronto Star*, 1 August 1930, 15; 11 August 1930, 3.

22. Burney, "Aviation and the Empire," 4–5; ad for Buckingham's cigarettes, *Vancouver Sun*, 29 July 1930, 11.

23. Beverley Baxter, "By Clipper," in *Maclean's*, 15 October 1941, 49–50.

24. Quoted in James Eayrs, *In Defence of Canada: From the Great War to the Great Depression* (Toronto: University of Toronto Press, 1964), 89.

25. William Stewart Wallace, *A History of the Canadian People* (Toronto: Copp Clark, 1930), 327.

26. Dickie and Palk, *Pages from Canada's Story*, 434–36.

27. Quoted in Eayrs, *In Defence of Canada*, 105.

28. Clifford H. Bowering, *Service: The Story of the Canadian Legion, 1925–1970* (Ottawa: Canadian Legion, 1960), 31.

29. W.W. Murray, *The Epic of Vimy* (Ottawa: The Legionary, n.d.), 62.

30. Quoted in Arthur Bousfield and Garry Toffoli, *Royal Spring: The Royal Tour of 1939 and the Queen Mother in Canada* (Toronto: Dundurn Press, 1989), 73.

31. Much of this material on the 1939 Royal Visit comes from a scrapbook of newspaper articles and other material collected by Hilda Hemstreet of Montreal, in the author's collection.

32. James Reaney, "The Royal Visit," in *The Red Heart* (Toronto: McClelland & Stewart, 1949), 23.

33. Hemstreet scrapbook.

CHAPTER FIVE A New Generation in the Old Country

1. Stephen Leacock, "Canada and the Monarchy" in *On the Front Line of Life: Memories and Reflections, 1935–1944* (Toronto: Dundurn Group, 2004), 185. I am grateful to Terry Copp for this reference.

2. Charles Ritchie, *The Siren Years: A Canadian Diplomat Abroad, 1937–1945* (Toronto: McClelland & Stewart, 1974), 42.

3. Letter of 6 June 1940, at http://www.canadianletters.ca.

4. *We Have Been There* (Toronto: CBC Publications Branch, 1941), 12–13.

5. "'London Calling'—news letter delivered by W. Garfield Weston M.P. over B.B.C. & C.B.C.," 29 August 1940, Weston Corporate Archives.

6. *Globe and Mail*, 8 July 1939.

7. Quoted in Travis L. Crosby, *The Impact of Civilian Evacuation in the Second World War* (London: Croom Helm, 1986), 106.

8. Quoted in Patricia Y. Lin, "National Identity and Social Mobility: Class, Empire and the British Government Overseas Evacuation of Children during the Second World War," in *Twentieth-Century British History* 7/3 (1996): 313–14.

9. *Times*, 29 June 1940, 7.

10. Quoted in Lin, "National Identity and Social Mobility," 313, 321.

11. Quoted in Ralph Barker, *Children of the Benares: A War Crime and Its Victims* (London: Methuen, 1987), 30.

12. C.H.J. Snider, "Blinds Up in Britain," address given 8 January 1942, in *The Empire Club of Canada: Addresses Delivered to the Members during the Year 1941–42* (Toronto: Warwick Bros. & Rutter, 1942).

13. *Daily Express*, 10 August 1940.

14. *Globe and Mail*, 26 August 1940.

15. *Rushden Echo and Argus*, 15 November 1940.

16. Jenni Mortin, *A Prairie Town Goes to War* (Shelburne, ON: Battered Silicon Dispatch Box, 2003), 29.

17. Vincent Massey, *The Sword of Lionheart and other Wartime Speeches* (London: Hodder & Stoughton, 1942), 26.

18. Letter of 4 April 1944, at http://www.canadianletters.ca.

19. Garfield Weston to R.A. Robertson, 16 November 1940; 18 July 1941; 29 December 1943, Weston Corporate Archives.

20. Letter of 6 June 1940, at http://www.canadianletters.ca.

21. "Fifth fortnightly report of the Field Censors (Home) on Canadian Army mail (27 Oct–9 Nov 41)," at http://www.cmp-cpm.forces.gc.ca.

22. Letter of 17 December 1944, at http://www.canadianletters.ca.

23. Letter of 25 January 1942, at http://www.canadianletters.ca.

24. Quoted in Wilfred I. Smith, *Code Word CANLOAN* (Toronto: Dundurn Press, 1992), 55.

25. Mortin, *A Prairie Town Goes to War*, 30.

26. Letter of 24 July 1942, at http://www.canadianletters.ca.

27. Ritchie, *The Siren Years*, 83, 102.

28. Letter of 4 April 1944, at http://www.canadianletters.ca.

29. G.R. Stevens, *A City Goes to War* (Edmonton: Edmonton Regiment Associates, 1964), 205.

30. Quoted in C.P. Stacey and Barbara M. Wilson, *The Half-Million: The Canadians in Britain, 1939–1946* (Toronto: University of Toronto Press, 1987), 58.

31. "Tenth fortnightly report (8–21 Dec 41)," at http://www.cmp-cpm.forces.gc.ca.

32. Quoted in Stacey and Wilson, *The Half-Million*, 46.

33. William C. Wonders, *The Sawdust Fusiliers: The Canadian Forestry Corps in the Scottish Highlands in World War Two* (Montreal: Canadian Pulp and Paper Association, 1991), 78.

34. *News of the World*, 25 January 1942.

35. Letter by Harvey Burnard of 5 December 1943, at http://www.canadianletters.ca.

36. Report No. 119, Historical Officer, CMHQ, "Canadian Relations with the People of the United Kingdom, and General Problems of Morale, 1939–44," 30 June 1944, at http://www.cmp-cpm. forces .gc.ca.

CHAPTER SIX They Came, They Saw, They Conquered

1. Report No. 119 Historical Officer CMHQ, Canadian Relations with the People of the United Kingdom, at http://www.cmp-cpm.forces.gc.ca.

2. Charles J.V. Murphy, "The First Canadian Army," *Fortune*, January 1944.

3. *Some Letters and other Writings of Donald Albert Duncan* (privately published, 1945), 150, 155.

4. Letter of 6 September 1942, at http://www.canadianletters.ca.

5. Ritchie, *The Siren Years*, 173.

6. Murphy, "The First Canadian Army," 239.

7. Quoted in Stacey and Wilson, *The Half-Million*, vii–ix.
8. War Diary for 25 December 1943, quoted in Robert L. Fraser, *Black Yesterdays: The Argylls' War* (Hamilton: Argylls Regimental Foundation, 1996), 171–72.
9. Maclay, *Aldershot's Canadians*, 97, 131.
10. *We Have Been There*, vol. 2 (Toronto: CBC, 1942), 113.
11. Massey, *Sword of Lionheart*, 37.
12. Letter of 17 February 1942, at http://www.canadianletters.ca.
13. Stacey and Wilson, *The Half-Million*, 92.
14. Quoted in Canada, National Defence, Historical Section, *The Canadians in Britain, 1939–1944* (Ottawa: King's Printer, 1945), 167.
15. Michael Whitby, ed., *Commanding Canadians: The Second World War Diaries of A.F.C. Layard* (Vancouver: UBC Press, 2005), 588.
16. Quoted in Brereton Greenhous et al., *The Crucible of War: The Official History of the Royal Canadian Air Force*, vol. 3 (Toronto: University of Toronto Press, 1994), 45.
17. Letter of 17 March 1945, at http://www.canadianletters.ca.
18. Quoted in Reginald H. Roy, *The Seaforth Highlanders of Canada, 1919–1965* (Vancouver: Evergreen Press, 1969), 144–45.
19. Quoted in G.R. Stevens, *The Royal Canadian Regiment*, vol. 2, *1933–1966* (London, ON: London Printing, 1967), 66.
20. Stevens, *The Royal Canadian Regiment*, 70.
21. Quoted in Stevens, *A City Goes to War*, 249.
22. Stevens, *A City Goes to War*, 279.
23. Quoted in Roy, *The Seaforth Highlanders of Canada*, 311.
24. Roy, *The Seaforth Highlanders of Canada*, 332.
25. Garfield Weston to R.A. Robertson, 9 May 1944, Weston Corporate Archives.
26. Ritchie, *The Siren Years*, 186.
27. Quoted in Bruce Tascona and Eric Wells, *Little Black Devils: A History of the Royal Winnipeg Rifles* (Winnipeg: Frye Publishing, 1983), 144.
28. Quoted in Fraser, *Black Yesterdays*, 250.
29. W.T. Barnard, *The Queen's Own Rifles of Canada, 1860–1960: One Hundred Years of Canada* (Don Mills: Ontario Publishing, 1960), 234.
30. W.L. Mackenzie King diary, 18 May 1944.
31. *The Legionary* 19/2 (August 1943), 20.
32. Quoted in Paul Dickson, *A Thoroughly Canadian General: A Biography of General H.D.G. Crerar* (Toronto: University of Toronto Press, 2007), 427.
33. The text of the addresses can be found in *Freedom of the Borough of Aldershot, reprinted from "Aldershot News" of Friday, 28 Sept., 1945*, in author's collection.
34. Carlile, *Folkestone during the War*, 170–71.

EPILOGUE

1. Beverley Baxter, "London Letter" in *Maclean's*, 26 October 1957, 12, 82–83. I am grateful to Neville Thompson for this reference.
2. Ritchie, *The Siren Years*, 102.
3. Letter of 4 June 1944, in *Some Letters and Other Writings of Donald Albert Duncan*, 161.
4. Fleming, *The Wartime Letters of Leslie and Cecil Frost*, 92.
5. Mortin, *A Prairie Town Goes to War*, 37.

FURTHER READING

Most of the research for this book was done through primary sources, some of which are mentioned in the endnotes. I have kept these notes to a minimum to avoid distracting readers, but am quite happy to provide full citations for any references. Most regimental and squadron histories contain wonderful details about time spent in Britain, and there is a large and growing body of material written by Canadian soldiers in Britain during both world wars, some of it published and much more available online. The best of these websites is The Canadian Letters and Images Project, at http://www.canadianletters.ca. In making suggestions for further reading, I have tried not to duplicate sources that appear in the endnotes, and have confined myself to published works that are easily accessible.

Abraham, Dorothy. *Lone Cone: A Journal of Life on the West Coast of Vancouver Island, B.C.* Victoria: Tiritea Press, 1945.

Barker, Ralph. *Children of the Benares: A War Crime and its Victims.* London: Methuen, 1987.

Berger, Carl. *The Sense of Power: Studies in the Ideas of Canadian Imperialism, 1867–1914.* Toronto: University of Toronto Press, 1970.

Bernier, Serge, et al. *Military History of Quebec, 1608–2008.* Montreal: Art Global, 2007.

Bishop, Charles W. *The Canadian YMCA in the Great War.* Toronto: National Council of YMCAs of Canada, 1924.

Bourassa, Rollie, ed. *One Family's War: The Wartime Letters of Clarence Bourassa, 1940–1944.* Regina: Canadian Plains Research Center, 2010.

Bousfield, Arthur and Garry Toffoli. *Royal Spring: The Royal Tour of 1939 and the Queen Mother in Canada.* Toronto: Dundurn Press, 1989.

Clifford H. Bowering. *Service: The Story of the Canadian Legion, 1925–1970.* Ottawa: Canadian Legion, 1960.

Buckner, Phillip and R. Douglas Francis, eds. *Rediscovering the British World.* Calgary: University of Calgary Press, 2005.

———. *Canada and the British World: Culture, Migration and Identity.* Vancouver: UBC Press, 2006.

Buckner, Phillip, ed. *Canada and the British Empire.* New York: Oxford University Press, 2008.

Canada, National Defence, Historical Section. *The Canadians in Britain, 1939–1944.* Ottawa: King's Printer, 1945.

Carlile, J.C. *Folkestone during the War: A Record of the Town's Life and Work.* Folkestone: F.J. Parsons, 1919.

Champion, C.P. *The Strange Demise of British Canada: The Liberals and Canadian Nationalism, 1964–1968*. Montreal: McGill-Queen's University Press, 2010.

Cook, Tim. *At the Sharp End: Canadians Fighting the Great War, 1914–1916*. Toronto: Penguin, 2007.

———. *Shock Troops: Canadians Fighting the Great War, 1917–1918*. Toronto: Penguin, 2008.

Coombs, Howard G. *Dimensions of Military Leadership: The Kinmel Park Mutiny of 4–5 March 1919*. Kingston, ON: Canadian Forces Leadership Institute, 2004.

Cowley, Deborah, ed. *Georges Vanier: Soldier. The Wartime Letters and Diaries, 1915–1919*. Toronto: Dundurn Press, 2000.

Cozzi, Sarah. "'When you're a long, long way from home': The Establishment of Canadian-Only Social Clubs for CEF Soldiers in London, 1915–1919." *Canadian Military History* 20/1 (winter 2011): 45–60.

Crosby, Travis. *The Impact of Civilian Evacuation in the Second World War*. London: Croom Helm, 1986.

Daniel, I.J.E. and D.A. Casey. *A History of the Canadian Knights of Columbus Catholic Army Huts*. 1922.

Critchley, A.C. *Critch!: The Memoirs of Brigadier A.C. Critchley*. London: Hutchinson, 1961.

Dickson Paul. *A Thoroughly Canadian General: A Biography of General H.D.G. Crerar*. Toronto: University of Toronto Press, 2007.

Duguid, A. Fortescue. *Official History of the Canadian Forces in the Great War, 1914–1919*. Ottawa: King's Printer, 1938.

Duthie, William Smith. *Letters from the Front: Being a Record of the Part Played by Officers of the Bank in the Great War, 1914–1919*. Toronto: Canadian Bank of Commerce, 1920.

Eayrs, James. *In Defence of Canada: From the Great War to the Great Depression*. Toronto: University of Toronto Press, 1964.

Fetherstonhaugh, R.C. *The Royal Montreal Regiment, 14th Battalion, C.E.F., 1914–1925*. Montreal: Gazette Printing, 1927.

Fleming, R.B., ed. *The Wartime Letters of Leslie and Cecil Frost, 1915–1919*. Waterloo: Wilfrid Laurier University Press, 2007.

Fraser, Robert L. *Black Yesterdays: The Argylls' War*. Hamilton: Argylls Regimental Foundation, 1996.

Giles, L.C. *Liphook, Bramshott and the Canadians*. Liphook: Bramshott and Liphook Preservation Society, 1986.

Greenhous, Brereton, et al. *The Crucible of War: The Official History of the Royal Canadian Air Force*, vol. 3. Toronto: University of Toronto Press, 1994.

Harper, Marjory. "Cossar's Colonists: Juvenile Migration to New Brunswick in the 1920s." *Acadiensis* 28/1 (autumn 1988): 47–65.

Hitsman, J. Mackay. *Safeguarding Canada, 1763–1871*. Toronto: University of Toronto Press, 1968.

Holmes, Peggy. *It Could Have Been Worse*. Toronto: Collins, 1980.

Hopkins, J. Castell. *Canada at War: A Record of Heroism and Achievement*. New York: George H. Doran, 1919.

———. *The Province of Ontario in the War: A Record of Government and People*. Toronto: Warwick Bros. & Rutter, 1919.

Hughes, John R., ed. *The Unwanted: Great War Letters from the Field*. Edmonton: University of Alberta Press, 2005.

Iarocci, Andrew. *Shoestring Soldiers: The 1st Canadian Division at War, 1914–1915*. Toronto: University of Toronto Press, 2008.

Jarratt, Melynda. *Captured Hearts: New Brunswick's War Brides*. Fredericton: Goose Lane Editions, 2008.

Knight, Martin. *We Are Not Manslaughterers: The Murder of Station Sergeant Thomas Green*. Newcastle: Tonto Books, 2010.

Lambert, R.S. *Old Country Mail*. Toronto: CBC, 1941.

Lashbrook, Harley. *West Elgin at War: Letters, Stories and Pictures of Local Men and Women in Our Armed Forces in the 1st World War*. West Lorne, ON: privately published, 2007.

Leggett, Joe. *Growing Up in Griggs Green: Recollections of Life at the Time of the First World War and the Canadian Army*. Liphook: Bramshott and Liphook Preservation Society, 1999.

Lin, Patricia Y. "National Identity and Social Mobility: Class, Empire and the British Government Overseas Evacuation of Children during the Second World War." *Twentieth-Century British History* 7/3 (1996): 310–44.

MacDonnell, Tom. *Daylight upon Magic: The Royal Tour of Canada, 1939*. Toronto: Macmillan, 1989.

MacLaren, Roy. *Canadians on the Nile, 1882–1898*. Vancouver: UBC Press, 1978.

Maclay, Mark. *Aldershot's Canadians in Love and War, 1939–1945*. Farnborough: Appin Publications, 1997.

Macpherson, Donald Stuart. *A Soldier's Diary: The WWI Diaries of Donald Macpherson*. St Catharines: Vanwell, 2001.

Mann, Alan. *"No Return Ticket": Wallaceburg's War Casualties and Selected War Memories*. Wallaceburg, ON: Mann Historical Files, 2002.

Masefield, Peter. *To Ride the Storm: The Story of the Airship R101*. London: Kimber, 1982.

Massey, Vincent. *The Sword of Lionheart and Other Wartime Speeches*. London: Hodder & Stoughton, 1942.

McClare, Dale, ed. *The Letters of a Young Canadian Soldier during World War I: P. Winthrop McClare of Mount Uniacke, N.S.* Dartmouth: Brook House Press, 2000.

McKenna, M. Olga. *Micmac by Choice: Elsie Sark—An Island Legend*. Halifax: Formac Publishing, 1990.

Miller, Carman. *Painting the Map Red: Canada and the South African War, 1899–1902*. Montreal: McGill-Queen's University Press, 1998.

Moore, Mary Macleod. *The Maple Leaf's Red Cross: The War Story of the Canadian Red Cross Overseas*. London: Skeffington & Son, 1919.

Morgan, Cecilia. *"A Happy Holiday": English Canadians and Transatlantic Tourism, 1870–1930*. Toronto: University of Toronto Press, 2008.

Morrison, J. Clinton, Jr. *Hell upon Earth: A Personal Account of Prince Edward Island Soldiers in the Great War, 1914–1918*. Published by the author, 1995.

Mortin, Jenni. *A Prairie Town Goes to War*. Shelburne, ON: Battered Silicon Dispatch Box, 2003.

Morton, Desmond. "Kicking and Complaining: Demobilization Riots in the Canadian Expeditionary Force, 1918–1919." *Canadian Historical Review* 61/3 (1980): 334–60.

Motiuk, Laurence. *Thunderbirds at War: Diary of a Bomber Squadron*. Nepean, ON: Larmot Associates, 1995.

Murray, W.W. *The History of the 2nd Canadian Battalion (East Ontario Regiment), Canadian Expeditionary Force, in the Great War, 1914–1919*. Ottawa: Mortimer, 1947.

Nicholson, G.W.L. *Canadian Expeditionary Force, 1914–1919: Official History of the Canadian Army in the First World War*. Ottawa: Queen's Printer, 1964.

Norris, Marjorie Barron, ed. *Medicine and Duty: The World War I Memoirs of Captain Harold W. McGill, Medical Officer, 31st Battalion C.E.F.* Calgary: University of Calgary Press, 2007.

Perkins Bull, William. *From Brock to Currie: The Military Development and Exploits of Canadians in General and of the Men of Peel in Particular, 1791 to 1930*. Toronto: Perkins Bull Foundation, 1935.

Pollock, J.P., ed. *Letters from Angus, 1915–1916*. Victoria: Trafford Publishing, 2005.

Rhodes, Robert James. *Memoirs of a Conservative: J.C.C. Davidson's Memoirs and Papers, 1910–37*. London: Weidenfeld and Nicolson, 1969.

Ritchie, Charles. *The Siren Years: A Canadian Diplomat Abroad, 1937–1945*. Toronto: McClelland & Stewart, 1974.

Roy, Reginald H. *The Seaforth Highlanders of Canada, 1919–1965.* Vancouver: Evergreen Press, 1969.

Senior, Elinor Kyte. *British Regulars in Montreal: An Imperial Garrison, 1832–1854.* Montreal: McGill-Queen's University Press, 1981.

———. *Roots of The Canadian Army: Montreal District 1846–1870.* Montreal: The Society of the Montreal Military & Maritime Museum, 1981.

Shephard, Norma Hillyer. *Dear Harry: The Firsthand Account of a World War I Infantryman.* Burlington: Brigham Press, 2003.

Six Years and a Day: The Story of the Beaver Club, 1940–46. London, 1946.

Smith, John Owen. *All Tanked Up: The Canadians in Headley during World War II.* Bordon: privately published, 2004.

Smith, Wilfred I. *Code Word CANLOAN.* Toronto: Dundurn Press, 1992.

Some Letters and other Writings of Donald Albert Duncan. Privately published, 1945.

Stacey, C.P. *Canada and the British Army, 1846–1871: A Study in the Practice of Responsible Government.* Toronto: Longmans, Green & Co., 1936.

———, ed. *Records of the Nile Voyageurs, 1884–1885: The Canadian Voyageur Contingent in the Gordon Relief Expedition.* Toronto: Champlain Society, 1959.

——— and Barbara M. Wilson. *The Half-Million: The Canadians in Britain, 1939–1946.* Toronto: University of Toronto Press, 1987.

Stanley, George. *Canada's Soldiers: The Military History of an Unmilitary People.* Toronto: Macmillan, 1974.

Stevens, G.R. *A City Goes to War.* Edmonton: Loyal Edmonton Regiment Associates, 1964.

Tascona, Bruce and Eric Wells. *Little Black Devils: A History of the Royal Winnipeg Rifles.* Winnipeg: Frye Publishing, 1983.

Templin, Hugh. *Assignment to Britain.* Privately published, 1941.

Voeltz, Richard A. "The British Boy Scout Migration Plan, 1922–1932." *Social Science Journal* 40 (2003): 143–51.

Walsh, Milly and John Callan, eds. *We're Not Dead Yet: The First World War Diary of Private Bert Cooke.* St Catharines: Vanwell, 2004.

We Have Been There. 2 vols. Toronto: CBC, 1941 and 1942.

Whalen, Dwight, ed. *War Christmas: Letters to Niagara.* Eugenia, ON: Battered Silicon Dispatch Box, 2010.

Whitby, Michael, ed. *Commanding Canadians: The Second World War Diaries of A.F.C. Layard.* Vancouver: UBC Press, 2005.

Whyte, King. *Letters Home, 1944–1946.* Toronto: Seraphim Editions, 2007.

Wonders, William C. *The Sawdust Fusiliers: The Canadian Forestry Corps in the Scottish Highlands in World War Two.* Montreal: Canadian Pulp and Paper Association, 1991.

ILLUSTRATION CREDITS

The publisher is grateful to the following for their permission to reproduce the illustrations. Any illustrations not noted here are from the author's private collection; although every effort has been made to contact copyright holders, it has not been possible in every case, and we apologize for any that have been omitted. Should the copyright holders wish to contact us after publication, we would be happy to include an acknowledgement in subsequent reprints.

Colour Plates

PLATE 6. "If Ye Break Faith We Shall Not Sleep." Library and Archives Canada, Acc. No. 1983-28-619.

PLATE 7. "Be Yours to Hold it High." Library and Archives Canada, Acc. No. 1983-28-469.

PLATE 8. "Our Export Trade Is Vital." Library and Archives Canada, Acc. No. 1983-28-451.

PLATE 10. "Canada's Pork Opportunity." Library and Archives Canada, Acc. No. 1983-28-684.

PLATE 11. "Fight for Her Come with the Irish Canadian Rangers Overseas Battalion." Library and Archives Canada, Acc. No. 1983-28-1017.

PLATE 13. "Canada and the Call." Library and Archives Canada, R11274-606.

PLATE 15. "Lick Them Over There!" Library and Archives Canada, Acc. No. 1983-30-236.

PLATE 16. "Can't You See? You Must Buy Victory Bonds." CWM 19900348-009. © Canadian War Museum.

PLATE 17. "Men of Valor—They Fight for You." Library and Archives Canada, Acc. No. 1983-30-224.

PLATE 19. "Eux aussi achètent des obligations de la victoire." Library and Archives Canada, Acc. No. 1983-30-348.

PLATE 20. "To Victory." Library and Archives Canada, Acc. No. 1983-30-243.

PLATE 21. "Give Us the Tools and We Will Finish the Job—Help Finish the Job—Buy Victory Bonds." Library and Archives Canada, Acc. No. 1983-30-585.

INDEX